Righteous Sisterhood

SARAH L. HOILAND

RIGHTEOUS SISTERHOOD

*The Politics and Power of an All-Women's
Motorcycle Club*

TEMPLE UNIVERSITY PRESS
Philadelphia • Rome • Tokyo

TEMPLE UNIVERSITY PRESS
Philadelphia, Pennsylvania 19122
tupress.temple.edu

Copyright © 2025 by Sarah L. Hoiland
All rights reserved
Published 2025

Library of Congress Cataloging-in-Publication Data

Names: Hoiland, Sarah L., 1978- author.
Title: Righteous sisterhood : the politics and power of an all-women's motorcycle club / Sarah L. Hoiland.
Description: Philadelphia : Temple University Press, 2025. | Includes bibliographical references and index. | Summary: "In this book, the author rides along with an all-women motorcycle club and observes their lifestyles and rituals of membership. She theorizes the sense of belonging they derive alongside their reactionary politics, their desire for relevance, and their alienation from male-focused right-wing spaces"—Provided by publisher.
Identifiers: LCCN 2024029451 (print) | LCCN 2024029452 (ebook) | ISBN 9781439925928 (cloth) | ISBN 9781439925935 (paperback) | ISBN 9781439925942 (pdf)
Subjects: LCSH: Women motorcyclists—United States. | Motorcycle clubs—United States. | Motorcycling—Social aspects—United States.
Classification: LCC GV1059.52 .H65 2025 (print) | LCC GV1059.52 (ebook) | DDC 796.7/5082—dc23/eng/20240917
LC record available at https://lccn.loc.gov/2024029451
LC ebook record available at https://lccn.loc.gov/2024029452

♾ The paper used in this publication meets the requirements of the American National Standard for Information Sciences—Permanence of Paper for Printed Library Materials, ANSI Z39.48-1992

Printed in the United States of America

9 8 7 6 5 4 3 2 1

To the Righteous Sisterhood Motorcycle Club and the women who made this book possible: Mom, Ria, Julia, and Megan.

Contents

Acknowledgments	ix
Introduction	1
The 1960s and the Biker Outlaw	4
Women Bikers and Righteous Sisters	8
Methodology and Authorship	11
Biker Semiotics and Semantics	14
Breakdown of the Parts	17
1. Citizenship in the Biker Nation	20
A Patching Ceremony	20
A Brief History of RSMC	25
Patches as Sacred Symbols	27
A Political Community	34
Bodies and Structures	38
Conclusion	48
2. Becoming a Righteous Sister	49
Spirit Ride	49
Theorizing Righteous Sisterhood	53
Dreaming of Righteous Sisterhood	57
Initiation	59
Marrying In	66
Conclusion	70

3.	Righteousness and the Realm of Action	71
	An Awards Ceremony	71
	Achieving Arete	74
	The Public Space of Appearances	77
	Gifts and the Space of Appearances	88
	Conclusion	99
4.	From Righteous Sister to Civil Death	101
	A Beginning and an Ending	101
	"She's Dead to Me"	110
	Life Changes	116
	Until Death Do Us Part	123
	Ex-Ethnographer	127
Epilogue		135
Notes		141
References		145
Index		151

Acknowledgments

My initial interviews with the Righteous Sisterhood Motorcycle Club (RSMC) took place when my son, David, was in pre-K; he will be a senior in high school when this book is published. David, you were my first research assistant, my road trip companion, and my best friend. Thank you for your love, support, insights, and for all the laughs.

Mom, your unceasing support and enthusiasm, including innumerable flights to stay with David when I was still in graduate school, and the ever-present question, "How is your book coming?" when the book was dozens of pages of field notes kept me going. Thank you Mom, Dad, Aaron, Nicole, Zoe, Sebastian, Ani, and Lake.

From the first pages to the last, Drs. María Julia Rossi, Megan Behrent, and Ria Banerjee have provided insightful comments, much-needed criticism, and endless encouragement. Thank you for the hundreds of hours you have poured into this book, the encouragement, love, and most of all your friendship. Thank you for convincing me to keep writing when I wanted to quit—more than once. I love you all.

Thank you to "Sandy" and the women of RSMC who opened their doors and their lives and saved me a seat on their bikes. Sandy, you are the harshest critic and you entrusted me to write about your life's work. Thank you. Thank you to "Apples," "Diesel," "Winona," "Skully," and the many women of RSMC that rode me around the back roads and highways, fed me, welcomed my son, and allowed "the Writer" to interview you.

Dave, you were with me during the first set of interviews and gave me immeasurable insight into bikers and MCs. A decade later, you listened to the first and final drafts of this book. Thank you.

The City University of New York's (CUNY's) Faculty Fellowship Publication Program (FFPP) provided crucial support for this book. My FFPP mentor Dr. Matthew Brim and my original writing group—Drs. Ria Banerjee, Megan Behrent, Alison Better, Allison Curseen, María Julia Rossi, and Henry Welcome—changed the trajectory of my research and writing. Matt, thank you for your mentorship then and now, and Maryanne McKenzie, thank you for advocating for CUNY faculty. Beth Harpaz, who led CUNY SUM, and Kathleen Collins at John Jay's Indoor Voices Podcast, provided early publicity for an article I wrote about the Hollister Gypsy Tour—thank you both!

Funding for *RS* came from the American Community of Learned Societies (ACLS) / Mellon Community College Faculty Fellowship (2019–2020), Professional Staff Congress (PSC) CUNY Awards in 2014–2015, 2016–2017, 2019–2020, and 2020–2021. In 2022, I was given a research fund for a National Science Foundation grant. This drastically accelerated the completion of *RS*—thank you to Senior Vice President Esther Rodríguez-Chardavoyne for the research support and to Amanda Howard in the Hostos Grants Office.

The *International Journal of Motorcycle Studies* and their annual conference has been a pivotal place for me to share ideas with scholars from around the world. Thank you to the journal editors and conference organizers.

Thank you to the New School for Social Research, and my mentor Dr. Terry Williams, who has supported me since my first ethnography class in 2003. Dr. Elzbieta Matynia, thank you for all of your encouragement and support. Thank you Jules Vivid, for your early edits and continued enthusiasm for *RS*.

The team at Temple University Press is outstanding. Thank you to my editor, Ryan Mulligan, for taking a chance on a first-time author and a book about bikers. You made this entire process supportive and generative. For the entire team, thank you for your attention to detail, especially my copyeditor.

My developmental editor, Dr. Trevor Perri, has been pivotal. My favorite recurring comment is "This might disorient your reader." Indeed! Thank you for helping me to become a stronger writer and for your timely and spot-on comments and edits.

Andrew Hubner and I were reading and writing partners for nearly a decade. We collaborated in a folder titled "The Good, the Bad, and the Ugly." His "spaghetti Western" and the first messy pages of *Righteous Sisterhood* are still there. Andrew, I finally did it. Rest in peace, my friend. I wish you were here.

Guy Cohen, thank you.

To my students who are currently or formerly incarcerated in New York State prisons (Greenhaven, Fishkill, Otisville, and Taconic), thank you for teaching me to talk about my research and thank you for your careful reading, comments, and enthusiasm. You are brilliant scholars and bring out the best in me (my "A" game) and I see the best in all of you. Together we have created spaces where we can big-belly laugh *and* get uncomfortable. To my Holistic Oasis for Parents' Education (HOPE) Scholars: the sisterhood that so many of you freely talk about (I was careful to never use the word!) that forms through the HOPE Program, mom-to-mom (one father-to-moms), scholar-to-scholar, is inspiring. You are all incredible. Many of you (mom scholars and incarcerated scholars) have entrusted me with your stories; *Righteous Sisterhood* lays bare some of my story. It takes courage to be vulnerable. Thank you for showing me the way. These tools that we are using to build community—in prisons and in the South Bronx—entail dreaming and co-creating. We need this now more than ever.

Righteous Sisterhood

Introduction

"Cobra" was a regular customer at a Brooklyn bar and owned a tattoo parlor around the corner. Standing five feet, five inches with a shaved head, trimmed goatee, green eyes, and a body covered in tattoos, Cobra was a neighborhood fixture and one of the few white non-Hispanics in that part of the neighborhood. Rapid gentrification was ensuing, and I was part of it, but my friendships with Brooklynites gave me some of the backstory I was not reading about in school. His family home and his business were across the street from each other, and both were a hundred yards from the bar. A year into our friendship, as I saw him limp around the pool table we were playing at, I asked, "What happened? Did you hurt yourself?" He looked at me with incredulity. "Are you serious?" he asked and then laughed. We both knew he was usually sitting in his tattoo chair or on a barstool. He told me he had been hit by a garbage truck on his motorcycle four years earlier, which "tore off [his] leg." Cobra described a gruesome process in which his leg was "fused back together," leaving him with no mobility in one knee joint. That was all he ever said about it.

Cobra's annual Thanksgiving weekend shop party was a big moneymaking event for the bar and was sure to be busy, but I was scheduled to bartend alone because Cobra made that request to the bar owner. "People are going to have to wait for their drinks," I said to Cobra. He said, "No problem. The most important thing is that every guest is respected." Later, he added, "Some of the bikers might show up—maybe two or maybe a hundred—put anything they want on my tab." "How will I know who they are?" I asked. Most of his friends looked similar—heavily tattooed. He laughed. "Oh, you'll know. You'll see their patches. If Davey Dirt[1] shows up, he'll burn the bar down with everyone in it if he gets pissed off," he said with another hearty laugh and a twinkle in his green eyes. Davey Dirt had been best friends with Cobra since childhood, but I had never met him. The bikers were indeed impossible to miss. Around midnight, two walked in and went straight through the bar into the backyard. One of the bikers was enormous, standing around six feet, four inches and weighing at least 250 pounds, and the biker he was with was a foot shorter and a hundred pounds lighter. They wore the same black leather vests with three-piece club patches. I assumed the bigger biker was Davey Dirt. I was wrong.

Cobra was approved to tattoo members of the motorcycle club (MC)[2] Davey Dirt was a member of, and he went to their clubhouse parties. He was extraordinarily generous and frequently paid for everyone's drinks, so his offer to pay for members of the club at the shop party was not unusual; however, I later found out that Cobra felt indebted to the club. After his motorcycle accident, Cobra spent a year in the hospital and was bedridden for another year. During his two-year recovery, the club threw benefit parties for him and paid his rent at the tattoo shop, allowing him to keep his business. Cobra's sense of loyalty ran deep, and although he did not "patch in" (become a member of the MC), he was a "friend of the club" and a "brother," which is a term of respect that is usually reserved for members. A nonmember brother, then, marks a liminal space. A "friend" is not an insider (a patched member) or an outsider (a civilian). This outlaw[3] MC was predominantly Latino, with most members being of Puerto Rican descent, so Cobra stood out as a white guy, but he occupied a special place, having known many members his entire life. Davey Dirt had a Sicilian background, with dark skin and long black hair, and he appeared Latino or Native American. He did not consider himself white, and neither did his brothers.

Davey Dirt did not burn the bar down, and he and I ended up spending a lot of time together in the months following that night. We fell in love, but the biker lifestyle was not for me, and I told him that I had no intention of becoming an "ol' lady."[4] He assured me he was relocating and getting out of the club. He moved to Florida in 2006, I followed six months later, and we got married in 2007 in a small church. On that day, the left side was populated by white Lutherans from Washington, North Dakota, Texas, and Minnesota, and the right side was filled with Puerto Rican bikers from Brooklyn and Florida. Getting married and inviting both sides to our wedding had been my idea. Davey's family of origin was not coming to the wedding, so I encouraged him to invite his club brothers. He said on a few occasions, "Maybe it's not a good idea. You know how they can get." He retold a story I'd heard several times: "Cement," the national president of the club, had started a fistfight at another biker's wedding and knocked out the bride's father. "It'll be fine," I said. I considered many of the bikers friends and earnestly believed we had some control over the wedding and reception.

It was not fine. Cement did not punch out my dad, but he destroyed our reception. It ended hours earlier than it should have when he cursed out my family during his impromptu speech on the mic, threatened the DJ, drank the bar dry, and wrote "Fuck You" on a wedding present, signed his name, and then denied it. Cement's position in the club made him untouchable, and his outsize role continued to permeate our family life for years after the wedding. He blocked Davey's retirement, piling up more things for him to do before he could retire, increasing the minimum number of years for retirement, and flying him back to New York City to do things for the club. The threat of violence was always there, permeating our life; the threats were from other clubs in Florida and from his club brothers. The penalty for exiting early without permission was a beating that would lead to hospitalization or worse. The lifestyle coupled with an economy that was tanking made it difficult for Davey to find employment,[5] and I found myself working full-time, writing a dissertation, and raising our baby. My new husband was not able to keep his promise of starting a new life, and it took its toll on our marriage. He was still at the mercy of the club in New York City, and we lived 1,200 miles away. In 2010, my son and I moved out. When I completed a required online parenting class for divorcing parents, it said something akin to "Congratulations. You are getting out of an emotionally abusive relationship, and that's the best thing you can do for your child." I was stunned by the matter-of-factness of that statement. Davey was a loving husband—albeit absent in many ways—and a good father; however, the MC was violent, and he was inextricably part of it, which meant my son and I were part of it.

My own struggle to understand the contradictions in my married life coupled with the need to move forward with my dissertation led me to interview women who had various affiliations with MCs—including ol' ladies, adult children of bikers, and a clubhouse stripper—to better understand their roles and my own. I also interviewed a few male bikers about the role of women because they were always more willing to talk to me than any of the women were. Each interview provided new insights into this world, but it felt incomplete. In 2011, my dissertation defense date loomed, and a $10,000 raise depended on the completion of my degree. I just wanted to finish and had nearly three hundred pages written, but I could not ignore the nagging feeling that I was not done. Six months before my defense, I saw a video clip of an interview with a woman biker who had started an all-women MC. These women wore patches. I found the contact information online and sent an email requesting an interview. I was told no. I tried again and was told no again. I tried a third time and asserted my position vis-à-vis my husband's involvement in a club. Shortly thereafter, "Sandy," the national president of "Righteous Sisterhood Motorcycle Club" (RSMC),[6] replied and invited me to her birthday party at her home. Accustomed to club parties in New York City, I asked her if it would be kid-friendly (assuming it would not be) because my son went everywhere with me. In an email and in a follow-up phone call, she assured me it would be. Nevertheless, I asked Dave (his name shortened for me when we separated) to accompany us, and he agreed.

At the party, Sandy relayed a story from her 1960s childhood. She asked her mother, "Can girls ride motorcycles?" She said her single white midwestern mother responded, "Girls can do anything they want, baby." This anecdote encapsulated the story Sandy wanted to convey to me about her and the club. It seemed to suggest that for her and other women, riding motorcycles was an act of rebellion and liberation—a version of the American dream dipped in girl power. I wanted to believe this narrative, and it was easy to see it play out because Sandy was the gatekeeper; however, the contradictions and complexities of life for Sandy's mom, for Sandy, for the women in the club, and for my own personal life as well as my ethnographic work necessitated rigorous reflexivity. In Sandy's version of her childhood story, it seemed apparent that she did not see women riding motorcycles; however, Sandy later told me that her grandmother rode a motorcycle. Sandy's mother lived an extremely difficult life and faced tremendous structural constraints. Sandy also faced structural constraints within the one-percenter[7] world as an adolescent bride and young mother, then as a single mother, and again as the founder and national president of one of the first all-women MCs. Although she would deftly traverse the men's MCs to create RSMC and provide a space for women to exist independently in the MC world, the club ultimately reproduced many of the practices from the larger misogynist biker subculture.

The history of one-percenters and the "outlaw" biker has been documented (and is outlined in what follows); however, the history of biker culture as it pertains to biker women is far less known and researched. The 1960s were formative years for Sandy and are essential to understanding her and also the MC dynamics that emerged during that time, particularly as they pertain to women.

The 1960s and the Biker Outlaw

MCs originated in the United States in the 1930s and made international headlines in 1947 with the Hollister riot, which was immortalized in U.S. popular culture with *The Wild One* (1953) and which presented an image of bikers as rebellious and quintessentially masculine.[8] In the 1960s—a decade marked with state-sanctioned violence against Black people, Latino people, Native

Americans, women, gays and lesbians, incarcerated people, people with disabilities, and Vietnamese and Cambodian people abroad—the public image of bikers and clubs as lawbreaking, masculine, and violent was reinforced when four Hells Angels[9] were charged with raping two adolescent girls on Labor Day weekend in 1964 in Monterey, California. Hunter S. Thompson interviewed several Hells Angels who were present that weekend. These interviews, which Thompson published in the *Nation* in 1965 and later in his first book, *Hells Angels: A Strange and Terrible Saga* ([1966] 1999), included details of a gang rape of these two adolescent girls, one white and pregnant and the other Black, and sensationalized the rapes by including the Hells Angels' accounts and not any court records or victim reports. The charged bikers were released because of witness intimidation and critiques of witness credibility. Thompson famously referred to these bikers as the "all-American bogeyman" (Thompson [1966] 1999:38).

In response to the Monterey rape case, on September 18, 1964, the California attorney general Thomas C. Lynch submitted a circular letter to all district attorneys, sheriffs, and police chiefs "requesting information concerning the Hell's Angels and also soliciting any suggestions as to methods to control them" (Lynch 1965: enc 2). This sixteen-page report, released to the public in March 1965, detailed myriad crimes, including fraud, forgery, motorcycle thefts, narcotics (marijuana and "dangerous pills"), and assault and battery. Several instances describe racially motivated assaults against "Negroes." Eighteen instances of rape are detailed along with initiation rites, some of which include "heterosexual perversions . . . performed primarily for the shock impact on others" (Lynch 1965:3). In these reported "perversions," new members performed cunnilingus on a woman in front of other club members. Thompson describes the effect of the released report as "coast-to-coast infamy and a raft of new possibilities" in which the Hells Angels began issuing statements, posing for photos, and arranging news and media coverage for a price from $100 to $1,000 ([1966] 1999:38–39). William Dulaney (2005: para. 28), a professor and biker often interviewed in popular press about outlaw motorcycle clubs, describes what became known as the Lynch Report as the "first bureaucratic attempt to portray motorcycle clubs as a clear and present danger to the local, state, and ultimately international constituencies." The Australian sociologist Arthur Veno argues that the report led to a drop in membership but an increase in crime and violence, with incarceration leading to prison recruitment and eventually a more hardened membership ([2002] 2003:189). Dulaney (2005: para. 28) calls the report "little more than law enforcement urban legends" including "unsubstantiated absurdities such as gang raping of innocent young women and the plundering of small California townships"; however, Dulaney does not provide any evidence for his critique and asserts that "outlaws" are men.

Although the Lynch Report is reviled by bikers and its trustworthiness questioned, a close reading of the report offers a complex picture of biker culture in the sixties, especially as it pertains to the topics of gender, race, and sexuality. For example, it describes female associates of the Hells Angels who threatened other women; for example, one told a rape victim "she would be cut on the face with a razor" if she cooperated with police (1965:9). Instances of female criminality from assaults to thefts and aiding and abetting, in addition to witness intimidation, among "females wearing Hell's Angels jackets" are detailed (1965:12). For a relatively short period of time, women could be members of the Hells Angels and other MCs. My archival research in Hollister, California, uncovered dozens of photographs of patch-wearing women at the 1947 Hollister Gypsy Tour, which suggests that women were wearing patches and participating in some areas and clubs from the late 1940s through the 1960s. The assumptions about social class and sexuality remained fairly constant from the popular press coverage of Hollister to the Lynch Report. Lynch notes the Monterey rape victims' lack of willingness to testify to their social class and writes that they "are not of a higher social strata and thus are vulnerable to the mores of the 'saloon society'" (1965:14); this reflects not only the attorney general's assumptions about the "*mores of saloon society*" but surely also those of the lower court judges across California. He refers to the "general filthy condition" of both men and women, who seem "badly in need of a bath" (1965:4). The "dirtiness" of bodies and of values also marks class, gender, and race.

A closer reading of the Lynch Report also shows the significance of race and racism for biker culture in the sixties. The report recounts several instances of racially motivated violence. For example, on May 17, 1964, "two white motorcyclists" were arrested after they assaulted "a group of Negroes, damaging their vehicle and breaking a toll gate" (1965:9). The report states that the bikers "decided that a Negro girl in the car was Spanish and attempted to speak to her in that language" and later "tried to pull the girl from the car" (1965:9). Bystanders apprehended the two bikers, who were arrested, convicted, charged small fines ($110 and damages to the car), and given jail time (thirty days), with one year of probation for one. Another example involves a "Negro customer who was at the time reaching into the refrigerator for a bottle of soda water" and was "punched in the face and pushed against the refrigerator with such force as to break the door" (1965:9). The five bikers stole cigarettes, beer, and wine and left the liquor store. In response to the Hells Angels' use of symbols such as iron crosses, swastikas, and other Nazi symbolism in the post–World War II era, the Anti-Defamation League (ADL) has concluded that they "tended to use many of these symbols to show their nonconformist nature and for 'shock and awe,'" adding that although many of the clubs have had many (and even a majority of) racist members, they do not necessarily harbor "group-wide white supremacist ideology" (2011:5). However, countless racially motivated attacks, predominantly segregated MCs, and racist symbols suggest a different story.

Anti-Black violence within biker culture was immortalized in 1969 at a concert headlined by the Rolling Stones at the Altamont Speedway when eighteen-year-old concertgoer Meredith Hunter, a young Black man wearing a lime-green suit, who was with his white girlfriend, was brutally beaten and fatally stabbed by members of the Hells Angels, who had been hired to provide stage security. The attack was caught on video and appears in the 1970 documentary *Gimme Shelter*, but what is highlighted in the documentary is a close-up of Hunter holding a gun in the air, juxtaposed against the white crocheted dress of his girlfriend, and Mick Jagger's reaction. As Sasha Frere-Jones (2019) aptly states, "Altamont is where Hunter lost his life. 'Gimme Shelter' is where he lost his story" because Altamont became a symbol for the end of the 1960s rather than the public murder of a young Black man. The music critic Greil Marcus, who attended the event, said, "The murder crystallized the event. A young black man murdered in the midst of a white crowd by white thugs as white men played their version of black music—it was too much to kiss off as a mere unpleasantness" ([1977] 2015). The Hells Angel Alan Passaro was charged with murder but was acquitted on self-defense. While this event has been widely written about and analyzed, the attack of an eighteen-year-old Black man with a white girlfriend by a gang of white bikers empowered to provide security and the subsequent acquittal illustrate the power of white masculinity, even in a stigmatized subculture. While the California government "reacted" to the 1964 Monterey rapes, producing the Lynch Report, the Angels were emboldened by Altamont and positioned to leverage their power globally and commercialize it even more.

In *Gimme Shelter*, women can be seen riding on the backs of Hells Angels motorcycles, but they were not wearing patches and had no role in the security detail. Turf wars between clubs became increasingly common, particularly in urban areas in the 1970s. As a result, MCs became men-only. Patches were prized possessions, and women were viewed as not being able to "defend their patches" in physical confrontations, which had become more prevalent and lethal. Women in the 1960s biker subculture were either "dirty" (physically and morally) and "criminal" because they willfully associated with bikers or innocent victims of biker violence—and similar to the coverage of Hollister nearly twenty years earlier, women bikers are underexamined, mostly ignored, or decontextualized. I draw on these limited historical depictions and roles of women and create new language and new categories for women bikers.

Women Bikers and Righteous Sisters

In Randy McBee's (2015) historical account of the American motorcyclist, one page of the three-hundred-page tome discusses "women as outlaws," and although outlaws and bikers are not McBee's primary focus, they are featured predominantly throughout the book. In *Bike Lust: Harleys, Women, and American Society* (2001), the anthropologist Barbara Joans debunks many of the stereotypes and myths about women riders and identifies three categories: *lady biker, woman biker,* and *woman rider*. Most pertinent for this ethnographic exploration are the woman bikers, who ride and maintain their own bikes (motorcycles), expect to be treated as equals, prefer to ride with men, and "may present a variety of demeanors, anything from sexy broad to hard-living biker, but she never makes nice" (2001:104). Joans's research is predominantly on lady bikers and woman riders, but she interviews a few woman bikers. Before Joans's work, there were three long-standing categories, established by men, for women who associated with men's clubs—ol' ladies, mamas, and broads. Debunking these categories is a major contribution of Joans's work.

Righteous Sisterhood builds upon Joans's woman biker category with an additional category that I call the *righteous sister* to describe women bikers who join MCs. A righteous sister identifies herself as a biker; might wrench, or maintain her own bike, or might not; and prefers to ride with other righteous sisters. Like biker women and one-percenter women, righteous sisters are notoriously difficult to observe. Many have the attitude of bikers and even one-percenters and are also doubly guarded by their club. There is little scholarly information about all-women MCs in the United States or elsewhere, and there are no ethnographic accounts prior to *Righteous Sisterhood*. Motorcycle clubs are notoriously difficult to access; initiation processes for potential members are long and challenging, and access for outsiders is very limited. Several academic books have been written about all-men motorcycle clubs and bikers who are men.[10] The anthropologist Daniel Wolf's fieldwork and ethnography of the Rebels MC ([1991] 2000) had the greatest impact on my work, along with the anthropologist Philippe Bourgois's ethnography *In Search of Respect* (1995). Ann Ferrar is a notable writer on women motorcyclists,[11] but the differences are vast between the women she describes and the women in Righteous Sisterhood Motorcycle Club (either "RSMC" or the "club") whom this book focuses on.

From 2011 to 2019, I engaged in ethnographic research and was granted access to RSMC's initiation rituals, annual ceremonies, and extensive socialization process. I observed how righteous sisterhood is constructed and maintained over time, why women choose to join, and what happens when the sisterhood bond is severed by the individual member or by the club. This study is the first of its kind, and although RSMC is a unique group, as were Thompson's Hells Angels in the 1960s, these women tell us a lot more about gender and politics than they do about an obscure subcultural group or about motorcycling. The characteristics of the club and the built spaces of appearances create alternative political spaces for libertarian and conservative ideas, primarily among middle-aged white women, as well as spaces for these women to serve their communities, heal their own traumas, and bond with other women. This political community is informed by and informs the larger populist turn in the United States. "Unskilled and uneducated," Thompson pointed out, "the outlaw motorcyclist views the future with the baleful eye of a man with no upward mobility at all. In a world increasingly geared to specialists, technicians and fantastically complicated machinery, the Hell's Angels are obvious losers and it bugs them" ([1966] 1999:52). Unlike their one-percenter counterparts, who today are still similar to what Thompson described in the 1960s, righteous sisters are not unskilled, and many have college educations; however, they have experienced systemic sexism, and many have suffered physical, sexual, and emotional abuse. Like many of their male counterparts, many served the United States military in a series of endless wars.

The kind of freedom and ideal of "girl power" described by Sandy is observable throughout my research and is highlighted with a variety of stories, interviews, and analysis; however, Sandy eschews the term "feminist" to describe her club, and its policies and practices are far from promoting equality among all gendered members. In fact, several instances highlight homophobia and transphobia in the club's words, actions, and policies. The many contradictions inherent in closed groups that espouse freedom and independence while demanding dependence and obedience trouble the one-dimensional views of this club and its righteous sister members. This matriarchal political community must be examined within a political context, particularly since Sandy is the national president of the RSMC nation. They are sovereign within the biker subculture, which is discussed at length, and they have several elements of nationhood, including their own national symbol (a trademarked three-piece patch), formal governing documents, internal economy and currency (RSMC coins), and processes for citizenship (or membership). Significant attention is drawn to how members of the club can achieve excellence, or righteousness. The philosopher and political theorist Hannah Arendt made a crucial ontological connection between the "space of appearances" and the realm of the political as something created by people who speak and act together and "can find its proper location almost any time and anywhere" ([1958] 1998:198). As Arendt points out, many do not live in this space of appearances and therefore are "deprived of reality," quoting Aristotle "for what appears to all, this we call Being" ([1958] 1998:199). Through membership in the club, women can become righteous sisters, distinguishing themselves within RSMC in ways that complement their roles in society, and some can surpass any type of excellence they could achieve outside of their club. The solidarity they feel and enact as a group also gives them political power and agency within the subculture that extends into other areas of their lives.

Women bikers have largely been omitted from the plethora of biker origin stories, most of which began after World War II. Through archival research in Hollister, California, I was able to uncover and piece together a new origin story for the American "outlaw" biker that included women who rode motorcycles and wore patches (Hoiland 2018). By contextualizing RSMC within a larger historical context of women who transgressed societal gender constraints, I am rewriting the male-centric biker history. Throughout the book, I leverage both micro- and macrosociological approaches to examine the meaning attached to one's patches or "colors," which are sacred symbols in the biker world and analogous to a nation's flag. The creation of the all-women MC was a very political act within the outlaw MC subculture, in which one-percenter clubs assert territorial control over large swaths of the globe and proclaim it on their patches. The kinds of values and norms associated with being a righteous sister and proclaiming membership by becoming a full-patch member are detailed through a lengthy initiation process, rites of passage, and annual events. All of these function as spaces of appearances, reaffirming the camaraderie and sisterhood as well as providing a unique view of a white, predominantly politically conservative, quasi-international group of righteous sisters. Perhaps most importantly, *Righteous Sisterhood* attends to exit and exile—topics that are nearly absent from accounts of clubs and other related closed societies—both of which result in members being stripped of their biker citizenship and sisterhood.

Most books about motorcycling or motorcycle clubs are written by authors who are motorcyclists or bikers, and the epistemology is phenomenological. There are tensions between motorcyclists and bikers, the latter easily distinguishable by their demeanor and patches ("MC" and sometimes "1%"). For the former, the emphasis is on *riding* and on the relationship between the *motorcyclist, the motorcycle,* and *the road*; for the latter, the emphasis is on the *brotherhood* and *the club*. While motorcycle scholars, almost all of whom ride themselves, have successfully turned motorcycle studies into a growing field with its own journal and a global network of scholars and riders, there is no complementary biker studies subfield or recognized field of scholarship. Motorcycle studies has increasingly become a mixed-gender field for scholarship, thanks in part to organizations like the *International Journal of Motorcycle Studies*, which has a peer-reviewed academic journal and an annual conference both of which feature an international academic community of scholars and frequently an intersectional lens. In the journal, scholars theorize the performative aspects of riding, where, for example at the Pride Parade, "The motorcycle and the body produce a cyborgian relationship that resists gender bifurcation and synthesizes pleasure and politics through vibrational resonance that is only possible when machine and body come together as collaborating objects" (Malone 2013: para. 1) or of the "bike-biker in terms of connective unions" and "the endless possibilities of re-organ-ising our identities" (Miyake 2015: para. 19). The semantics of "dykes" is explored in an article detailing the legal battle of the San Francisco Women's Motorcycle Contingent (SFWMC), better known as Dykes on Bikes, to trademark their name, as "dyke" was initially thought to be disparaging and the patent application denied (Ilyasova 2006). M. Shelly Conner (2009: para. 14) provides a critical look into the "Black MC set" by leveraging her own experience as a member in a coed MC, describing her experience as a coalition meeting in which "the presiding coalition president announced, 'All right, time for the real business. Bitches leave!'" Conner explores the sexism in Black MCs and contends Black women members "are subjugated to men in relationships that resemble that of pimp to prostitute, instead of their professed relationship of club brother to club sister. Similarly, the female motorcycle club member is both victimized and protected by her associations with male club members" (2009: para. 15).

Journalists continue to be enthralled with bikers, and in 2018, the *New York Times* featured New Orleans's all-women Caramel Curves MC (Simms), but the article does not attenuate to the deeply political nature of calling oneself an MC, particularly in the U.S. South. More scholarship in this area is needed to further examine the ways in which these women-only or mixed-gender MCs negotiate race, gender, sexuality, power, space, and respect in this male-dominated subculture.

Methodology and Authorship

Righteous Sisterhood grew from a chapter in my dissertation that was based on a set of interviews with Sandy conducted in 2011. Much of the dissertation aimed to refute existing stereotypes and add women's perspectives, collapsing distinctions between the biker world and the larger patriarchal society (Hoiland 2012). I decided to revisit the chapter on Sandy a few years later and approached her about writing a book on her and her club. In a short period of time, I had a small research grant from the City University of New York (CUNY), Internal Review Board (IRB) approval for the study of human subjects, and, most importantly for the research to commence and move forward, Sandy's approval. She granted me unprecedented access to the club, I met some of the members and attended a few events, and by 2015 I was attending the annual gathering they refer to as nationals.

I tried to capture things as I saw them when I saw them. This was challenging since I did not use audio recordings and sometimes could not take field notes in situ, especially if I was on the back of a motorcycle. I hung around, watched, and listened, and whenever I had the opportunity, I spent time with women in RSMC and got to know them. I met their children and grandchildren, went to their homes, and worked alongside them on a variety of clubhouse projects. On several occasions, I asked for permission to formally interview members, and I typed while they talked, doing my best to transcribe live in accordance with my IRB. In total, I observed from July 2014 until July 2019, and I conducted fifteen formal interviews with members and three with immediate family members. Sandy was my key informant, and we had dozens of conversations over the years, both formal and informal. Informal conversations numbered in the hundreds. During this five-year period, I attended many club events and took notes in my notebook or on my phone. I relied on emails and texts for dates and places. Sandy gave me access to primary source materials including photographs, the RSMC Sponsorship Manual, and three-ring binders filled with articles about the club, all of which were housed at national headquarters. Through individual stories and observable behaviors and events, I interpret the club and its members and make some generalizations. Although the stories are very particular and nuanced, they convey in a general way the stories of similarly situated women—women who seek to be part of something bigger than themselves; to have a place, or space of appearances, in which their speech and actions are recognized as *righteousness*; and to have the support of a hundred women at any given moment in a *sisterhood*.

I am not a motorcyclist or a biker, and although I rode as a passenger on many motorcycles over the past twenty years, I did not begin this research with the intention of becoming either. While one does not have to smoke crack or take opioids to study drug culture, and while distancing oneself from the activities themselves is a sound ethnographic technique in these cases, there has been criticism for my nonphenomenological approach from bikers, motorcycle studies scholars, and biker scholars. For a woman researcher who had extensive experience around MCs, my prior knowledge was key. I wanted to stand out as a nonbiker, non–righteous sister, so I didn't wear any club T-shirts or biker clothing, and I never rode a motorcycle. In a sea of one hundred biker women, I could be instantaneously spotted. No prospect (someone looking to join the club) would mistake me for another newcomer and share something they would not want shared, and no member could ever forget who I was and why I was there. I was "the Writer."

Professionally, this type of research was challenging. Community college teaching loads are heavy, with minimal time allotted to "junior" faculty to conduct the research required for reappointment and tenure. Small research grants were available, and I received several from CUNY, which made it possible to travel to various RSMC events. When I applied for an enhanced internal grant, a reviewer shared their "concern" for my "personal safety." I interpreted it as sexist and paternal and doubted any of my male colleagues were dissuaded from their research because of personal safety concerns. When I told Sandy, we both laughed, and she told me about the time they were busted selling Girl Scout cookies as the most illegal club activity they engaged in. So little was known about righteous sisters, even among other scholars in my field, that the importance of writing this book and challenging assumptions about "biker gangs" and "outlaws"—and also challenging stereotypes about women ethnographers in fields that are traditionally male dominated—became increasingly important. In 2016, I became part of a CUNY diversity initiative, the CUNY Faculty Fellowship Publication Program, and began working with a mentor and a group of colleagues. The chapter I wrote and revised with that group provided me with structure and the confidence to write an academic book. Four of the seven original members still meet monthly. Their rigorous support, critique, and friendship are invaluable. In 2019, I received an American Council of Learned Societies (ACLS) Fellowship, which changed the trajectory of this research and made it possible for me to complete the first draft of the book. In 2021, I was awarded a $2.3 million National Science Foundation grant, and my institution gave me a small percentage to advance my own research, some of which I used to hire a developmental editor, and in 2022, I used a sabbatical year to initiate the grant-funded research and to work on this manuscript. For the unacclimated, writing an academic book is a lengthy process that requires time and money.

Motorcycle clubs are notoriously insular. Sandy's invitation and approval of the research meant that I had club approval. Notwithstanding the official processes for human subject research, which were adhered to, Sandy was the gatekeeper. The importance of a confidential, ethical research process remained one of my primary concerns, particularly because RSMC is unique, and even with the most rigorous deidentification strategies, RSMC might be known to those who are familiar with the subculture. Motorcycle clubs deem a wide array of things to be club business, and club business is strictly off-limits to anyone who is not a patched member. This kind of secrecy serves as a bonding agent, reinforcing the in-group of the club and the out-group of all nonclub members. I was afforded unprecedented access to club business, and I strive to balance secrecy with a full ethnographic rendering. There are many things I do not know about RSMC. One example is the kind of deliberation I imagine occurred behind closed doors among national officers about new prospects, the awarding of one of the three club patches, especially the coveted "center" patch, and exit and exile.

The annual business meeting was the pinnacle of club business, so when Sandy invited me to attend in 2015, I was shocked. Several members were so shocked that I was escorted *out* of my first national business meeting, only to be escorted *back in* by Sandy just before she made her entrance. When I attended again in 2016, the only woman in the room without a black leather vest, shock registered on the faces of those who were new to RSMC and were attending their first business meeting and of those who did not attend in 2015. Business meetings were *all* club business, but few, if any, details were provided regarding decisions to award or not award patches and or exit and exile, which were reserved for full-patch members or officers. I attended the annual ritual patching ceremony on three occasions, a highly restricted ceremony. Private, informal conversations with Sandy allowed me to understand things I observed, and they also allowed her to remain in control of the information I received.

Biker Semiotics and Semantics

One of the reasons this research was perceived as dangerous ethnography was that I initially used the term "outlaw motorcycle club" or "OMC" to describe my research. Among bikers, "Outlaws" refers to the one-percenter Outlaws Motorcycle Club, founded in 1936, and no other MC would want to be mistaken for or claim to be part of the Outlaws when they mean an "outlaw." In scholarship, OMCs include any motorcycle clubs that are not affiliated with the American Motorcycling Association (AMA).[12] However, all-women MCs that are not affiliated with the AMA are not counted or recognized by scholars or bikers. Women cannot be *outlaws*.

There are competing tensions regarding terminology within a niche group of individuals—motorcycle scholars and bikers. In 2015, I copresented with two members of RSMC at a motorcycle studies conference. I purposely used "outlaw" in my presentation. Motorcycle studies scholars and Dulaney, who studied OMCs and wrote a much-cited article on biker terminology, were in the room. When the question-and-answer portion of the presentation began, a male biker, who was a guest attendee, stood up and sneered, "Well, I have a big problem with *you* referring to *them* as *outlaws*." Small in stature with a scruffy gray beard, he was wearing a well-known MC patch. Since it was more a comment than a question, I responded with an explanation of why I used the terminology and recited Dulaney's definition, nodding toward Dulaney. The biker continued his rant and sat back down. Other attendees raised their hands and objected to using "veteran" and "outlaw" in the same presentation, which I did to discuss the many women veterans in RSMC, including one of the copresenters. This was a striking criticism since veterans and MCs have been inextricably linked, particularly after World War II. "You are using the term 'outlaw,' and that is precisely what we are trying to distance ourselves from at this conference," a lady biker, to use Jones's term, whispered to me later that day. While motorcycle studies might not embrace a non-established field I am referring to as "biker studies," it became abundantly clear that the problem was adding "female" or "woman" to outlaw and that it was an act of resistance.

My righteous sister copresenters also didn't like the term "outlaw" because it is too close to the name of the Outlaws Motorcycle Club. Unaccustomed to this type of presentation and venue, they seemed a bit uneasy during the question-and-answer period. After the presentation, I called Sandy and relayed the story, which I am certain she had already heard. Bikers are known for their tests of new recruits—or in this case, of the Writer and the way I would present the club and myself. Sandy was uncharacteristically congratulatory when I told her what had happened. She suggested I come up with my own terminology if the existing term "outlaw MC" did not fit, and eventually I did: "righteous sister" and "women's motorcycle club."

The lady biker's comment also verbalized something that was deeply rooted in popular culture—women can be (respectable) motorcyclists and be part of riding clubs like the Motor Maids or Harley Owners Group (HOG) chapters, but they cannot be *outlaws* or *bikers*. This distancing began with the press surrounding the 1947 Hollister Gypsy Motorcycle Tour, which erased women bikers and righteous sisters from the birth of the bad boy / motorcycle outlaw. The quest for respectability and separation of the "good" motorcyclists from the "bad" bikers was an articulated motive of some of the conference organizers. The latter is a domain restricted to men. Dulaney, a biker and a professor, was highly respected by the conference organizers and journal editors and appears as an "expert" in a variety of news outlets. He used "outlaw" to describe a wide range of men-only MCs. A few other male presenters used the term to describe men's outlaw motorcycle clubs (OMCs), and there was no contestation or debate. One presenter used "outlaw motorcycle gangs" (OMGs) to refer to one-percenter MCs. No protests. What seemed to rile nearly everyone up was referring to an all-women motorcycle club as an *outlaw* motorcycle club and providing an origin story strikingly similar in form and function to the one told of the post–World War II MCs.

When descriptive labels previously only applied to men are applied to women, they take on new meaning. The conference also laid bare the gendered nature of who has the power to apply these labels. Similar to studies on women punks (LeBlanc [1999] 2006), women racist groups (Blee [1991] 1992, 2002), and sororities (Turk 2004), *Righteous Sisterhood* presents women's motorcycle clubs as realms of action within a male-dominated subculture; they appear like nodes of feminist resistance while also reifying some of the troubling aspects of MCs. These groups rose up, adopting many of the male counterparts' argot, norms, rites and rituals, and identities, and they have lasted as outliers in some cases (righteous sisters, punks, and racists), while sororities became mainstream counterparts to fraternities much more rapidly. Such groups embrace *sisterhood* as a gatekeeping mechanism and as a way to impress lifelong solidarity among its members. In this book, I chose to move the focus away from "outlaw" and instead use "righteous sister." I claim "righteous," a term of respect within all-male MCs, as an adjective and a noun as resistance.

Although Sandy and I agreed with respect to the term "outlaw" in 2015, our relationship evolved from 2011. At that time, she had been exasperated with what she perceived as my inattention to semiotics and semantics. She said, "You're all over the place. You're confusing one-percenter women with biker women. They're two totally different things. You're going to get two totally different answers. Women don't matter in the one-percenter world. Seriously." I pushed her on the issue, and she described her socialization as a young wife of a one-percenter by saying,

> I learned to be quiet and stay in the background, but it just became too hard to be quiet. "YOU! IN THE POOL," a club member shouts. "Really? I had no plans to go there." Then my husband ran over and said, "What did you do now? Just get in the pool."

Sandy's transformation from a one-percenter woman to a righteous sister who runs an international all-women's motorcycle club (in both cases married to a one-percenter) is highlighted in this book. In her first marriage, she was a one-percenter woman, and in the second, she was a righteous sister. This could not have occurred on her own—through her words and actions and the participation of hundreds of women over the years, she created a space of appearances, a political sphere for herself and other women to ride their motorcycles; engage in "Sister Time" through myriad rites of passage, ceremonies, events, and communication channels; and have political agency. Today, she jumps in the pool for no biker.

Nicknames, inside jokes, and club rituals that are closed off to nonmembers are all mechanisms through which individual members can exhibit righteousness and by which the sisterhood is strengthened. Many bikers say MC life is "simple" and based on "respect," "righteousness," or "brotherhood/sisterhood," but I challenge this rhetorical simplicity. It is a highly regimented, nuanced social world that is incredibly difficult to navigate and purposely so because this helps to maintain the solidarity of the group while providing a lifelong quest for righteousness among its members and a promise of lifelong commitment. In RSMC, the language of marriage is used to describe the permanent union between an individual and the club, but there are almost constant transgressions leading to sanctions, exits, and even exiles, all of which reaffirm righteousness and sisterhood.

In an era of heightened awareness of sexual harassment, catapulted into mainstream media with the #MeToo movement, and a national racial reckoning in the summer of 2020, in the wake of the murder of George Floyd in Minneapolis, how does a group of women who have seemingly acquiesced to the patriarchal and racist structure of the MC world show us anything outside of the stereotypical, and well-documented, racist misogyny already synonymous with bikers? As a group, RSMC reaffirms many of the troublesome tenets of this world simply by being part of it, but they have also been able to negotiate a distinctively womanly space within this world that is both recognized and respected, albeit limited in crucial ways. These righteous sisters provide a lens through which to understand class, race, and structural changes in the United States and also within their own political sphere and space of appearances.

Disrupting the predominant dualism of the hard-bitten one-percenter woman and the respectable woman motorcyclist, *Righteous Sisterhood* posits a new category—the righteous sister—and also provides an in-depth look at white, heterosexual, middle-aged, and senior women with varying educations and professions, who mostly lean politically libertarian or Republican, some of whom have varying disabilities. Although the members of the RSMC are diverse in education, class, background, geographic origin, and family structure, the draw of both righteousness and sisterhood is a prime motivating factor. Few had criminal records or backgrounds, and few wanted to patch in for protection; rather, the quest for *righteous sisterhood* is about finding individual excellence and camaraderie. For RSMC, members serve the club's interests by raising money, garnering publicity for philanthropy and activism, increasing membership, and solidifying an all-women MC that is recognized and accepted in the larger male-dominated subculture.

Breakdown of the Parts

In Chapter 1, I argue that the biker patches serve as sacred objects necessary to the material culture of the club and its concept of nationhood and citizenship. The patches create and reinforce social solidarity and loyalty to the biker nation. Through the lens of political sociology and political theory, RSMC is examined as a nation-state with citizenship requirements, ritual ceremonies, a hierarchy, and an electoral process. I argue that RSMC provides a space of appearances for women who might not otherwise have access to this space and reproduces the same kind of stratification and inequality found in contemporary society.

Chapter 2 centers on the initiation and sponsorship processes and the path to becoming a full member of RSMC. I develop a conceptual framework of sisterhood by critically examining other types of citizenship in all-female groups, particularly those that developed as responses to being excluded from male-only groups. Sisterhood becomes a mechanism of social solidarity but also one of social control. The stages of socialization and sponsorship are described and analyzed through primary sources and ethnographic research.

In Chapter 3, relying on extensive participant observation, I describe the structure of RSMC by delineating a number of elements required for righteous sisters. These elements include traditional biker and motorcycle events like annual rides, philanthropic events, and motorcycle awareness, as well as elements that are unique to RSMC, such as elaborate gift-giving ceremonies, modes of communication, and awards. Play and work are threaded throughout and together form an overarching concept of what it means for a group of women with a common interest to create such a tightly knit social bond within a highly regimented structural apparatus.

In Chapter 4, I examine political exile from RSMC, a relatively unexplored topic across groups and subcultures. The severing of the sisterhood is profound, and although ex–righteous sisters are not stateless in a literal sense, they have lost both their space of appearances and their sisterhood. Using ethnographic strategies and autoethnography to describe my own exile, I systematically situate exile within a larger theoretical framework and expand it.

The epilogue examines the lessons learned from this ethnographic project and broadens the lessons about righteous sisters to the broader demographic RSMC overwhelmingly represents. I briefly look at RSMC during the COVID-19 pandemic in 2020–2021, tying RSMC's public communications and responses to the pandemic as well as the future of RSMC into the larger political theory underlying this group. A brief discussion of the spaces needed for further research and the future of RSMC concludes *Righteous Sisterhood*.

Righteous Sisterhood blurs boundaries and dichotomies by describing a group of women who have created an all-women biker nation, but a central question is the group's success as an equal in the MC world and as a liberatory female space. In many ways, the women remain outsiders with somewhat muted political voices. It seems fitting then that several of Hannah Arendt's key theoretical contributions shape *Righteous Sisterhood*. Arendt's legacy at the New School for Social Research (NSSR), my alma mater, where she was a philosophy professor from 1967 until her death in 1975, is vast. She understood being an outsider. Arendt's then chair actively campaigned against her appointment, in spite of the fact that she studied with Martin Heidegger, because she had not "remained faithful to her teacher's orthodox approach to phenomenology" (Freidlander 2019:273). According to the late Richard Bernstein, eminent Arendt scholar, NSSR philosophy professor, and then dean for whom I worked as a work-study graduate student, "Arendt expresses what was always fundamental for her and should be fundamental for us—the desire of people to have their voices heard in public, to become genuine participants in shaping their political life" (2018:115). Through extensive ethnography, I examine the political life of one club and the public they create for righteous sisters, and while many things I uncovered call into question Arendt's ideal realm of action, through a creative and constitutive process, RSMC formed and has lasted for four decades as a political community, multiplying the occasions for women to win "immortal fame" and offering a "remedy for the futility of action and speech" (Arendt [1958] 1998:197). While RSMC is not a feminist organization (indeed, they would not use the term to describe themselves), it can be seen as a response to women seeking recognition and immortality among their peers.

1

CITIZENSHIP IN THE BIKER NATION

A Patching Ceremony

A woman puts her hand on *The Book of Sisters*, recites an oath of allegiance, solemnly signs her name in *The Book*, and is handed a lit candle before she takes her place among a short line of newly inducted women who stand in the middle of a large circle. The circumference is made up of full-patch members, who have all been patched in the same way. A group of women sit in folding chairs in rows outside one side of the circle; these women are either "support" members or women who have been accepted as members and hope to someday gain the full patch and entrance to the inner circle. These initiates are referred to as "prospects" in the MC world. The large industrial space is totally dark except for the candles held by those in the circle and a small light off to the side for the mistress of ceremonies, who performs off-stage (behind the bar) and functions as a "voice of God" narrator. The silence is deafening. Her voice, low and ceremonious, guides the participants through a scripted series of steps to perform the initiation ritual. In this sacred and closed ceremony, initiates receive the large center patch that displays RSMC's trademarked logo and marks their new status as full-patch members.

Women who are approved for membership through an online application and review process are immediately considered a "sister" and part of the community of women, but full-patch sisters have more status and are given more respect. The patching ceremony is closed to outsiders, and my approval to observe was fraught: I was seated inside and then asked to leave, until

Sandy confirmed that I could observe as she made her grand entrance, and I was hurried back inside. I observed three patching ceremonies between 2016 and 2019. The first time I observed, I hardly took a breath. The level of solemnity is akin to a funeral, but the simultaneous anticipation of those in the rows who do not know if they will be called up and initiated is perhaps more like a Women's National Basketball Association draft pick as women anxiously wait to hear their names called. The anxious anticipation is part of the performance all the women engage in, knowingly and unknowingly.

Once the doors are reopened and the sunlight floods back into the space, many women have tearstained faces, and a receiving line forms, with each newly inducted member awaiting hugs and kisses from the other full-patch members and the prospects whose names were not called. Festivities follow, with music, dancing, food, and drinks. The newly inducted members use safety pins to pin their center patches on until it's their turn at the sewing machine, which is operated by the club seamstress and placed in the corner of the clubhouse. Each newly patched woman walks a bit taller. Her three, four, five, or more years of proving herself worthy have been formally and publicly recognized by the nation. A small cadre of women who were eligible in years to become full-patch members but were not called into the circle try not to show their disappointment as they congratulate their full-patch sisters. They will have to wait another year because full patches are only awarded at nationals, an annual gathering of all members of the nation. Prospects with only one or two years of membership enter the ceremony knowing they will not be patched, and the ceremony reinforces their commitment to be patched in. New prospects witnessing their first patching are overwhelmed with emotion. Although some prospects are meeting the other sisters for the first time at nationals, they feel part of the secret society and the sisterhood.

This ritual appears pagan, occultist, and at odds with the overarching mainstream Christian practices prevalent in the club, and the ritual and space can be likened to several forms of religious practices. It is a rebirth, of sorts, and the "body" of RSMC welcomes its newest members, as they might in a baptism ceremony. Like the mikvah where women bathe in sacred waters in an Orthodox Jewish conversion, this is a female-held space, and once the ritual is completed, a new identity is conferred and made visible. There is no water or blood, nor are there other bodily fluids, such as the excrement and urine in Thompson's ([1966] 1999) description of a Hells Angels MC initiation ritual. Rather, the candle's flickering flame in the darkness symbolizes the women's place in the nation. Light and darkness are ritualized and starkly contrasted so that the patched women serve as the light amid the darkness. This elaborate patching ceremony formally marks a change in status within the club while simultaneously reaffirming each full-patch member's commitment and sense of belonging, and it highlights the secrecy, sanctity, and exclusivity of membership for both full members and those waiting their turn to enter the literal inner circle.

Despite the overt religious symbolism in the patching ceremony, this ritual is primarily a political ceremony that confers citizenship in the club. The seventy-five-year history of MC patching is one of exclusion, specifically racial and gender exclusion under the guise of brotherhood or, more recently, sisterhood, where the familial terms mask a rigid nationalist approach to group membership. In the early days of MCs in the United States, iron crosses and swastikas were displayed by outlaw bikers, and many, perhaps most, MCs are still racially segregated in the twenty-first century. Moreover, racial and gender violence has long been attributed to clubs. Some women wear "property of" patches to indicate their relationship to a specific club member (the individual's name would be underneath the top rocker) or a specific club (the club's name would be underneath the top rocker). This type of "ol' lady" proclaims her allegiance through ownership to the individual man or the club as a whole. Although the MC I discuss in this book has come a long way from the property patch, it mirrors societal shifts toward libertarianism, white supremacy, isolationism, and populism, which complicate a narrative of progress and sisterhood. To situate it neatly as a feminist turn for women in the MC world would be to ignore the actions and stated thoughts of group members, and my use of the term "citizenship" here indicates a deeper commitment to statist thinking that is not openly acknowledged but that nevertheless rules their beliefs and actions.

The interdependencies between MCs have a yearslong and complex history. The increasingly violent MC subculture of the 1960s paved the way for decades of violence among one-percenters and solidified the importance of the accompanying symbols of one-percenter clubs. Three-piece patches, one-percenter patches, MC cubes, and other such symbols sewn onto biker gear were at the center of this identity. Patches were the most visible symbols of citizenship in these nations, and they were tightly controlled. For RSMC to become a three-piece patch MC—in other words, for the RSMC to set itself up as a legitimate "nation" and political equal among others—a significant amount of interclub politicking was required. Nearly twenty years after it was founded (this time frame is intentionally vague), RSMC changed from a one-patch club to a three-patch MC, indicating the constraints on these women's actions and the importance they place on being acknowledged by MCs. The two decades of lead time gave RSMC time to establish themselves and avoid the extremely violent turf wars that occurred between MCs in the 1980s and early 1990s. Once the interpersonal situations between other MCs became favorable, the RSMC adhered to the established protocols and requested to separate their patches into a three-piece patch, which involved approval by the regional Coalition of Clubs (COC), a group that consists of MCs, one-percenter MCs, and riding clubs (RCs).[1] A three-piece patch is deeply symbolic, demanding that its wearers be respected by other bikers and project an appropriate biker persona. The parallels to many kinds of group formations are clear, but the comparison to nation-states is particularly appropriate given the history of the RSMC's establishment. One path to a three-piece patch in the MC world is to align one's club with a larger, three-piece MC; smaller MCs, both men's and women's clubs, operate as satellite biker nations whose members wear the colors of the dominant MC and are under its jurisdiction and protection. In the biker world, these are referred to as "bitch clubs," and in governmental parlance, these clubs are akin to protectorates, colonies, or other kinds of nonsovereign occupied territories. In contrast, Sandy wanted RSMC to be established as a sovereign nation. Since there were few, if any, other stand-alone three-piece-patch women-only clubs, this required negotiations, political maneuvering, and biding time for Sandy and her sisters. Changes had to be made to their original plans; for example, instead of a geographic location, as would be typical for men's clubs, the MC claims an ideal on its bottom rocker.[2] Legitimacy within the world of MCs was important to Sandy, and in order to be legitimate, she had to have her own seat at the tables where regional and national club presidents gathered. Territorial exclusivity was out of the question, so she made a brilliant compromise and claimed an ideal instead of a place, and despite being uninterested in and even opposed to larger feminist conversations, she placed a feminist ideal at the center of their club identity.

While RSMC wearing a three-piece patch challenges the patriarchal structure that was cemented in the 1960s, it also reifies and legitimates this structure by its very participation. Other well-known women's clubs that were also established in the 1980s, such as Dykes on Bikes and the Sirens, wear one-piece patches and work to actively separate themselves from the territorial nature of MCs by avoiding altogether the bottom rocker and what it signifies. The RSMC is distinct from those other women-centric groups because it remains within the purview of, and exists with the permission of, men's clubs without appearing to seriously question their authority or standing. However, the move to claim an ideal instead of a geographic location has within it the seeds of a real usurpation of power. Sandy said at one point that she would like to have "worldwide" embroidered on the RSMC bottom rocker. I raised my eyebrow, skeptical, questioning. She said flatly, "We could do that now." This signals a consolidation of power and membership, flouting the territorial notion of claiming a particular space and rather laying the RSMC's claim on the world. This rogue nation, which established itself meekly, circumvented future expansion issues by avoiding territory altogether.

Sandy and her RSMC are products of our times and reflections of larger global political trends that we can track from the club's inception to today.

Chapter 1 draws connections between RSMC and a wave of global populism and explores the lived experience of women bikers as citizens of a biker nation by virtue of their membership in RSMC. The use of a feminist ideal in the RSMC's terms remains separate from any broadening of gender, sexual, and political identity formations; at the same time, its use, and the adoption of a three-piece patch described earlier, gives an incredible power to populist movements against the established status quo, allowing RSMC to dream of putting a term as big (but still narrowly and apolitically defined) as "worldwide" on their patch, which would challenge the hegemony of every MC at once. But we must acknowledge that this particular populist movement derives its power from leaving the governing hierarchies of power unquestioned. It derives its strength from the same system that it seeks to disrupt. This is not political revolution or change but a kind of reestablishment of conservative social and hierarchical values. Sandy, as the new queen of such a system, would be, and is, not much different from the old kings she seeks to dislodge.

Like conceptions of the nation and belonging in global populism, MCs tend to have a strong us-versus-them mentality—what the Nazi theorist Carl Schmitt ([1932] 1966:26) described as the distinction between "friend and enemy." For the RSMC, this mentality became apparent with respect to perceived internal and external threats. The populist conception of the nation and the "friend and enemy" distinction also became apparent with the exclusion of members because of their racial or ethnic background or their sexual orientation. Participant observation research from 2010 to 2019 gave me insight into the political beliefs of RSMC's members during two transformative U.S. presidential administrations—the Obama and Trump administrations—and into the ways that national political trends are reflected in RSMC policies, procedures, and membership.

In contrast to other books and articles on the subject of biker culture in the United States, this analysis focuses on the women-focused RSMC, and male-centric MCs broadly are a point of comparison in discussions of the rituals and paths toward full citizenship. I broadly avoid repeating the well-known abuses of power, particularly sexual but broadly violent, that characterize the world of men bikers. The RSMC is not a feminist ideal, but it does operate as a corrective to the kinds of stereotypical biker cultures still governing the norms of the predominantly male-only MCs today. In this sense, my own politics and analytic decisions are integral to this depiction of women in a quasi-national, patch-oriented, male-dominated world. Briefly, the abuses of male power in a plethora of sectors have been highlighted by the #MeToo movement, and the misogyny within MCs has been documented in film and television as well as through descriptions of sexual acts in some of the one-percenter MCs (Queen 2005; Thompson [1966] 1999). A multitude of examples of rape and sexual abuse within the subculture have been commercialized for public consumption in articles, books, and films. Women's presence at key historical events, such as the 1947 Hollister Gypsy Tour, was minimized and sexualized by the national press (Hoiland 2018), setting the stage for decades of erasure. Through extensive participation observation research, this monograph centers the experiences of righteous sisters and sisterhood and in doing so highlights the contradictions that emerge between freedom and constraint, women's power and subservience, and belonging and exile, to name a few, which both individuals and RSMC face. It also troubles the simplistic binaries that have characterized biker women for nearly a century. Unlike popular conceptions of bikers and women involved in the biker world, members of RSMC are encouraged to nurture other identities outside their status as a righteous sister, such as mother, grandmother, employee, and romantic partner, and to maintain dual citizenship between their biker life and their civilian life. And yet their complete commitment to the club at the cost of other kinds of loyalties, the rigid culture of exclusion when club rules are even mildly questioned, and their overall adherence to cultural groups like the COC indicate that any advances this rogue nation makes are tempered by their loyalty to the extant structures of the biker world.

A Brief History of RSMC

At various points in history, women have fought for their own counterparts to fraternal associations such as fraternities, racist organizations, and different sports teams, including soccer, basketball, and baseball. Scholars have examined *sisterhoods* in sororities (Gillan 2016; Bauer 2005; Handler 1995; Turk 2004), sorority rituals (Callais 2002), and racist organizations, such as the Ku Klux Klan (Blee [1991] 1992:129) and contemporary neo-Nazi groups like United White Sisters (Blee 2002:142), as well as among punks (LeBlanc [1999] 2006:92). Women's MCs are relatively new and have not yet been studied or examined. The anthropologist Barbara Joans, author of *Bike Lust*, writes, "According to male writers, women are peripheral to the biker world. Necessary but peripheral. They are also classified in relation to men, rather than in relation to bikes" (2001:89). Angela McRobbie and Jenny Garber describe a similar phenomenon among motorbike girls who "remained excluded from the central core of the subculture—the motorbike itself" ([1977] [1993] 2006: 216). The peripheral status of these organizations helped RSMC get its start as a women's riding club in the 1980s, with the full support of Sandy's then husband, a one-percenter in an MC who was engaged in some of the violent turf wars of the 1980s and 1990s. Creating a women's riding club was a safe and less controversial way to enter into the violent masculinist world Sandy knew so well as an ol' lady. She put an advertisement in the paper with her phone number and garnered several interested women.

These original members were *bikers*; they had their own motorcycles, they were skilled riders, and several could wrench, or tune up and fix, their own bikes. Like its founder, many came to RSMC with experiences with male MCs as ol' ladies, hangarounds, or friends of the club. The original members were working-class women—women who lived Dolly Parton's "9 to 5" (1980) and then worked a "second shift" (Hoschild [1989] 2012) at home, were married, and had children. As blue- and pink-collar workers, these women found freedom and escape through motorcycling and connected with other similarly situated women on the road, at restaurants, and at weekend getaways for a few minutes, a few hours, or a few days. Most garnered the tacit approval of their ol' men / biker partners, who operated within an entirely misogynist subculture. Most of the original members were in their twenties and thirties when they joined, and photographs of youthful biker women in leather chaps with their motorcycles and huge smiles pervade the clubhouse and photo albums.

From its onset, RS was dedicated to philanthropic endeavors that benefited women and children, with the stated goal of a "greater purpose" as a group than just riding together, as described by Sandy. Nationals and the patching ceremony were part of the early days; the club was smaller, it was less formal, and by all accounts it seemed to center on riding. A longtime member said that members were "patched within a year" when RS was still a one-piece patch club. Another said, "Back then, we did a lot of probating. You didn't necessarily have to wait until nationals. Patches were given out as deserved. [Sandy] would watch and make sure." Many stories of the early rides and nationals were shared during interviews and are delineated in Chapter 3, but righteousness in the early days revolved around riding and laughing, with an endless array of jokes, stunts, and near arrests that are depicted in dozens of photo albums and readily conveyed in interviews.

As the club grew in number and in new and ever-expanding geographic locations, it became more formalized, and the political stakes grew as RS had to negotiate with MCs in new states and in new countries over the ensuing decades. The club added a three-piece patch and the MC cube to their vests in the early 2000s, as the result of a lengthy negotiated process with other MCs and tacit approval from the one-percenter clubs. From the documents and several formal and informal interviews, I can infer the presence of bureaucratization and rationalization in initiation and hierarchy. Initiation could take place in one year for a riding club, but for an MC, it became four to five years on paper and often two to three years in reality. This shift to being an MC led to a more public profile for RSMC, with some very public dismissals. Male bikers and biker scholars have publicly said that female patch clubs are "not *real* three-piece patch clubs" (my emphasis).[3]

The three-piece patch also caused new tensions for members in states and countries in which the approval did not extend; while there are regional and national bodies, these agreements often end up relying solely on the approval of a handful of one-percenter MCs. Because the MC world is so heavily masculinist and misogynist, observing and understanding how gender and sisterhood operate daily is crucial to understanding what it means to the women to be righteous, what that looks like within the larger subcultural world, and why women would want to become righteous sisters.

Patches as Sacred Symbols

Initiation into a biker nation is often a lengthy and tedious process; in the United States, it typically includes an application, a waiting period of one-to-five years, an interview, and someone (usually a patched member) to vouch for the initiate and/or sponsor them. During the initiation period, prospects are visibly not yet citizens because their leather vest does not have a completed set of patches. In some one-percenter MCs, a prospect patch is sewn on the backs of their vests. There are also many tests of character and a series of tests regarding knowledge of the club and club rules, which take many different forms in MCs; Chapter 2 gives several examples to describe the gauntlet bikers go through before they are made full members through the socialization process. It is the duty of full-patch members to pass the knowledge of the club and its rules along to prospects, and a prospect is often assigned a full-patch mentor, who is jointly responsible for the prospect's actions and behavior. After a period of time, the top patch, or "rocker," which includes the name of the MC, is issued. The next patch to be issued is the bottom rocker, which includes the location of the MC chapter (or in the case of RSMC, an ideal). Clubs claim a city, state or province, or a country. As recorded in police actions, news reports, and historical archives in small towns across the United States, territorial disputes have led to serious conflicts—for example, the violence in Waco, Texas, in May 2015. In that case, one club added Texas to their bottom rocker without the approval of the dominant one-percenter club in the state, and the act was viewed as one of aggression and disrespect. The incident ended with nine deaths and 177 arrests, which underscores the significance attached to patches, claims to geographic territory, and biker protocol regarding other clubs. Sandy's delicate and savvy handling of the bottom rocker becomes more significant in light of the intensely violent history of such "nations."

As more patches are added, one's status increases within the club, and they are also an outward symbol, particularly to other clubs, of one's time and commitment. The final back patch is the center patch, which is the trademarked (in most cases) club logo that indicates full membership. While U.S. citizenship is conferred through a public ceremony, biker citizenship is conferred through private ritualistic ceremonies whose only audience is the club itself, such as the one described at the beginning of this chapter. While the citizenship ceremonies in New York became severely limited during the pandemic, the biker ceremonies went on as usual, but there are more similarities than differences between the two kinds of "patching ceremonies." As many new citizens pose in front of the American flag with their Certificate of Citizenship, bikers also pose for photographs with their newly full-patched vests and their brothers or sisters in the MCs. The investment in belonging is palpable, as is the relief when the induction is complete. And, as in any such ritual, there are sometimes surprising upsets that, rather than reducing the power of the ritual, further cement its importance to the group as a whole. In what follows, one such incident is described, highlighting the secrecy and power inherent within RSMC's hierarchy and its ability to create citizens and maintain noncitizens.

Like national flags, every element on a biker's vest is deeply symbolic. Besides the top rocker indicating the club name and the bottom rocker with the location, other patches such as the MC cube, the one-percenter patch, and other club-specific indicators further differentiate the individual and the type of club. In biker subcultures a one-percenter patch indicates the highest status, and wearers include the Hells Angels MC, the Bandidos MC, the Pagans MC, and the Outlaws MC, to name a few of the largest one-percenter MC clubs with home bases in the United States and subsidiary global chapters (with a history that supersedes the more recent use of one-percenter to criticize the elites). Patches indicate status not only pictorially but also materially. The back patches convey the group status as an MC within the subculture and a general measure of the individual's time in the club. The degree of fading or sun bleaching of the patch and jacket indicates how much the individual rides and how long someone has been a member. Vibrantly colored patches are the sure sign of a newcomer or a member who doesn't spend time riding in the sun. Also, both front and back patches convey individual standing within the group. Thus, patches and the jackets they are on are considered sacrosanct and inviolate.

Further echoing the constructions of the modern nation-state, front patches are modeled after military uniforms. Front patches show an individual's name, which is almost always a club nickname, rank (if any), and accolades (some clubs have special patches for the number of years served), as well as different bike runs and events one has attended. National ranks include national president, national vice president, national sergeant-at-arms, national road captain, national enforcer, and chapter ranks with the same titles. There are state chapters (e.g., Texas), city chapters (e.g., Los Angeles), and regional chapters (e.g., a combination of states if there are not enough members to form a chapter in a city or if proximity is an issue). The governing structure is similar to the federal and state system in the United States, except there are many different MC nations within any given state, territory, or country, and each chapter answers to its own national president and executive board.

Bikers have described "property of" patches as social/cultural symbols akin to wedding rings, but they are much more visible. A ring or a property patch is an outward symbol of commitment, they say. Some male and female bikers defend the "property of" patch as something that prevents conflicts between members. Several of the women in RSMC were ol' ladies who had worn property patches and now wear their own three-piece patches. This transformation from second-class citizenship with no rights and privileges to full citizenship is generally viewed as growth and transformation. I observed a few women who wore "property of" patches at events and spoke to several who used to wear a property patch. One woman wearing a "property of" an Outlaws MC patch (it included the member's name) attended a National Coalition of Clubs (NCOM) meeting in 2019. She appeared to be significantly younger than her ol' man, wore her long blond hair in low pigtails, and had high platform shoes. I did not see her utter a word to anyone other than him, nor did she leave his side except to use the restroom. This stood in stark contrast to the righteous sisters who were at NCOM. The "property of" patch commanded respect, but it also ensured the woman would be totally isolated. The RSMC patches did not command the same respect, but they ensured one would never see a sister alone.

In the accounts of one-percenter clubs, there are no quality interviews or observations of women who wear the "property of" patch, and the most extensive descriptions come from men who were members of one-percenter clubs. William Queen, undercover FBI agent and former Mongol, said, "For many of these women, being 'property' of the gang is the one thing that gives their lives meaning. . . . For all the sexual abuse and beatings they're subjected to, there's also a sense of belonging, a sense of power" (2005:66–67). He described the protective mechanism of the patch as being "untouchable to the world at large" because wearers have the "whole Mongol Nation" behind them (2005:66–67). Throughout his book, Queen describes the singular importance of being a Mongol and the extensive physical and emotional abuse male Mongols are subjected to, so the key differentiating factor seems to be the sexual abuse, not the property patch itself. By virtue of wearing any three-piece MC patch, all members become "property" of the club. Queen's gendered characterization is troubling precisely because his undercover work subjected him firsthand to what club members go through. Men as well as women, patch holders and "property of" patch holders are protected by the patch, but it also makes them vulnerable. While the violence of one-percenter clubs like the Mongols and the all-male MC I observed is quite different from that of RSMC, the sense of being untouchable is observable, and many full-patch members describe it as a dominant emotion.

Anthropologist Daniel Wolf, who like Queen became a patched member of an MC but with the club's full understanding that he was a social scientist writing a book about the MC lifestyle from the inside, said of the "property of" patch: "An ol' lady wears a property badge as a matter of choice and prestige," and "an exceptional ol' lady may go so far as to have the property badge tattooed on her shoulder or some other area of her anatomy" ([1991] 2000: 153). Wolf's synopsis followed a lengthy chapter on the role of ol' ladies within MCs as both "the dominant female force in the outlaw-club subculture" and also "the principal threat to the solidarity of the brotherhood because of the competition she offers" ([1991] 2000:150). Wolf's observations run counter to mine, as I noticed a distinct lack of agency in the "property of" patch wearers, which mirrors the overall lack of free will and strict adherence to group norms that I saw within the MC world overall. He refers to the patch as a "badge" rather than its usual nomenclature, which might reflect the argot of Canadian MCs more than an academic word choice, but he also describes patching as "a matter of choice and prestige," showing that in an extremely hierarchical social world, adopting this outward symbol of loyalty to one particular member and club as a whole is a rational choice according to the values and norms of MCs. Furthermore, Wolf ascribes respect to the term "ol' ladies" and finds those with a tattoo to be "exceptional." In my decades-long close observation and hours of conversations with bikers from different clubs, fear was the biggest motivator, not status or prestige. Women feared their "outlaw" partner, but they also feared not being under the protection of that partner.

When I asked about the "property of" patches, Sandy responded, "Some of the women, yeah, the women do get out of it the same things that guys do, but on a different level. They have cliques, just like the guys. It's nice to have somebody that has your back. People don't fuck with you because they know you're connected. Being where I am, running my own nation, nobody has got my back but me and my sisters." The protective element of the patches is illustrated by club mottos: "All on One and One on All" for the Hells Angels (Thompson [1966] 1999:68), although today "Angels Forever, Forever Angels" is more commonly seen; "Respect Few, Fear None" for the Mongols; "God Forgives / Outlaws Don't" for the Outlaws. Thompson said the "belief in total retaliation for any offense or insult is what makes the Angels such a problem for police and so morbidly fascinating to the general public" ([1966] 1999:68). He continues: "Yet they have a very simple rule of thumb; in any argument a fellow Angel is *always right* and disagreement is an open challenge." This is written into the club charter as bylaw number 10: "'When an Angel punches a non-Angel, all other Angels will participate'" ([1966] 1999:68). The sisterhood in RSMC is less predicated on violence, although willingness and ability are ever present, so the effect is similar—untouchability and protection from the nation. And yet "property of" patches put wearers at a secondary status to full club members. Sandy proudly separates herself from such "property of" patch wearers while reiterating the protection of MCs in saying, "Nobody has got my back *but* me and my sisters" (emphasis added). This bold statement of independence from the dominant male structures of power within the biker world is complicated by her personal ties to several powerful one-percenters. As I discuss in greater detail in coming pages, Sandy's unique position within the biker world prepared and allowed her to rise to her current ability to challenge biker norms while reiterating several of the most toxic aspects of that world.

Patches provide a lens through which we can see many facets of club life, and like other sacred objects, they come with a plethora of formal and informal norms. Many of the patch rules are similar to rules for national flags: who can touch or handle them, how they are displayed and stored, and how they are retired. Crucially important to anyone encountering a one-percenter or typical MC member is that people who are not patch holders, which includes friends of the club and family members, cannot touch the patches, even during a hug, or casually brush against them. Patches can never be out of the patch holder's immediate control. For example, at a clubhouse, if it's hot and members remove their patches and hang them on the back of a chair or a coat rack, they must maintain visual contact with the patches or entrust them to another patch holder. Patches cannot touch the ground. If a club member is traveling by airplane, patches cannot go into a checked bag. Patched club members (male or female) can never be on the back of a motorcycle; they must always be riding their own motorcycles while wearing patches. If that is not possible and they have to ride on someone else's motorcycle, for whatever reason, they either turn their vest inside out or put it in the saddlebag. Only women who wear property patches can ride on the back of a bike, once again underlining their essentially second-class and dependent status within the group and to outsiders. Special protocols are in place for arrests or roadside accidents, and these vary from club to club, but the common quotient is the high level of ritualistic respect that must be shown toward the patches and any garment they are sewn onto.

One representative instance of widespread respect informs my previous comments. I interviewed a national enforcer, and he told a story about being hit by a car while riding his motorcycle with his patches on. Oddly, the driver of the car was a club brother who had run a red light while arguing with his wife in the car. The enforcer was lying on the pavement underneath his bike, and it was obvious to him and the driver of the car that his shoulder was dislocated. To tend to his club brother, the driver first called the national president, then called 911, so that half a dozen club members arrived right behind the ambulance. The enforcer described the following scene:

> The EMTs took out scissors to cut my full-patch T-shirt, but I said, "Don't fucking cut the shirt!" My brothers had already helped me take off my colors (vest), but it was a full-patch shirt, and I didn't want them to disrespect the patch like that. It hurt like hell getting that T-shirt off over my shoulder. It [shoulder] was hanging. Once it was cut off, I went onto the stretcher with no shirt on. My brothers took my colors and loaded my bike onto a trailer.

The biker responsible for the crash was chastised but not punished; the two had been friends for decades, and it was clearly an accident; most importantly, no respect was lost even though the biker was grievously injured and continued to have shoulder troubles. The incident became an ongoing joke between the two men, particularly because the driver later got divorced and his now ex-wife, an easy scapegoat, was blamed for the entire accident.

Such incidents are somewhat routine and are documented in other professional spaces. For instance, a 2014 article provides information for medical personnel who arrive at a scene similar to the one above, explaining how to identify the various types of bikers, the importance of the colors, and the potential for violence. The manual reads, "If a gang member perceives disrespect from anyone, including ED [emergency department] staff, the outcome can be deadly." It adds, "Outlaw bikers should always be treated with respect, regardless of whether their behavior warrants it" (Bosmia, Quinn, and Peterson 2014:526). The latter statement is fascinating. Shouldn't all people who come into contact with the ED be treated with respect irrespective of their behavior, whether it be fueled by drugs, alcohol, rage, mental illness, or club (or gang) affiliation? The possibility of violence is alluded to in the interview with the enforcer—if the EMTs had cut the T-shirt, there likely would have been words or potential violence between the club members and the emergency personnel. The same article describes women, in one paragraph, as "support" and says they are "generally forced into prostitution or street-level drug trafficking" and may "carry weapons or drugs for the biker or members of his club" (2014:526). It is not clear where any of these "facts" are derived from, and neither the authors or the emergency personnel quoted in the article leave any space for an all-women's MC or righteous sisters who crash while wearing their patches. Sandy and her road captains, for example, have an elaborate emergency protocol that includes a calling tree and on-site assistance whenever possible. Several high-ranking members with extensive ED experience from service in the military, from fire service, or as EMTs created these RSMC protocols to protect the women bikers and their patches.

This episode underlines the importance of club regalia, but it also points to the ways in which a club operates as a commercial concern. Club colors are highly regulated once members are approved by leadership for a patch or patches. For RSMC, what the price one pays for patches to who sews the patches themselves and who sews them onto the vests, it's a business within a business. One of its national officers is an embroiderer who sews all club patches. They must be identical, and the colors must be perfect. She also receives orders through her business from other clubs. There is a markup so MCs can make money on the patches after paying the embroiderer, and prices range from ten to fifty dollars. The club embroiderer does screen printing and produces T-shirts, tank tops, sweatshirts, and all kinds of merchandise for full-patch members, regular members, and friends of the club, and a small store opens for business during club events, parties, and nationals. Prices are similar to other biker apparel, but there is a total monopoly on the economy of patched apparel. Many clubs sell items through their websites and at their parties for members and outsiders. One popular item for friends of the club and guests at one MC was an "I Survived a Night at the [name of the MC] Clubhouse." Because of the otherwise exclusive nature of clubs, such items are popular among nonmembers.

The RSMC promoted and pushed merchandise in a way the all-men MCs did not. One example is the possibility of layaway in the RSMC store. Women could purchase items on credit and then make payments. Additionally, newer members could purchase full-patch items in advance, and the store would hold them until they gained that rank. As mentioned, all full-patch items (those with the center patch) were meticulously tracked as inventory.

When any of the rules or protocols are violated, one highly visual sanction can be for the club to take back a member's patches. This publicly shames the individual since all members wear their patches during club business meetings, parties, runs, and so on, and it also operates as a strong deterrent to the rest of the members. A one-percenter said this about his violent past and the repercussions with his club: "I was hitting presidents from other clubs, VPs, sergeants-at-arms, like I am supposed to go back and tell my prez that you said something. At one point, I put them on Velcro. After like fuckin' ten years, they were like, 'Let's just give him his fucking patches. He cannot stop hitting people—he has a problem.'" He was revered and feared by his own club because of his unpredictable, violent outbursts, which simultaneously made him a valuable asset as an enforcer. He called it a Catch-22 in the interview, referring to the fact that although his behavior served the club, they didn't like their lack of control over him. This is analogous to Jeremy Bentham's concept of "deep play," as described by Clifford Geertz in the classic anthropological study on Balinese cockfighting, "in which the stakes are so high that it is, from his utilitarian standpoint, irrational for men to engage in it at all" (1973:7)—and yet, as in Geertz's example, here too this man not only engaged and enjoyed "deep play," but he also recognized the Catch-22 of his violent outbursts. The stakes are indeed high, and death is an accepted and probable outcome for these types. Some clubs have created nomad chapters or what one biker referred to as "prison chapters," referring to the large numbers of bikers who have spent time in prison, to counteract the benefits and risks of having such maverick members. Nomads have no home chapter, no geographic location. In many cases, the bottom rocker reads "Nomad." They are accountable to the club's national president, but they have significantly more freedom and less club protection.

Patches are an outward representation of one's commitment to a particular biker nation, as represented by the center patch, and also of a larger biker ethos. Patches communicate status, rank, and time in the club, as well as different activities such as fundraisers, rides, and rallies. For the handful of women who once donned a property patch and now sport their own three-piece patch, the difference is monumental, and their commitment to their new nation is consequently stronger. Consumerism supports RSMC and the club members who produce the club-approved items, and the norms surrounding club merchandise ensure a solid business, a monopoly over production and sales, and total control over club merchandise. Egregious violations of club norms can result in losing one's patches temporarily or permanently; thus patches are positive sanctions for behavior that is beneficial to the nation and also can be taken away as a negative sanction.

A Political Community

For Benedict Anderson, a nation "is an imagined political community—and imagined as both inherently limited and sovereign" ([1983] 2016:6). Motorcycle clubs use "nation" to describe themselves as a group, and the language and rituals surrounding all facets of this social world are analogous to those of citizens in a nation. They are political communities that control physical territories whose geographic boundaries are limited and often contested. Describing the Hells Angels, Victor Turner writes that although they have "opted out of the structural system," they nevertheless "constitute formal organization with complex initiation ceremonies and grades of membership emblematized by badges" ([1969] 1995:193–194). Turner states, "I prefer the Latin term 'communitas' to 'community,' to distinguish this modality of social relationship from an 'area of common living,'" and distinguishes "this 'sacred' component [that] is acquired by the incumbents of positions during the *rites de passage*, through which they changed positions" ([1969] 1995:96–97). In the case of RSMC, however, it is not Sandy playing "the role of the humbled chief"; rather, the "neophytes," or prospects, are dressed identically, they are submissive and silent, and they "submit to an authority that is nothing less than that of the total community"; with the imparted wisdom having "ontological value, it refashions the very being of the neophyte" ([1969]

1995:103). The oath new members make solidifies their citizenship in the nation, a new but parallel structural system to the one they already occupy as U.S. citizens rendering them dual citizens.

Most three-piece patch clubs are racially homogenous, contain heterosexual members, and appear to be graying along with the rest of society, with many members over fifty years of age. While some prospects are as young as eighteen, others are retired or on disability; intergenerational diversity is touted as a strength. Longtime members are given the utmost respect even if they cannot ride their motorcycle any longer or have started riding a three-wheeled motorcycle. The wide and open acceptance of disabled bodies was a constant and included not only members who experienced disability later in life but also prospects who entered the club with mobility issues or other types of disability. Becoming a biker in an MC is generally viewed as a lifetime commitment founded on sisterhood and brotherhood, although in practice there is significant membership movement in and out of RSMC, which is elaborated upon in Chapter 4.

By succumbing to the demands of RSMC, women gain sisterhood within a group of like-minded women who ride motorcycles and the status that is awarded to patch holders and officers at various levels within the hierarchy. The centrality of patches, from their significance in the initiation ritual to their meaning as fundamental material cultural objects and symbols of the nation, cannot be overstated. When RSMC became a three-piece-patch MC, it became part of a complex web of other biker nations around the world who are competing for members, power, prestige, and geographic and economic resources. It stands out as an MC, strengthening the bond of sisterhood and also remaining separate from "civilians," a word commonly used to describe nonbikers; however, most RSMC members continue to play several roles in addition to biker, such as mother, grandmother, wife/partner, or employee. Many code-switch (E. Anderson 1999) and adjust their appearance accordingly, while others wear biker apparel such as black boots, jeans, and Harley-Davidson T-shirts most of the time and work as freelancers, small business owners, or service workers, for whom that is acceptable attire. Many members are successful by societal standards, in terms of occupation, income, or education. Most are conventionally employed and are more akin to weekend warriors, although this is never openly admitted. Others live more of a biker lifestyle, working various jobs with their Harley-Davidson as their primary (and sometimes only) form of transportation. A minority fit Deborah Paes de Barros's description of a road woman, who "rejects all universal rules and categories. Her actions are specific to her place and situation. She is at turns pretty, serene, caring, and rabid and schizophrenic and free. She paints her nails red or refuses to comb her hair. She disavows all behavioral codes; she looks at the road and 'plays it as it lays'" (2004:17). Like the one-percenter

"Velcro," a road woman is valuable to RSMC, but she is far less common. Conformity is prized and respect for hierarchy demanded, and I observed far fewer misfits in RSMC.

In this, there is more social variety among the women who are citizens in the RSMC nation than in the average men's biker club. Wolf describes becoming a (male) biker as "a class-specific response to the general problem of self-actualization" ([1991] 2000:30), and Thompson calls the Hells Angels "obvious losers" ([1966] 1999:52). Class differences are evident within RSMC, creating some intraclub issues less common in all-male MCs, but the types of women who join are not uneducated or underemployed, nor are they "obvious losers" distinct from women in the rest of society. Women bikers add (rather than replace) "biker" and "righteous sister" to their repertoire of roles and statuses, and the club does not force them to choose those roles over others as most one-percenter clubs do. This difference is especially pronounced around patches in public nonbiker spaces—some righteous sisters do not wear their patches outside RSMC events, to avoid interclub tensions and violence where there are active turf disputes between one-percenter clubs. For some of the women, riding is a means of transportation, and they put thousands of miles each year on their motorcycles with or without their patches, while others seem to hardly ride at all outside of chapter rides and annual rides as a club. Aside from the black vest and patches, a member of RSMC could be indistinguishable from nonbiker women. To the contrary, many men advertise their "outlaw" citizenship and are typically recognizable by their unkempt beards, long hair, and visible tattoos. They seem to wear their patches more and generally are less adept at code-switching; rather, many embrace "biker" as their master status and work in blue-collar jobs or are self-employed or, in some cases, underemployed, unemployed, or work "off-the-books." Although many are husbands, partners, fathers, and employees, their club comes first. The transformation, then, from "civilian" to "biker" is more apparent in all-male MCs. A biker woman complicates these boundaries and clear-cut delineations. "She possesses multiple identities and no identity. 'She has no passport and too many of them'" (Paes de Barros 2004:18, citing Rosi Braidotti). Observing RSMC over an extended period of time in their natural milieu, at their clubhouse and in their homes, allowed me to see the various women who choose to be part of it and who are selected and the various ways in which they occupy their dual citizenship. There is a real diversity of perspectives and attitudes despite the assumptions one might make about such women and their chosen allegiances.

A love of motorcycles draws very different people together as a biker nation, but what seems to really unite both club members and different clubs, even rival MCs, is a pervasive sense of being under attack by a common "enemy." The 2016 incident in Waco, Texas, has resulted in what bikers describe as increased "motorcycle profiling," which entails frequently being pulled over and searched. David "Double D" Devereaux founded the Motorcycle Profiling Project as an organization dedicated to legislation to address motorcycle profiling and discrimination.[4] Double D, a white biker from Washington, maintains an incredibly robust website with dozens of articles, white papers, and press releases coded and tagged with keywords, which makes it even more troublesome that the search term "race" showed no results. It is unclear whether the irony of an organization dedicated to eradicating profiling among predominantly white bikers is lost on Double D and indicative of his unchecked white male privilege. Predominantly Black one-percenter MCs like the Chosen Few and Hispanic one-percenter MCs like the Bandidos are included on the website in articles generalizable to motorcycle profiling, but the website makes no connection between racial profiling and motorcycle profiling; rather, the predominantly white MCs are outraged that their constitutional rights are being infringed and are successfully organizing at the state level, with four states (Washington [2011], Maryland [2016], Louisiana [2019], and Idaho [2020]) having adopted anti-motorcycle-profiling laws. It is notable that no additional states have been added after Idaho passed Senate Bill 1292 on March 18, 2020. The COVID-19 pandemic and the May 25, 2020, murder of George Floyd by a white police officer in Minneapolis likely tempered lawmakers' enthusiasm for the cause. Minorities in purported "gangs" have long been targets of racial profiling, and racketeering laws have been used as both federal and state weapons against Black and Latino gang members.

Despite the lack of acknowledgment, questions of race and ethnicity shape biker clubs as profoundly as they do U.S. society overall. The Mongols MC were founded in Montebello, California, in 1969, with some accounts stating that founding members were rejected from the Hells Angels because of their Hispanic ethnicity. Although worldwide, they are based in Southern California and are composed predominantly of Hispanic members. A federal case beginning in 2008 charged the Mongols MC with Racketeer Influenced and Corrupt Organizations (RICO) Act offenses, and seventy-nine Mongols were indicted. The case culminated in a RICO indictment of the entire Mongols nation in 2013 and a renewed attempt by the states' attorney general to confiscate the trademarked patch. In March 2019, U.S. District Judge David O. Carter saw the attempt to confiscate patches as a federal overreach and a violation of the First Amendment guarantee of freedom of association and the Eighth Amendment bar of cruel and unusual punishment, saying, "Regardless of how 'potent' a symbol may be, or how much 'fear' a symbol generates, the Government cannot justify the restriction of this speech, especially given the symbols' purely associative purpose.... Though the symbol may at times function as a mouthpiece for unlawful or violent behavior, this is not sufficient to strip speech of its First Amendment protection" (quoted in Barbash and Flynn 2019). Judge Carter fined the Mongols MC $500,000 ($250,000 per RICO charge) and put the entire Mongol nation (approximately twelve thousand members) on federal probation for five years after a federal jury found the Mongols guilty of racketeering and conspiracy to engage in racketeering under RICO.

The Motorcycle Profiling Project has several articles penned by Double D urging bikers to unify against these kinds of governmental intrusions and highlighting possible ramifications for the right to bear arms and for employment, since all members were found guilty. At the National Coalition of Motorcycles (NCOM), biker nations become unified political groups by seeing a common "enemy," albeit without addressing divisions within the nation or attenuating to the racism, sexism, misogyny, or violence that is endemic within it. This was an opportunity for RSMC to publicly side with MCs, aligning nations over an issue that rarely affects RSMC because of the limited times in which members ride with their patches outside of major events, which provide some protection against harassment. Similarly, other clubs not likely to be profiled rallied behind this motorcyclist rights movement with a populist, libertarian bent.

In the 2000s, the perceived attack on patches was translated into yet another attack on biker freedom through governmental overreach. Bikers aligned with former U.S. president Donald Trump in unprecedented ways: the political action committee (PAC) Bikers for Trump, Trump's numerous appearances at biker rallies, and the extreme commodification of the alliance through T-shirts and other merchandise. The women in RSMC widely disdained Barack Obama and supported Donald Trump, both of whom were in office during this research. To my knowledge, they were not politically active as a club, and Sandy made it a general policy to avoid politics because the membership of RSMC was not uniformly right-wing, although anyone considered left-wing, liberal, or even progressive was in the extreme minority. The political focus generally stayed on their own imagined community, RSMC, and the individuals within the nation—reiterating a simplistic us-versus-them binary to ensure cohesion among diverse women.

Bodies and Structures

Riding a motorcycle is a deeply embodied physical act, and bodies are political and economic units. Michel Foucault describes the "political investment of the body" as being "bound up, in accordance with reciprocal relations, with its economic use," and he writes that the "body becomes a useful force only if it is both a productive body and a subjected body" ([1977] 1995:25–26). Motorcycle clubs make political investments in their future citizens, or "prospects," by taking the time to vet a new member and risking the club's status with a new prospect who could undermine the club's prestige with their actions or behavior. During the liminal, or prospecting, stage, bikers undergo a variety of tests, including riding with the pack, working club parties and events, and being of service to the MC, particularly to its leadership. Any special skills will be harnessed and utilized, including physical strength; financial acumen; technological prowess; leadership skills; organizational skills; first aid or medical training; bartending; advertising; construction and trade skills (such as carpentry, electrical, plumbing, and HVAC); mechanical abilities; riding safety and road skills; and traditionally domestic skills such as sewing, cooking, and cleaning. Each member contributes to the nation; few MCs keep members who are proverbial deadweight. Some bikers are financial assets, or "cash cows," who spend significant amounts of money at club events or while purchasing club merchandise. Although the illegal activities of one-percenter MCs have been widely documented, scant attention has been paid to other, legal kinds of economic utility. Some members provide service to the nation by maintaining biker clubhouses and motorcycles. Righteous sisters were constantly in motion. From improvements to a massive clubhouse and adjoining property to pointless, repetitive tasks like moving tables and chairs and then putting them back in their original positions, these docile biker bodies were always moving.

Bikers' bodies are controlled in a number of ways. They are, in fact, docile citizens of their respective nations; while the "property of" members are clearly marked as such, regular members in all clubs meet many of the aspects of "control of activity," including establishing timetables with rhythmic activities such as weekly meetings, annual runs (rides) and fundraisers, and annual parties. The patch serves as identification of a docile citizen and is heavily gendered. Women who wear a three-piece patch are particularly docile—while paradoxically carrying out many kinds of activities not typically associated with docility or passivity—because they are scrutinized by outside MCs as women and the standards within RSMC are more stringent than within all-male MCs as a result of that scrutiny. Hence, these women are caught in a double bind of femininity-antifemininity, reiterating both and neither at the same time.

Esperanza Miyake questions why the motorcycle itself is used as a "visible and visual shorthand for 'masculine' and for masculinized deviant styles" ([2018] 2020:12). Her book *The Gendered Motorcycle* explores these representations in popular and visual culture and describes the motorcycle as a "mobile technology of gender" that "[engenders] identities, relations, and practices in often problematic ways, which reinforce meanings, reproduce and re-establish dominant, normative, ideologies surrounding gender (as well as class, race, and sexuality) that have significant material and political implications" ([2018] 2020:209). When RSMC rides together in formation, it is profoundly political.

In strict two-by-two formation by rank, the column of bikers can stretch as far as the eye can see. It is a public display of power and nationhood not only through the visual image but also through the auditory roar of the engines. The bonding mechanism of group rides is described in Chapter 2, but the political function reifies the existing ideologies within the club and an outlaw mentality that includes running red lights to stay in formation.

At NCOM, one can see a variety of clubs, from one-percenter MCs to other three-piece-patch MCs and one-piece clubs, such as veterans clubs or Christian clubs. I attended in 2019 as a RSMC guest. When I went to the registration desk, a woman looked at me and said, "You must have the wrong conference," but she was quite willing to take my registration fee when I assured her that I was there for NCOM. At several points during the three-day conference, the various groups of bikers appeared to be in lockstep, bowing their heads during numerous prayers, standing during the Pledge of Allegiance and the national anthem, and applauding veterans on a number of occasions. The master of ceremonies said the goal of the convention was "freedom," telling attendees, "Fight for the man to your left and the man to your right," in spite of the presence of at least three women's MCs and several women riders. He continued: "I'm fighting for our children, children's children." The "fight" included raising awareness of motorcyclists on the road and reducing the number killed each year, addressing police harassment for patch-wearing bikers (particularly motorcycle profiling), and opposing helmet laws.

RSMC was a visibly docile body within this larger group of bikers. Ahead of NCOM, they were asked to collect survey data for the Motorcycle Profiling Project, and while this put them in a highly visible position at the entrance of the banquet, it also made their bodies particularly vulnerable to the male gaze. The master of ceremonies referred to them as the "ladies" and "gals with the iPads." A few one-percenters scoffed at them outright. If the scoff had been directed at a male attendee, it would have been an open provocation, but RSMC ignored any outward signs of disrespect and stuck to the most rigid biker protocols of behavior. The protocols are endless, but a few examples illustrate the kind of performance one engages in at NCOM. Several hours before the three-hour banquet dinner, which took place in a large hotel ballroom and functioned as both an awards ceremony and a call to action regarding specific issues and concerns, a few women began to scope out the area and reserve their spots at the dozens of available white-tableclothed tables. They saved their tables by tilting the chairs forward onto the tables' edges. The tables were selected for their visibility and proximity to the exits on either side. It was important to secure at least two ten-seat tables so the entire club could sit together. Several members posted up before the banquet to ensure no one else sat there; however, a few male bikers sat at one of the saved tables. Club members didn't confront the men but moved quickly to tip the chairs at another table instead.

At public events such as NCOM, biker protocols are strictly adhered to and enforced. A national president is treated like a foreign dignitary—they are escorted to their seat, they are protected on all sides, and they dictate the movements of their entourage. If Sandy wanted to step outside to smoke a cigarette or use the restroom, for example, two national officers would immediately follow her. This happened several times during the nearly three-hour dinner and awards ceremony. There had to be eyes on Sandy at all times, with the sergeant-at-arms acting like a Secret Service agent and with frequent eye contact among the senior officers signaling her movements and the expected movements of the nation in response.

Sandy occupies a unique status with respect to the other MCs that is due in part to her connections to one-percenters via her two husbands, who were both one-percenters, and myriad connections she has made as national president of RSMC. She said, "Yeah, I rode my husband's coattails for a while, and then I earned respect on my own. We've [RSMC] been around almost thirty years [pause] that says something, doesn't it?" Being a national president comes first, with her days of being an ol' lady firmly in the past, but her decades of experience and contacts with several one-percenters garnered through her first husband uniquely position her in relation to the larger MC world. Her current status and ability to negotiate on behalf of RSMC are largely a result of the network she established as a biker and club president, but she acknowledges the role of her "husband's coattails" in the beginning. Her club members are not afforded the same respect by the one-percenters, and the subtle and sometimes not-so-subtle biker communication signaling respect is club business. This pattern of one minority group member receiving recognition and full participation is not unique, and the acceptance, or perhaps tolerance, of one woman biker does not nullify the continued misogyny found throughout the clubs and the general lack of respect relegated to all-women MCs. Still, what Sandy has accomplished is nothing short of miraculous given the extreme misogyny in the biker world.

Although Sandy's status at the national level is limited, her role in her regional Coalition of Clubs (COC or "coalition"), analogous to a Motorcycle Club United Nations, is more pronounced. Sandy is the only woman who sits on her regional coalition, and in all regional COCs, the one-percenter MCs are the most powerful and generally approve attendees and participation. According to Sandy, the COCs began in California "by a bunch of lawyers" to try to end the interclub violence. She said she wanted her club to serve as an example to the male clubs, and she rapidly described the following two incidents:

They [one-percenters] had a meltdown because I was there, but the boss [MC president] had beautiful blue eyes, and as he pinned me to the wall, I just thought, "I'm not hearing *any*thing you're saying." At the first coalition meeting, they were all getting up. It wasn't going to happen. I was outside, probably looking for something to drink....

At another coalition meeting, everybody was frisked before going in. I refused to be frisked, being the only female. I said, "If I want a feel, I'll call you later." I had a pager stuck between my breasts, and it went off [vibrated] in the middle of the meeting. I reached in to get the pager, and everybody fell to the floor except the [MC president], assuming I had a gun and was going to get revenge.... As I pulled out the pager, they all nervously laughed and began to get off the floor. I said to the prez, "Your bros have your back, brother."

While being physically restrained by a "boss," what many bikers call club presidents, she noticed his eye color. The way in which she conveyed this story to me illustrates her bravado and plays upon a kind of hypersexualized woman biker who is always in control. The one-percenters I interviewed often used a joke or a sexual comment to deflect the danger of a situation, and Sandy is no different in this regard (although she does not consider herself a one-percenter). The second anecdote highlights the outlaw quality of refusing to be frisked before entering the meeting space and sexualizing the experience; her storytelling capitalizes on her authority while undermining the authority of the men in the room. In her response, she illustrates contempt, which is the "greatest enemy of authority ... and the surest way to undermine it is laughter" (Arendt 1970: 45). The false alarm of the pager buzz and her quick verbal comeback to the boss highlight the obvious—members protect their president, no matter what, and in this case, they failed miserably and publicly. These two examples also illustrate the one-percenter mentality: violence would have been a normal response relatively easily carried out; Sandy could have refused to be frisked so that she could carry in a weapon and avenge a wrong committed by one of the clubs in attendance. Her presence and willingness to discuss peace and turf with this particular club also legitimized the coalition just as the coalition legitimized RSMC. For Arendt, power "derives its legitimacy from the initial getting together rather than from any action that might follow" (1970:52). In both the formation of RSMC, first as a single-patch riding club and later as a three-piece motorcycle club, and the formation of the coalition, we see legitimacy springing from the early "getting together." The bodies of individuals, as well as the body of the nation itself and the relationships of nations through the COCs and NCOM, provide a blueprint for examining the structure and hierarchies within and among MCs.

The anthropologist Victor Turner published *The Ritual Process* in 1969, and as Roger D. Abrahams writes in the foreword to the 1995 edition, "Turner's discussion of the 'betwixt and between' states became a way to teach about cultures radically different from the West in terms relevant to the present American situation" at a time when "students throughout the West were questioning the relevance of the educational project" ([1969] 1995:viii). Thus, Turner describes beats, hippies, and Hells Angels alongside circumcision rituals of the Ndembu and the monks of Saint Benedict, stating, "It becomes clear that the collective dimensions, communitas and structure, are to be found at all stages and levels of culture and society" and that the relationship between the two is dialectical ([1969] 1995:113). Further expanding to include even more diverse groups, Turner writes of this "ill-assorted bunch of social phenomena" that they "all have this common characteristic: they are persons or principles that (1) fall in the interstices of social structure, (2) are on its margins, or (3) occupy its lowest rungs" ([1969] 1995:125). The predominantly working-class white women in RSMC have white privilege that they unabashedly deny but many righteous sisters are at the interstices, margins, or lowest rungs of the U.S. social structures from the economy to the family to the MC world.

According to Turner, the Vice Lords, an adolescent gang in Chicago, and the Hells Angels are "pseudohierarchies" that "stress the values of communitas"; however, they "are playing the game of structure rather than engaging in the socioeconomic structure in real earnest" with a structure that is both expressive and instrumental ([1969] 1995:193–194). Adolescent street gangs and bikers leverage hierarchies to organize large numbers of members, and according to Turner, "the liminality of the poor or weak assumes the trappings of secular structure and is masked in parental power" ([1969] 1995:195). Turner describes the contradictions inherent in groups that "opted out of the structural system" but yet embraced strict internal hierarchies. These contradictions form the basis of this ethnography, which examines the instrumental and expressive aspects of RSMC's structure as well as the ways in which the internal hierarchy is "masked in parental power." RSMC replicates the vertical hierarchical structures of MCs including national officers, and adds additional roles such as media relations and event planning to their national executive board. RSMC chapters mirror the national hierarchical structure and are localized to a city or geographic region but each chapter must answer to the national executive board. Within each chapter, members have rank.

Foucault discussed the importance of rank in the following passage: "The unit is, therefore, neither the territory (unit of domination), nor the place (unit of residence), but the *rank*: the place one occupies in a classification.... Discipline is an art of rank, a technique for the transformation of arrangements. It individualizes bodies by a location that does not give them a fixed position, but distributes them and circulates them in a network of relations" ([1977] 1995:146). Discipline in the MC world is key, and while a club can support a few outliers like Velcro, the rank and file commit to an incredibly rigid internal hierarchy based on rank. This "network of relations" organizes and controls MCs locally, nationally, and globally. MC officers, like military officers, have better sleeping quarters, eat better food, and have significantly better work details. One's individual rank or status can be elevated by one's length of tenure with the "original" clubhouse, time with a specific chapter, and leadership on specific events or club problems. Chapters can have different ranks based on the size of their membership, which affects dues, the length of time the chapter has been established, and the amount of money a chapter earns through its fundraising activities and bar sales. One chapter had a lot of status in the club because its members included the national president, it was formed in the early days of the club and included several full-patch members, and it was close to national headquarters. A new chapter has to apply for a charter, be approved by the national officers, and will undergo a probationary period with heightened scrutiny. While increasing numbers can be beneficial for clubs, they can also increase problems if there are interclub rivalries in that location and can weaken the club overall if the new chapter does not last. As described earlier, regional governance occurs through COCs, which include representation from each of the major players in a given region, and NCOM also have to approve new chapters.

The role of a national president in a three-piece-patch club is central to the club's identity, its respect in the biker world, and its longevity. National presidents like Sandy who are also the club founders have even more status and authority. Although there are presidential elections each year at RSMC's national business meeting, Sandy said, "It's always uncontested at elections." She quickly added, "Women are devious and will eat you." She described a "coup that kind of happened but didn't" when one member wanted the presidency and "worked it hard," referring to her attempts to sway members to vote her into office. She said, "Nobody paid any attention to it, but I did. They plant seeds. That's how a coup works. I didn't have time. [Name of her bike] was down, but if you [one of her executive officers] would have taken the time and punched her out, we wouldn't have been dealing with it." This was one of the few times anyone referenced violence against a member, although there were often references to various members' shooting prowess and the guns they owned. She referred to the former member, a national officer whose patches were burned, as a "cunt" with "something to prove." Toward the end of the story, she said, "She had [the national vice president] so twisted, I divorced her [the national vice president]. Been together twenty years, and I'm done."

This particular coup attempt and the details surrounding it were not revealed until many years after it occurred. I had just started my period of observation shortly before the alleged attempt occurred, but I knew almost nothing about it until years later. Sandy used "divorce" to signify the end of her bond with her national vice president, but in this case, the national vice president was demoted but was not exiled completely. She was effectively silenced; while it was not clear whether she was *not* allowed to attend nationals or other club functions, I did not see her or hear from her for several years and no one spoke of their former vice president until her return. This rupture of the firmly entrenched hierarchy that had been in place for decades caused some longtime members to cry, according to Sandy, and others refused to talk about it. Although the national officer who was deemed responsible for this attempted coup was kicked out of RSMC (more in Chapter 4), Sandy said, "My hands are tied. I cannot just throw you out. That's rude. I don't have that kind of control. Well I do, but I don't." She ended by saying, "Believe it or not, they [members who resist] have their own underground, which is kind of fun. I dug them out a few years ago. It's every three months. We are on a certain cycle, and they hit the cell phones." Dissention is not tolerated, and Sandy has a difficult time defining her control and authority, but if we situate them within power, they make more sense. For Max Weber, power is "the chance of a man or of a number of men to realize their own will in a communal action even against the resistance of others who are participating in the same action" ([1968] 1978:926). Arendt distinguishes power as "the human ability not just to act but to act in concert" (1970:44). When Sandy makes a declaration—such as burning a member's patches or ending communication with someone—the entire RSMC nation follows suit.

Strength, for Arendt, is singular, "an individual entity" (1970:44). Much of Sandy's power is derived from strength and her accomplishments since founding RSMC, but she realizes that true power is achieved through a unified club. Although the challenger was not able to sway enough members to remove Sandy as president, the attempted coup shook her to her core, and I was dissuaded from speaking to the exiled member or any other members about the incident. This was part of an unspoken arrangement—club business would be conveyed to me by Sandy alone. According to Arendt, "[Authority's] hallmark is unquestioning recognition by those who are asked to obey; neither coercion nor persuasion is needed" (1970:45). Repeatedly, Sandy acknowledges her own authority in a way that is classical confusing biker argot—simultaneously contradictory and telling. Although Sandy loosely blames her national officers for not "punching [the challenger] out," I never witnessed any woman-to-woman violence. This is highly contrasted to other MCs where in a short period of time I saw a dozen incidents of man-to-man violence. In one case, a chapter president who was in his late fifties or early sixties, a Puerto Rican from New York City who had relocated to Florida, was slapped across the face just a few feet from me. He was humiliated, but he had to take it as punishment for some minor infraction or sign of disrespect to the member issuing the slap. He had a red mark across his cheek for the rest of the night.

Sandy's response to this kind of underground was to create her own secret advisory board made up of senior members with extensive institutional memory. They are briefed on emergency protocols in the case of a coup and are poised to assert control over the nation if necessary. This advisory group, referred to fondly as FOG, for "Fuckin' Old Gals," played a more public role early in its inception. They had their own table, officers referred to them as FOG, and all members knew who was in FOG. Sandy said members, especially new members, were "just sucking up because they were FOG." As a result of a separate incident that will be described later, FOG becomes secretive. Sandy She describes the "new" FOG as follows:

> They are set in place to take over in case anything happens to me. If [the national officer who started the coup] would have come in an[d won an] election and six months down the road the club starts taking a turn, they [FOG] would step in. They are underground. Nobody knows who is on the board except me. The VP knows there is FOG. They are the ones who have the right to stand up and say this isn't the way it was planned. They get all the reports. They can keep abreast of the situation. They interview [for FOG] at twenty years.

FOG on its surface acts as a table of elders, and all members show them respect, but their governing ability is not known; it is seemingly masked by their age and semiretirement status. Approximately eight to ten women form FOG. A few were extremely approachable and immediately agreed to be interviewed for this book, and they are included in Chapter 3's discussion of sisterhood; however, I did not ask questions about their FOG roles as double agents. These women, above all others, are bikers and would not talk about club business; furthermore, it would undermine my role as a researcher to out myself as knowing the internal workings. Much of what I observed refutes what Daniel Wolf described as "consensual politics" with personal relationships, "within the frame of brotherhood," in a Canadian club ([1991] 2000:300–301). While much of RSMC's business appeared to be formal and based on consensual politics, many decisions were made behind the scenes by Sandy and one or two of her trusted national officers. Voting items, particularly elections, often seemed pro forma.

Sandy's leadership style is charismatic in the Weberian sense, based on her ability to attract a following and "the marked tendency to become the center of a charismatic movement," and as Robert Tucker suggests, the evidence can be observed before one takes power (1968:740). From her initiative in the 1980s to form a regional women's riding club to her drive to create an international women's MC, Sandy has envisioned expanding RSMC to include "worldwide" on the bottom rocker and organizing a global conference for all-women MCs; she is "the center of a charismatic movement." This makes the question of succession vital. Although the next in line would be the national vice president, with FOG in place to ensure a peaceful transition, the question of whether anyone would be capable of taking over the helm of RSMC after more than three decades of Sandy's leadership hangs in the air. Sandy occasionally speaks of retirement and her legacy. During focused interviews, I inquired directly about succession with other members and with her husband and found it to be a very taboo subject. The question of succession is particularly challenging because of the politics surrounding other MC nations. The bottom rocker lays a political claim—to an ideal—and Sandy has a near-mythic status. Expansion depends on relationships and power within the larger structure, particularly with one-percenter clubs, and a willingness to support the organizational structure of the larger MC world, which remains segregated and misogynist. Sandy's strength translates into total power within RSMC, but it is limited to strength, not power, within the regional COCs and to little strength or power at the national level. These are concessions Sandy is willing to make to be part of the larger MC world.

In 2019, Sandy invited me to attend the NCOM Convention as her guest. This allowed me to see RSMC interact with other clubs in a male-dominated space and to observe racial and gender dynamics across many clubs. Reminiscent of many academic conferences, it took place in a hotel convention center and had different sessions. The majority of attendees were heterosexual white males, but the range included one-percenters, male MCs, riding clubs (i.e., religious and military), and a small minority of women who were affiliated with different types of clubs. Racial divisions are prevalent with the MC world both in diverse, urban contexts and in geographic areas that are more racially homogenous. One of the sessions I attended was for women riders, and approximately twenty women were in the room, with RSMC constituting the majority. A Black rider gave a presentation about riding and motorcycle repairs and interspersed stories of her own rides across the United States over the past decade. At one point, she described motorcycle profiling and talked about the precariousness of being a Black woman rider and her interactions with law enforcement. It was an excellent presentation that touched on a factor ignored by the larger Motorcycle Profiling Project. Later, an RSMC national officer said, "Why do *they* always have to bring up the race shit?" I tried to engage her in a conversation about racism and racial profiling, but she quickly ended it.

There were approximately eighteen women with three-piece MC patches from three different MCs, hundreds of men with MC patches, and several dozen one-percenters from two major international MCs. Although RSMC is overtly pro-woman, they do not consider themselves feminist. Their approach tries to erode constraints placed on women by men, particularly around three-piece patches and the MC cube. While they have earned the respect of some of the MCs, it is limited and often more attributed to the individual, Sandy as national president, than to the patch itself. One of the other women's MCs was from the West Coast (this NCOM was held on the East Coast), and Sandy and other members of RSMC were not friendly toward them. I overheard a few critical comments about their style and appearance. While Sandy and I had spoken about the importance of women's MCs being unified, there seemed to be little interest in unification at NCOM.

Conclusion

As an imagined community, RSMC adopts the patriarchal structure of its male MC counterparts, reproducing many of the most troubling aspects and rendering members not quite citizens in within the United Nations of the MC world. However, unlike their counterparts, the RSMC nation serves as the locus of a number of social narratives (of outsiders, family, motherhood) that generally do not interrupt one another but rather appear to seamlessly blend to create greater in-group cohesion among members. Sandy benefits from the singularity of her club, though, and utilizes her strength to gain power outside her nation that is doled out by the men in charge. The sacrifices and concessions members of RSMC make are pressed on their backs with a three-piece patch. Their imagined community is powerful, always creating, building, and dreaming. The kind of respect afforded to full-patch members is evident within the club and formalized through the patching ceremony. For many women, a full patch is one of many lifetime accomplishments, and they balance this role among many others. The patches themselves are quintessentially feminine and announce femininity and power within a masculinist biker world—and also within a larger world in which white women have power. Through the sisterhood that is created, these dual citizens discover a sense of belonging and a place for action previously unknown to most of them.

2

Becoming a Righteous Sister

Spirit Ride

It's a warm and sunny Thursday morning, and tens of thousands of motorcycles are converging nearby for Daytona Beach's Bike Week. The members of RSMC, dressed in boots, jeans, a club T-shirt, and their patches (black leather vests), are ready for the annual spirit ride, which takes place toward the end of nationals each year. There is a quiet excitement among the women that is a mixture of reverence, excitement, and, for the newcomers, fear. Whereas much of RSMC's weeklong nationals is casual and many bikers can be seen wearing shorts and flip-flops, the spirit ride is one of a few notable exceptions, like the business meeting and patching ceremony described in Chapter 1. The reverence signifies yet another initiation ritual for the newcomers and a reaffirmation of commitment to the sisterhood for veteran club members.

The ride starts at the national clubhouse, referred to as "Home," and anywhere from thirty to forty motorcycles are parked in the large U-shaped driveway in perfect formation, backed in, ready to go. Some members rode their motorcycles from across the country, and others trailered their bikes from across the United States to take part in this ride. A few international members store a bike at national headquarters. Dozens of cars and several trailers can be seen on a huge front lawn, which doubles as a parking lot. Those who cannot ride or do not have a motorcycle with them will ride in one of the many chaser cars behind the pack of riders. Fifteen minutes before the start time, sixty women fall silent. There is nervousness and fear in the air, and the road captains confidently step to the center and provide detailed instructions for the ride, including the route, safety protocols, and emphasis on the buddy system. Every stop sign, stoplight, turn, and potential hazard has been meticulously mapped out by the road captains. The neighboring Bike Week means thousands of other motorcyclists will be on the roads, in addition to many more cars, or "cages." The potential for an accident and the pressure to ride well so as not to endanger oneself or one's sisters adds to the drama of the pre-ride lecture. This is one of the few times in which the entire nation rides together with patches on, and members' performance can be scrutinized by outsiders as well as by insiders who are deciding who will get patches and who will wait another year.

The stated purpose of the annual spirit ride is to commemorate deceased sisters and collectively celebrate their lives through the ritual act of riding, but like many other parts of the initiation process, this is a deeply political act for each rider and for the group. The spirit ride generally includes a remote destination several miles away and some open road to provide an opportunity to "throttle down." From inside the pack, the roar of the bikes is all-encompassing, and the visual display of perfectly formed two-by-two columns is visually stunning and a powerful symbol of RSMC's unity and power. It is an opportunity for women bikers to appear as righteous sisters in an intensely public setting.

In 2016, I drove my rental car onto the clubhouse property and parked among the other cars just as the women were gathering in the U-shaped driveway for the informational meeting before the spirit ride. A few dozen women immediately greeted me with open arms. The national president, Sandy, gave me a huge hug, and I could feel dozens of pairs of eyes looking at us. Wearing street clothes in a sea of women with black leather vests, I stood out, but the sense of belonging was there. In my field notes, I wrote the following: "Best huggers. These women hug you like they mean it." Sandy said, "Find a car and take the ride." Wait, what? A car? Then "Diesel" saw me standing there and asked if I wanted to ride on the back of her bike. Someone mentioned that I probably shouldn't be without boots (I was wearing flip-flops). Diesel said, "No problem. Go put your sneakers on." I did and hopped on. As with most MCs, anyone wearing a patch on a motorcycle must meet strict requirements that range from what one can wear to whom one can have on the bike. Boots are one of the most common rules across all MCs, but the vast array of biker protocols didn't apply to me. Since I wasn't wearing a vest or RSMC patches, I wasn't representing the club. I was the Writer.

As I was observing and participating in initiation rituals, the bikers were also observing me, and I underwent my own initiation process, which lasted the entire duration of my observation. Diesel was a full-patch member who was well respected both for her tenure in the RSMC and for her riding ability. Likely in her late fifties or early sixties during my observation, she drove an eighteen-wheeler truck for a living and was one of the few women of color, displaying her Native American heritage with her faded forearm tattoos and with her black hair in traditional-style braids. Since she stood five foot one, her giant diesel truck and trailer and Harley-Davidson Road King would seem likely to dwarf her, but they did not; Diesel was always a capable driver and rider. It was through getting close to Diesel that I was able to observe slight acts of deviance. Diesel was known for her to-go mugs, which contained rum drinks made in her camper trailer, and she was often one of the sisters out the latest—two or three o'clock in the morning—talking and laughing and smoking cigarettes. When Sandy declared that all members would have to purchase their alcohol from the RSMC clubhouse bar, I noted that Diesel spent a bit more time in her trailer and on occasion with her infamous to-go mugs. These slight forms of rebellion broke through the impenetrable image of RSMC solidarity and illuminated the business side of the MC—there was money to be made when members were forced to buy not only their alcohol but their water and soda from the clubhouse bar.

From the beginning, I was able to connect and build rapport with certain members, and Diesel was one of the sisters whom I liked from the start and who liked me in return. Riding with her gave me an incredible feel and view of the spirit ride, and she said I was so light and stayed so still she didn't even remember I was there until we came to a stop and I hopped off. Riding on a big bike, especially one with a large window or plastic shield, is luxury riding—the wind and bugs are mostly blocked by the window—and the large passenger seat on a Road King is roomy. Her bike also included a backrest, which meant I could just lean back and enjoy the scenery or close my eyes and drowsily feel the fresh air and rest my feet on the back pegs. Spirit rides were generally pretty short distances—ten to fifteen miles—but when I was with Diesel, I wished they would go on for a hundred miles or more.

For many members, the spirit ride was a high-pressure situation. They were being watched, and they were actively learning to perform the role of a member of RSMC. When members ride in formation, certain rules of the road are suspended as in a funeral procession but without the police escort. Red lights will break up the pack, so there is a concerted effort to time them so that all might pass through; however, the latter part of the pack often ends up having to run red lights to keep the pack together. The first part of the spirit ride contained few, if any, such obstacles and ended in a nature preserve. The challenge for newer riders was to park their motorcycles by backing them into the perfect lines of bikes with the officers watching. This was the first space in which vastly different riding skills were on display—some sisters required significant assistance from others, who used the luggage rack on the back to pull the eight-hundred-pound bike into place. Righteous sisters are top-notch riders and are also quick to help other sisters park their bikes.

As the parking spots filled, a few women lit cigarettes and talked quietly. Most were silent as an outward display of reverence. The "spirit" portion of the ride had commenced; they were here to remember the dead, and they took on a very ceremonial tone. Some MCs have chaplains, members who are ordained pastors or other recognized religious figures, and RSMC had one who wore a member vest during the entirety of my observation. "Chaplain Mary" spoke about each of the deceased sisters and one big brother and concluded with prayer. "Big brother" is a term of respect and familiarity for men who are affiliated with RSMC. Typically, the familial relation is husband of a member, but the term was also used to describe Sandy's brother, among other men with ties to RSMC. Several sisters cried, and others leaned on or embraced one another during the makeshift memorial. It was emotional even for those of us who did not directly know those who had died. I didn't inquire as to the selection process regarding who was memorialized, but I can infer that only sisters who were active members in good standing at the time of their deaths are remembered during the spirit ride and included on their website. Sandy's first husband, deceased, was also included as a spirit big brother.

In this ceremony, as in the patching ceremony, the prospects were being watched. Did they show reverence and respect? Did they show that they felt the spiritual bond with those who had died? Both ceremonies serve crucial functions, and the spirit ride is always a few days before the patching ceremony—death before birth as a citizen of RSMC. These ceremonies strengthen social solidarity within the group because new members want to be part of the sisterhood—they want to be remembered after their deaths, and more than anything, they want to be full-patch members. For the members, especially the old-timers, these ceremonies not only serve as crucial spaces and places of reaffirmation to RSMC and to the sisterhood but also offer opportunities to observe new initiates and assess their worthiness of the kind of immortality that can be gained if one is a righteous sister.

After the somber and emotional part of the spirit ride ends with a moment of silence and a prayer, sisters cry and hug, and within moments one can hear laughter again as they tell stories for another thirty minutes or so. Then it is back to the bikes and on to the restaurant for food and fellowship. As with everything else related to the spirit ride, lunch has been meticulously planned and organized, and restaurant managers are always happy to see fifty to seventy-five women bikers walk in at the time of their reservation. Eating in community was one of the activities in which the rules of initiation and the performance of gender and power were the most poignant and, as it turns out, disputed. For lunches and dinners, the protocol was almost always the same: a literal bell was rung, a prayer was said, and Sandy lined up and ate first, followed by members in order of rank. Any male companions or outsiders like me ate last. Although this type of tiered eating is explicitly denounced in RSMC's written guidelines, in reality it was almost always followed. In restaurants with table service, it could create a great deal of confusion.

Like the initiation patching ritual in Chapter 1, the spirit ride reinforces belonging and reassures members, both new and longtime, that the righteous sister will never be forgotten. The patching ceremony always takes place a day or two after the spirit ride during nationals, so initiates first see the commemoration of deceased members before they witness the birth of full-patch members later in the week. The spirit ride is also a high-stakes public performance in which women have an opportunity to demonstrate righteousness through their riding prowess or prove their inadequacy. There is danger in motorcycling, particularly on these types of rides, where one false move could lead to serious injuries for not only that rider but all riders around them. The adrenaline one experiences while riding in a pack is invigorating, and for prospects it provides an on-ramp to sisterhood and righteousness. For the national officers in RSMC, the spirit ride provides a place to observe prospects' worthiness and a place for socialization into the rules and expectations of the RSMC nation.

Theorizing Righteous Sisterhood

The word "righteous" has a long history, originating in twelfth century Old English and indicating a moral or virtuous person (noun) with the combined "right" and "wise" to describe something that is just or rightful (adjective) ("Righteous, *Adj., N., Adv., Int.*"; *Oxford English Dictionary* 2023). In the sixteenth century, something that is "genuine; authentic; true; correct; exact" could be deemed "righteous" and in the 1930s, African Americans adapted "righteous" as slang to describe something as "excellent, wonderful; 'cool'" with frequent implications of "integrity or authenticity" ("Righteous, Adj., Sense 3.a."; *Oxford English Dictionary* 2023). The slang moved from the "hepcats" in the jazz world into other spaces including the "beats" and the "hippies." Given the overlap between the beats and the Hells Angels in the 1960s,[1] it is not surprising that this word was co-opted to distinguish excellence in the biker subculture. By the 2000s, "righteous" was the word I heard most in my participant observation and interviews with male bikers. When men write about men bikers, this is also the most common stamp of approval for objects such as motorcycles or for individual bikers (Hopper and Moore 1983: 61; Wolf [1991] 2000:43, 48), the single most important criterion for membership (Wolf [1991] 2000:35), and a particularly American biker adjective (Veno [2002] 2003:51).[2] Wolf, an anthropologist who studied the Canadian Rebels and patched in as a full member during his research, describes a righteous biker as a "collective identity that features an antihero image, that of a strong-willed individual participating in an unconventional lifestyle, subjected to both censure and moral condemnation," that also entails a "degree of commitment that leaves no room for compromise despite the inevitable adversity that accompanies it" ([1991] 2000:62). The hepcats, beats, hipsters, and bikers were part of unconventional lifestyles, but by all accounts, these were overwhelmingly male-dominated subcultures. "Righteous," then, denoted those who were particularly genuine, excellent, or cool *men*.

Each of these groups was censured and censored by society, and Chapter 2 centers women in the biker subculture as *righteous* within a three-piece-patch women's club and as a particular kind of rebellion against the larger male-dominated subculture and society. RSMC members are subject to dangers on the road, from drivers swerving at them to law enforcement profiling them as "outlaw" bikers because of their patches. American popular culture has long been fascinated and repulsed by bikers; women who put on a three-piece patch do so with the acknowledgment that they could be denied access to restaurants and bars and that they are assuming the same risks as their male counterparts. Women rebel against gender role norms the minute they straddle their motorcycles; as described in Chapter 1, "the riding woman is seen as a *gender traitor*" (Joans 2001:89). The prevalence of women riders who own motorcycles has more than doubled from Joans's research until now, but righteous sisters are the extreme minority, and they are subject to censure from all angles—the one-percenter will never see them as equals, men and women riders distance themselves from all MC subcultures, and nonrider/nonbiker citizens still hold on to "gender traitor" bias. White, heterosexual righteous sisters experience this type of sidelining; however, righteous sisters who also occupy a racial, gender, or sexual minority status are triply marginalized, and some of that marginalization occurs within the protective cloak of sisterhood. The deep sense of belonging to a *chosen* family, emphasized by matrimonial terms of a promise ring, engagement, and marriage as symbolic phases of the patches and close mentoring as part and parcel to sisterhood, but the cost is withholding marginalized identities. Sisterhood also functions as a filtration system; it has become increasingly heteronormative and is racially homogenous. According to Sandy, the sisterhood binds women for a lifetime, but that bind is short-lived for many RSMC members and can be just for a few months or years.

Being a righteous (Hells) Angel, according to Thompson, "requires loud obedience to the party line. They are intensely aware of *belonging*, of being able to depend on each other," and he later calls it a "desperate sense of unity" ([1966] 1999:72–73). Like sisterhood, brotherhood offers a protective force (Wolf [1991] 2000:16; Thompson [1966] 1999:68; Veno [2002] 2003:48) and a shared sense of being an outcast (Hopper and Moore 1983:59; Thompson

[1966] 1999:52). For Wolf ([1991] 2000:30), becoming a biker is a "class-specific response to the general problem of self-actualization." These twin pillars of brotherhood—protection from outside forces and a shared sense of being an outcast among outcasts—cement the in-group solidarity and group identity and hark back to the classic studies on street gangs that bonded through an us-versus-them mentality. The youth subcultural studies Wolf cites as he describes the adult male Canadian Rebels MC borrow the focus on "essential masculinity" and the "rogue male" from Albert Cohen's classic *Delinquent Boys* (1955:139–140). Cohen notes that "untrammeled masculinity" is "not without a certain aura of glamour and romance" and finds its way into "respectable culture" (1955:140), which is readily apparent in popular culture by the 1950s with films like *The Wild One* elevating this type of masculinity through a male biker lead. Female delinquency in these early studies is almost always sexual delinquency (Cohen 1955:45). These subcultural studies lauded and celebrated Cohen's "rogue male" while "images of 'deviant girls' have always been distorted be lenses of paternalism and misogyny" (LeBlanc [1999] 2006:67).

This kind of historical foregrounding operates at both conscious and subconscious levels in the RSMC nation. Sandy and other righteous sisters find it incumbent on them to educate prospects on the types of behaviors that are acceptable and to reinforce club values, which club literature explains simply: "The order of things in our life" is "God, Family, Club." What is unwritten and rarely spoken about is the gendered construction of righteousness, the ways in which members of RSMC negotiate the transition from a woman biker to a righteous sister, and the ways gender is omnipresent through the initiation phase. In Leslie Salzinger's ethnographic study of women working in *maquiladoras*, she states, "If gender is truly locally emergent and contextual, then there is *theoretical* work to be done in delineating where, when, and how this occurs. This requires bringing an ethnographic eye to bear on the ways that gender is practiced on a daily basis" (2003:22). For righteous sisters, as for factory workers, this is observable "in the strategies, common sense, and power struggles of the actors" (2003:24). Through extended participant observation fieldwork as well as secondary research using RSMC manuals and interviews with members, I examine sisterhood as a gendered construct that is constantly negotiated at the individual level, at the club level, and within the larger world of bikers through initiation.

The field of leisure studies provides some interesting comparisons, particularly work done surrounding the Red Hatters, a group of women who are immediately identifiable by their conspicuous red hats in public spaces. The Red Hatters are a spectacle and they exploit codes of female appearance to criticize dominant gender discourse and explore new identities (Kaplan and Stowell 1995). One study of the Red Hatter Society suggests:

> The oscillation between feminism and femininity apparent in the Red Hat Society can be understood as an expression of what we want to call radical femininities. The "radical" refers to an array of factors (exceptional activities, extreme appearance, shameless self-indulgence) that both endorse and challenge traditional gender relations; the plural "femininities" acknowledges that Red Hatters do this in many different ways. (Bohemen, Zoonen, and Aupers 2013:593)

Similarly, RSMC exploits traditional gender codes by highlighting femininity and sexuality with its center patch (details are withheld to protect the identity of the club) and club colors, its name (although RSMC is a pseudonym, it mirrors the masculine and feminine duality in the club's real name), and the motorcycles themselves, which appear and sound masculine or feminine through paint colors, size, make and model, and customization. Appearances vary widely, with some women wearing biker T-shirts bedazzled with rhinestones and other bling, blown-out hairstyles, and makeup while others wear low tight ponytails and traditional biker T-shirts, jeans, and boots (whether they are riding the bike or not). Although I will not ponder whether Red Hatters constitute radical femininities, bikers are full of contradictions, and this is most apparent when it comes to gender and sexuality. In RSMC, contradictions with respect to race are less apparent but even more taboo than gender and sexuality.

In *Women of the Klan*, Kathleen Blee describes "the sense of belonging and collective importance" that was reinforced through "camping in the woods for the three-day meeting and celebration," combining "pomp and pageantry with politics" ([1991] 1992:128). Blee continued: "The Klans' propaganda stressed klannishness and a sisterhood that transcends the petty divisions of the alien world" ([1991] 1992:129). In sororities, Amy Stone and Allison Gorga found that "while no specific practices of social exclusion were identified, lesbianism was found to be contained and managed through the practices of discursive strategies about diversity and 'good fit'" and the "creation of a separate sorority to contain pariah femininities" (2014:353). Anne Campbell's influential study of New York City gang girls (1987) showed the same kind of in-group solidarity among Puerto Rican gang members, who excluded girls who didn't fit their criteria of femininity and even *marianismo*. The Ku Klux Klan, sororities, and street gangs developed because of their exclusion from the male-only groups and consequently exclude from membership women from various status groups. RSMC expertly uses a complex initiation process to control membership and regulate its women prospects and its members. While the club emphasizes transcendence beyond "petty divisions" through its cardinal rule of "no gossip," gossip and surveillance are mechanisms to observe and communicate righteousness or lack thereof. Gender is at the core of both righteousness and sisterhood, and it is a crucial part of the larger socialization that takes place throughout the initiation process.

Dreaming of Righteous Sisterhood

I observed motorcycle clubs for over fifteen years, and the question of why individuals want to become part of these social worlds is still a conundrum. There are so many contradictions and a degree of irrationality. For example, one morning as a group of sisters were finishing breakfast, one of the national officers came in and asked them to move a few dozen tables and chairs, but once they were moved, Sandy did not like how they looked, so the same women were asked or told to move them back to their original position. I found it difficult to disguise my shock at these nonsensical acts, and since I was moving the tables along with the other women, I was physically engaged in the kind of performance required of both prospects and full-patch members. I was in my thirties during most of my observational period, and most of the sisters were *at least* fifteen to twenty years older than me, and part of my fascination and discomfort was watching elders take orders and perform manual labor; however, there was an overriding sense of empowerment and community, and women bonded over the nonsensical command. For women with a military background, this blind obedience to authority was second nature, but women like Diesel toed the line between conformity and independence. All women wanted to become part of the righteous sisterhood, though, and to obtain what they viewed as a greater form of excellence, they were willing to move chairs and tables back and forth until Sandy was satisfied.

Daniel Wolf noted this paradox and described it as "how to reconcile the biker freedom ethic with the necessity of group conformity." He later wrote, "Ironically, deviance from social norms on a group level requires conformity on a personal level" ([1991] 2000:271–272). Many of the female bikers are fiercely independent and struggle internally and externally to adhere to the club requirements. Like Velcro in the MC, their tendency is to rebel, but they are useful members of the club *because of that fiery independent streak*. The allure of the center patch and full membership coupled with the elements of sisterhood—jokes and pranks, nationals, Sister Time, and structured weekly communication—are sufficient to motivate women to pass through the lengthy initiation period; however, many quit or are forced to quit before they become full-patch members. Some find that the demands or outright disapproval of their family members, usually nonbiker husbands, are irreconcilable with the club's demands (more in Chapter 4), but others remain in an extended initiation period until their deviance can be put in check.

Of the righteous sisters' motivation, Sandy said, "I don't think they want to be like the guys. I just think they want something to belong to. I think when women bond, they bond for a lifetime." Within moments she said, "Just because you have a full patch on doesn't make you my sister." Characteristically, she presented me with contradictory statements. The full patch *creates sisterhood* through the initiation process, and bonds are maintained by annual rituals, such as the patching ceremony and the spirit ride, that reinforce their tantamount importance. Brotherhood and sisterhood denote a familial bond within the MC worlds, and as in other groups with a central allegiance, the familial bond is centered on a political community, RSMC. The language to describe that allegiance is not only sororal but also matrimonial. Examining the club through the lens of the family of origin (sisterhood) and the family of procreation (marriage) elicits more contradictions in a staunchly heteronormative group than examining these groups solely through the chosen family of orientation model with "big brothers" and "sisters." Family and nation are interchangeable in the RSMC lexicon, but the way in which the dream of righteous sisterhood is marketed remains the same—RSMC is terminally unique, exclusive, and superior to other clubs (both men's and women's). Perhaps the former U.S. Marines in the club helped to reinforce the elitist framing and loyalty demanded as a way of life, but Sandy, the nation's leader, is the figurehead for the pomp. One year at nationals, she proudly stated, "We are the only women's MC in the fucking world. You belong to the elite. We are recognized all over the fucking world. [*Pauses.*] It's only taken [states the number of years since RSMC was founded] [*laughs*]." This brazen and contestable first statement is tempered by a humbler conclusion and Sandy's laughter.

As a counterpart to the hard-line rhetoric of the club, there is also a softer side. One of the original members described the spiritual connection among righteous sisters. She stated, "Take me in your heart. Take me in your soul. Remember we are all our sister's keeper. When you think of me, think of everyone else too. They are with you." She went on to describe the practical side, saying, "We will be there when you need us. We don't trust our husbands for our funerals and other things that are important. When tragedy happens, such as an accident, we need to be notified." Of her own family, she said, "My child is forty-seven years old. That child has been with [RSMC] a very long time." She reached over the table, touching my arm, and said, "You are in my heart and spirit. . . . Yes, yes. Not only the sisters." This ethos is widely known and called "sister's keeper." It can be seen as a patch on women's vests and is often heard in conversation, and it likely comes from the "brother's keeper" designation in MCs. At the most practical level possible, most members entrust their wills, medical decision-making, and funeral arrangements to Sandy or other club members.

Given the demographics of motorcycle owners[3] and my estimated median age for righteous sisters of fifty-eight years, the promises of righteous sisterhood are increasingly important as one ages. Some of these women find themselves alone for the first time or retired. Many of the RSMC prospects have more time on their hands, but the kinds of demands RSMC places are not for the faint of heart or those who are looking for a place to donate their time and money. Rather, what RSMC offers is a path toward righteousness that many have not achieved in other stages of life. That path to excellence has many elements and, for the spiritually inclined, being a sister's keeper and being a member of a nation provides a sense of security for older women.

Signing in and out at nationals, asking permission to leave the premises, and only being allowed to leave with permission and with a "buddy" are some of the requirements RSMC uses to control and monitor its members; however, these same rules that restrict one's freedom of movement and test members' willingness to comply also create opportunities for bonding and for observing righteous sisterhood through small daily acts. Dozens of women have come and gone from RSMC since I began observing the club, but the power of the patch and the dream of righteous sisterhood and all its promises entice women to join and provide enough benefits that many stay.

Initiation

According to the RSMC bylaws, membership is open to "all women 21 years of age and older who own and operate a motorcycle of 750 cc or greater on date of Full Membership." The club's website invites women to fill out an online application for membership. As in many MCs, new members often hear about membership through word of mouth or through a formal introduction by an existing member. When a woman fills out the application, the official vetting process begins. If a member brings a prospect to a club function, the vetting process begins immediately regardless of whether she has completed an application or expressed interest in becoming a member. In the former case, the RSMC executive board reviews the application, and the sergeant-at-arms is responsible for screening and identifying any potential security issues. Applicants are asked about any MC affiliations to see if their husbands, boyfriends, or sons are involved in one-percenter MCs as that could pose a security risk. The application fee is fully refundable if the applicant is denied; otherwise, the fee goes toward the first year's membership dues. Promotional materials emphasize the multiple roles women play—motorcyclists, mothers, sisters, wives, and daughters—which stands in sharp contrast to the emphasis of a singular identity in male MCs, especially in one-percenter MCs, where the MC is *the* family—one's family of orientation or family of procreation becomes secondary in all ways. In practice, however,

RSMC can become a singular identity and also shape individual members' decisions regarding where to live, for example—a fact that positions it much closer to one-percenter clubs.

Part of my research involved access to RSMC's giant collection of three-ring binders, which included a section called "The Vetting Process"; "Form A: New Applicant Interview"; "Form B: Background Check"; and a detailed chart of who does what at the national level to vet a new applicant *before* the woman is accepted as a prospect. The membership application asks all kinds of questions and presupposes heterosexuality: "Husband Name," "His Date of Birth," "Are you a member of any other motorcycle organization?" and "Is your husband/-Ol' Man a member of any other organization or club?" as well as more specific questions such as club names, years as members, and officer positions held for both the applicant and male partner. Form A includes the following instructions:

> These are questions used by the Membership Director to get to know the applicant, as well as write the new member announcement to the nation. It is important to be friendly—she will be more willing to volunteer information that way. Reviewing the application and asking questions about her family, and job, opens the door to what her other obligations are and how much time she has to commit to [RSMC].

The reminder "to be friendly" as a tactic to get prospects to "volunteer [more] information that way" is a common strategy to elicit information in myriad contexts; however, it seemed at odds with the virtues of sisterhood. One commonality across MCs is that prospects must have a use value to the club to which they are trying to patch in and must also be able to devote significant amounts of time.

All bikers want to both intimidate and impress, to some extent, to show that they are *real bikers*, but the prioritization of information about prospects and by extension their family and friends is common in other closed subcultures. The background check includes a perusal of social media accounts, a criminal background check, a search through the National Sex Offender Registry, and verification of the initial application and interview. Although I do not think a criminal background would preclude anyone from being accepted as a member to a women's motorcycle club, sex offenses would preclude membership. I did not have access to the completed membership applications, so I have no way of knowing if and how the application changed over time or how gay members completed it, especially the couples who were members of RSMC. Without this access, I was also not privy to grounds for rejection at the application stage.

Once the initial vetting process is complete, new members sign a Bylaws Agreement, asserting that they have read the bylaws and reviewed them with a sponsor; an Irrevocable Consent Agreement, which states that the club logo is trademarked and belongs to RSMC; an Events Release Form that includes a "holds harmless" clause for club events; and a Policy Agreement Form. Once a prospect is approved, they are sent a welcome packet and assigned a sponsor.

As the Writer, I was vetted by the national president, Sandy. As described earlier, I was twice denied an interview with Sandy, and then I was invited to her home, which also doubled as national headquarters for RSMC, in 2010. My personal connection to MCs got me in, but I would be regularly vetted over the next ten years. I have no doubt that Sandy kept me close to have as much influence as possible on what I *saw* and *who* I interviewed as on what I *didn't see* and *didn't hear*. During dozens of conversations, Sandy did most of the questioning, and she frequently disagreed with my understanding and evaluation. The vetting of male researchers has been described by other participant observers of male-only MCs (Wolf [1991] 2000), journalists (Thompson [1966] 1999), and undercover agents (Queen 2005), but none of them were shepherded in by the national president, and none of them remained as clearly marked nonbikers. One exception occurred in Australia when applied community psychologist Arthur Veno was sought out by an OMC to provide guidance on de-escalating a violent conflict between the OMC, the police, and the government.[4] The female (Julie van den Eynde) and male (Veno) research team engaged in participatory action research and described an "insider-outsider methodology" in which van den Eynde, the "outsider," "had to overcome strong 'mutual suspicions'" before proceeding, whereas Veno gained "immediate access" on the basis of his "previous earned credibility by OMC leadership" (2013:496). While van den Eynde "became an 'invisible person,'" Veno "eased into the OMC culture" and "took on many of the attributes of an OMC member" (2013:497). My vetting mirrored my presence in RSMC: I did not attempt to blend in or take on biker attributes, nor was I invisible. As a woman researching women, I worked to establish trust and develop rapport by being transparent and finding a balance between trying to fit in as a biker and becoming a completely detached observer. I was Sarah, the Writer.

Sponsorship in RSMC is a muted but important part of becoming a righteous sister, and a sponsor is assigned as soon as the background check is completed. Wolf's anthropological study of the Rebels MC in Canada highlights the role of sponsorship: "With more extreme outlaw clubs, especially those involved in organized crime, the boundaries are drawn even tighter in terms of the screening process, and the prospect will require an official sponsor. The sponsoring members accepts full responsibility for the striker's future actions" ([1991] 2000:80). Although RSMC is not an "extreme outlaw club" and does not partake in organized crime, prospects are assigned a sponsor as part of the initiation. In RSMC, the sponsoring member serves the dual role of a mentor to the prospect and an informer to the club on the prospect. The dual function of sponsors also serves to deepen their commitment; they are invested in the success of their prospects, but their loyalty to RSMC always trumps any affection toward a prospect, and they will report any misconduct or concerns to club leadership.

In the summer of 2018, the national president told me to "take a look" at the photo albums and binders that are housed in the "Big House" at the national headquarters. The full-time residents were away for the summer, and as in the preceding summers, I went to national headquarters and stayed for a week or two. Confidential documents such as intake and exit interviews that included personal information, the club membership roll, and other club documents were kept in Sandy's home office, but in several large three-ring binders alongside photo albums, near the bar and the large L-shaped leather couch where I slept, was the Sponsor Manual, a treasure trove of information about the structure of initiation and the role of sponsors. The only indications of a full-patch member having a special bond with a member was during the patching ceremony, where I heard, on occasion, a full-patch member saying, "She is my sponsee!" about a newly patched member. Throughout ten years of participant observation, I heard very little about sponsorship, knew of few sponsor-prospect pairs, and was not invited to closed-door meetings about prospects. The three-ring binder, like all RSMC documents, was extremely organized. Among old biker adages such as "It's not the patch that makes the person; it's the person that makes the patch," it clearly laid out an elaborate structure for tiered sponsorship and named levels of membership. Although I observed and heard a lot over the years, this binder consolidated information that I could only piece together from various conversations; sponsorship is club business, and members are not allowed to talk to outsiders about club business. Sandy said little of sponsorship over the dozens of conversations we had about the club.

According to the Sponsorship Manual, an RSMC sponsor is a full-patch member who is asked to teach a prospect about the history of RSMC and its values and norms; she "skools and help them learn what is expected of [an RSMC] Sister." Sponsors themselves are vetted and fill out forms with questions like "Do I look for opportunities to further my own growth? Yes/No Why?" and "Do I find it energizing to work with others who are different from me? Yes/No Why? What is my biggest motivation for being a sponsor?" A section titled "Self-Awareness Chapter 1 and Chapter 2" includes worksheets on listening, goals, and character traits as well as dozens of questions. Interspersed are motivational stories and a few poems.

Sponsors are reminded that "not everyone applying for membership is a 'biker'... please keep that in mind. Our Nation needs to grow so don't be so quick to throw people away because they don't fit a certain mold. Our differences make us who we are." This is not a statement highlighting diversity. It is designed to increase membership—"Our Nation needs to grow"—and implicitly acknowledges the graying of the biker world as well as the rise of motorcycling among nonbikers. The "certain mold" is the biker woman who wears black boots, jeans, and black biker T-shirts. She has long hair and likely some tattoos. She is an experienced rider and a Harley-Davidson enthusiast. The "mold" is female, white, middle-aged, and heterosexual. The warning "don't be so quick to throw people away" suggests that it has been an issue in the past. Although pages did not have dates, some of the sections appeared to be more recently updated than others.

Throughout the manual, sponsors are reminded to look for potential and to serve as an example of a committed sister, or righteous sister. From the start, sponsors are directed to instill accountability into prospects with weekly phone calls at a specific day and time, and sponsors report bimonthly updates and participate in bimonthly chats with other sponsors. Each phase of sponsorship has specific learning objectives or goals that include checklists. Sponsors are required to write letters of recommendation before the prospect is awarded her rockers (top and bottom) and the center patch. A cosponsor, who is outside of the prospect's chapter, is assigned to each prospect to increase objectivity. Likely the cosponsor would have less direct contact with the prospect because of geographic distance, but the communication loop keeps everyone abreast of the prospect's activities and also maintains social ties among sponsors, Sandy, and other national officers. The various levels of sponsorship provide a sorting mechanism, providing paths to cultivate righteousness among individual sisters as well as RSMC as a club while at the same time weeding out sisters, prospects, and sometimes even sponsors themselves.

Initiates are subjected to trials and tests to determine their character, tenacity, and ability to both take orders and act independently as a member of the sisterhood. Will a prospect gossip if given an opportunity to do so? Will she talk about club business with outsiders, including but not limited to her significant other? Will she leap into action if she sees a full-patch member moving a piece of furniture or notice if Sandy is looking for a lighter for her cigarette? Sponsors are guides during this process, but they also serve a reporting role for RSMC.

Of the initiation period, Sandy said, "It takes five years minimum to become a full-patch holder. She must have her own life together before she can fully give to the club." During my period of observation, most members earned their full patch in three to four years, but at least one took five years or even longer, and the holdup did not seem to be whether a prospect had "her own life together" but rather how well she could work the tiered system of sponsorship, how much time she devoted to RSMC, how many events she attended, how much money she directed to club activities, and how much labor she gave to national headquarters. All sponsors and the national officers deliberate on the decision to patch someone in, but obedience, likability, and collegiality seem to be major unwritten factors. The time itself is also something that makes RSMC *righteous*, particularly in the eyes of other MCs. The getting-in process is both instrumental and symbolic. Several times, I heard Sandy tout the length of time as being something the male bikers, especially the high-ranking officers, respected about RSMC. Another time, a male guest at a public RSMC event said, "Didn't she have two rockers at this time last year? What's taking so long?" Sandy and other national officers took this as a compliment of the highest order.

Victor Turner's notion of liminality can be used to describe the period of initiation in "outlaw" motorcycle clubs as a period of ambiguity, "betwixt and between the positions assigned and arrayed by law, custom, convention, and ceremonial" (Hoiland 2012:107–109, citing Turner [1969] 1995:95), because the initiate is neither a biker nor a citizen—she is a prospect. As a noun, "prospect" originated in the early fifteenth century from the Latin *prospectus*, meaning "distant view, look out; sight; faculty of sight," with *pro-* meaning "forward" and *specere* meaning "look at"; only in 1922 did a prospect signify a "person or thing considered promising" ("Prospect"; *Online Etymology Dictionary* 2024). In RSMC, several marked stages require both knowledge and actions, leading to sponsor recommendations and national executive board approval for a full patch. Of his initiation, Velcro, who had a different pseudonym in my earlier writings, told me, "I beat a prospect—that's everyone's initiation. First, I was a hangout, so the club members can get a feel for [my] background. You have to obey everybody who is a full patch or an officer—obey what they say, clean bikes, and show up for all of the parties, and usually do security or bar work" (Hoiland 2012:170). In MCs, members have to be able to give back to the club. For some, the contribution is financial, for others it is technical (e.g., providing website help or sewing patches), and for others it is sheer brute force, as described previously. He added, "They brought me in because of what I can do," and he went on to describe several violent encounters that made him valuable in the eyes of his club (Hoiland 2012:170). In one-percenter MCs, prospects might have to do something illegal to prove they are not cops and to reinforce club loyalty (Queen 2005). Gypsy, a road captain with one of the Satan's Choice MC chapters in Ontario, says:

> When you become a striker [prospect] you are characterized as nothing but dirt. You have no say concerning club activities; and you are

always wrong no matter what you are talking about, even if you're 100 per cent right. It's during this time that you have to start proving yourself to the club. Many times the other members will razz you because you're a striker. He will have to take shit from any member in any chapter; he will have to do whatever he is told by any member, and still do whatever his sponsor tells him to do. (Quoted in Wolf [1991] 2000:91)

This type of extreme liminality is much less pronounced in RSMC. In the Sponsorship Manual, "prospect" is used throughout all stages of initiation, but in practice, many new members are referred to as "sis" or "sister" even before they earn their first patch. Support sisters are also referred to as "sis" and "sister," and many women referred to me as "sis." While some members of RSMC, particularly those who fall on the *biker* spectrum, keep their distance, those on the *rider* spectrum are eager to welcome new members. Trust is hard to come by, and "one's initiation into the Club, like initiation into a [wolf] pack, is lifelong and most [members] believe their very survival depends upon their relationship to the pack" (Hoiland 2012:260). There is a wide spectrum of members' attitudes toward new initiates. Some maintain distance until the newcomer proves themselves by sticking around for a period (months or even a year or more); until they show their riding capabilities during one of the national runs; or until their behavior is observed to indicate their character and temperament.

Sandy assumed the role of being my sponsor, and at times, she encouraged me to get a motorcycle and join. Several members of FOG and a few officers watched me very closely, and some members flat-out ignored me. A few members who were trying to prove their own merit in order to patch up created situations where I was tested. On the other end of the spectrum, at least a dozen righteous sisters hugged me and warmly welcomed me year after year. They invited me into their homes and onto the backs of their motorcycles and treated me like a "sister" from the beginning. These women texted and called me, offered to share space with me, and always asked about my son. In 2014, the national president said, "You will never know what the club is about without joining," but over time, my relationship to the club deepened. Only a few nonmembers attended RSMC's patching ceremony, and I was the only nonmember in the business meeting, to my knowledge. Although there are things that I would never be privy to, primary documents coupled with nearly a decade of participant observation gave me a unique vantage point. Hunter S. Thompson's account of the Hells Angels ([1966] 1999), based on one year of what he calls "gonzo journalism," provided little if any information on the socialization process that both grooms loyal citizens of the club's nation and weeds out potentially problematic members. Daniel Wolf ([1991]

2000), who became a patched member of the Rebels MC, provides one of the few detailed accounts of initiation and the tremendous amount of socialization that occurs in a Canadian MC, which he breaks into two distinct periods: Friend of the Club and Striker. There were few, if any, "friends of the club" in RSMC. Generally, that role, common in MCs, became somewhat more formalized in RSMC—as a support sister—and also allowed the massive bureaucratization of membership to include those who didn't want to be full members. Chapter 2 focuses the processes to "strike" or "prospect." The Sponsorship Manual breaks it down into two categories of knowledge items (KIs), which are what full members have to *know*, and action items (AIs) which include what full members have to *do*. These items are broken down throughout the various stages of initiation and are discussed in detail.

Marrying In

Although I heard various references to being "married" to the club throughout the years, seeing the large three-ring binder with the official stages of initiation "The Promise Ring," "The Engagement Ring," and "Marriage is Forever" surprised me because RSMC is deeply conservative, with the expectation of heteronormative relations and monogamy, and the sister-wives vibe of the initiation stages was shocking. The Sponsorship Manual gave me unprecedented details of the inner workings of initiation. In nearly a decade of participant observation, there was only one instance in which I heard a member describe the dissolution of the tie between a sister and RSMC as "divorce." Men's clubs do not speak in these terms—they speak strictly about *brotherhood*, not marriage—and since RSMC so closely mirrors one-percenter MCs, the shift to heterosexist *marriage* was shocking, particularly given the formal exclusion of nonheterosexual women. This exclusion, however, was not documented, and the only information I could obtain about the switch from the RSMC that admitted gay, lesbian, and queer women when I started my research to the RSMC that no longer admitted gay, lesbian, and queer women halfway through was through Sandy and my own observations.

Before a new prospect enters one of three numbered stages of initiation, they are assigned a "Starter Sponsor" and enter the "Gel Seat Rider" Stage. This four-to-six-week initiation marks the beginning of "Basic Training." Starter Sponsors are given total guidance, from the questions that should be asked in five separate conversations to specific elements on the KI and AI checklists. This stage is a "soft" gel introduction, particularly for those that don't fit "the mold." Prospects sign several agreement and release forms and pay their dues. The most important KIs for Gel Seat Riders are knowing (1) the difference between a motorcycle club (MC) and a riding club (RC) and (2) the Golden or #1-Rule and the difference between "speaking badly about a Sister [violating the Golden Rule] and reporting internal issues detrimental to the club [not violating the Golden Rule];" The AIs revolve around an elaborate system of communication that includes regular phone calls to one's sponsor, to Sandy, and participation in RSMC's private online chat room, and posting in a RSMC online forum. Sponsors go over the RSMC Code of Ethics and personal conduct. Prospects are encouraged to consider how they can give back to RSMC. The sponsor is expected to take detailed notes and to pass the information along to senior leadership, national officers, who will assign the next sponsor.

In stage 1 and 2, prospects are assigned two sponsors, and the completion of each stage results in the acquisition of a "rocker," or one part of the three-piece patch. According to the Sponsorship Manual, it takes between seven months and eleven months, with forty-eight phone calls and forty-eight hours, which is distributed between two sponsors for each stage. At the end of the "skooling period" of each stage, the sponsors must write letters of recommendation for the prospect to receive her patch (bottom rocker and top rocker).

In stage 1, the "Promise Ring," there are a total of thirty-eight KIs and six AIs. The "Navigator" sponsors the prospect for four to twenty-four weeks and the "Co-Navigator" sponsors the prospect for an additional twenty-four weeks. The "Promise Ring Navigators" are responsible for providing a recap of the Gel Seat Rider information, especially what constitutes "club business" and a nuanced understanding of MCs; maintaining call logs; and "Bottom Rocker Skooling," with KIs such as riding protocols; knowledge of RSMC history, traditions, and values; patch protocols and etiquette; and knowledge of several symbols specific to RSMC. Club tattoos are a great example of a KI. They must be approved by the Nationals Executive Board *and* "shared with a Sister." Although I did not hear about any specific club tattoo artists (this is a big business in other MCs) or placement of the club tattoo, the requirement for two women to get tattooed together evidences the centrality of the sisterhood. Club tattoos for RSMC are its center patch. While many women in RSMC did not get a club tattoo, several had prominent (and matching) club tattoos on their forearms. During this stage, prospects also learn about trademark and copyright. While it seems unlikely any lay person would be able to "skool" on these topics given the tremendous complexities surrounding copyright and trademark law, prospects are expected to report any signs of copyright or trademark violation. Sandy registered a trademark of the club's name without the "MC" (RS is a pseudonym) and center patch logo and copyrighted a drawing (presumably the center patch). Tattoos are considered trademarked and copyrighted items, and like full-patch t-shirts and other items "which must be returned to the National Office" if a member leaves the club, members who get club tattoos demonstrate their commitment in a particularly visible way and engage in a potentially risky standoff if they ever resign or are forced to leave RSMC. Another KI is the "no contact rule," or "out means out," which will be discussed in detail in Chapter 4 but is an important part of the early initiation process.

The checklist of AIs includes attendance at one RSMC event in addition to all of the communication requirements. The emphasis on communication can be seen throughout this stage of initiation. Call logs document prospects' participation in the mandatory communication forums, which include weekly online chats, weekly phone calls to sponsors, and monthly phone calls to Sandy. Communication also takes the form of using an emergency text tree and informing road captains when traveling certain distances on one's motorcycle. When the Promise Ring stage is completed, the second sponsor presents the prospect to leadership with a recommendation letter, and a bottom rocker is either awarded or not awarded.

Many times, bottom rockers are surprises—I observed more than a dozen women receiving their bottom rocker at fundraising events for individual chapters or more commonly at club events outside of nationals. It was always quite dramatic, with surprise as a key factor, as well as lots of emotion and affection. Prospects use safety pins to immediately attach the newly earned patches to their leather vests, and other sisters help them with temporary placement until they can be properly sewn on. The surprise factor also serves as a motivation to attend club events outside of nationals, but it also necessitates additional time and money to travel.

In stage 2, the "Engagement Ring," there are a total of twenty-two KIs and fifteen AIs. Two sponsors share the responsibilities of this stage for one month to six months in each of the two phases, "1st Gear" and "Cruising." At the conclusion of this stage of initiation, the top rocker, which is the club's name, is awarded to the prospect. The 1st gear sponsor and cruising sponsor are responsible for a stage 1 recap; call logs; and "top rocker skooling," which includes more about several areas that have already been covered including tattoos, symbols that are unique to RSMC, center patch meaning and history, trademark and copyright, national business meeting, national clubhouse history, reading list, and MC websites. The cruising stage noticeably requires the prospects to get into action by attending all events within a hundred-mile radius of their homes and attending Nationals or the annual family summer gathering. The AIs that the cruising sponsor oversees include more contact with leadership and interactions with national officers, as well as a visit to the national office. Some prospects live as far as 4,500 miles (about 7,242 kilometers) from the national office, so this action item requires significant time and money for some, while others might live in the same state or in a neighboring state for a day or weekend trip. The top rocker is more significant and is the last patch before the center patch, and since it contains the club's name, it is a powerful testament of one's commitment to and acceptance by RSMC. Interestingly, stage 2 could be completed in as few as eight weeks, according to the Sponsor Manual, or as long as forty-eight weeks. Top rockers have been awarded at nationals and at other regional and national club events and are also frequently "surprises" to unsuspecting prospects. Although the conferral of the bottom and top rocker patches is not ceremonial or sacred like that of the center patch, the surprise nature and the drama surrounding it serve the same function: they keep other prospects eager to earn the same patches, and full-patch members are invested in the progress of their prospects and want to be present during these impromptu events. Clearly, they are only impromptu for members who are not privy to inside discussions between sponsors and national officers.

In stage 3, "Marriage is Forever!" there are twenty-four KIs and eight AIs. Two sponsors have the initiate for a total of twelve months split between "6th Gear" and "Hammer Down," This is the longest stage of initiation, and as the title indicates, it is the most important because it is the last stage before a prospect receives her center patch, which makes her a full member of RSMC. The language for the KIs shifts at this stage and becomes more biker and less motorcycle rider. For example, in stages 1 and 2, the KI is "Knows to never discuss club business with anyone other than full members of RSMC." In stage 3, the KI is "Knows and understands the consequences of running her mouth to prospects or citizens." "Discuss" is replaced with "running her mouth." Added to the same norm are consequences. In MCs, the consequences can be immediate and violent—a slap across the face—but in RSMC, the same kind of humiliation can be verbal and public and can also include having one's patches pulled (taken). The time it takes to earn pulled patches back depends on the club, but the public punishment is a form of shaming designed to lead members into submission. The sponsors are responsible for the following: a recap of all info, call logs, and "center patch skooling," including specific artifacts related to the history of RSMC, current RSMC chapters, one-percenters in her area, and the club constitution and bylaws. The final sponsor must make a recommendation, and center patches are only awarded annually at Nationals.

During several interviews, Sandy made statements like "You can come from a bad background, and some stay with us a short period of time, and others stay with us for good. God sends them our way, and we help them along. They say, 'I've been raped, or I've done this.'" Through many conversations with Sandy and members, RSMC provides an elaborate support network, and as with other recovery programs that also work within a sponsorship framework and specific phases or steps of recovery, survivors of rape, domestic violence, and other types of trauma find a home in RSMC. The initiation structure provides a way for prospects to connect with sponsors, but it increasingly becomes more MC and less supportive hub. Unlike many other types of supportive women-centered communities, "out means out" in RSMC. With very few exceptions, Sandy was extremely detached when it came to "divorce," or members leaving the club; the seemingly free-flowing exit with no reentry contradicts both familiar structures—sisterhood and marriage—and exit was not always voluntary as it appears in the Sponsorship Manual.

Conclusion

Becoming a righteous sister and being awarded the three-piece patch is a long and arduous process. Events like the spirit ride are more than an "action item" on a checklist. They serve multiple functions from the political socialization about brothers and sisters lost to technical socialization related to riding in formation with dozens of other women to the social components of the club, which are largely absent from the formalities discussed through the various stages of initiation. The spirit ride and the patching ceremony also provide glimpses of the immortality that awaits full citizenship and membership. Throughout these stages of initiation, which take several years of a woman's life, there are also games, laughter, pranks, and inside jokes. There is also gossip and rivalry and aggression. Sisterhood is a gendered construct that is constantly negotiated at multiple levels—at the individual level, at the club level, and within the larger world of bikers—through initiation. The next chapter delves into the many facets of "being a sister" that are part of the stages of initiation and part of the sisterhood that encompasses the dozens of full-patch sisters.

3

RIGHTEOUSNESS AND THE REALM OF ACTION

An Awards Ceremony

The Sister of the Year Award is given on the last night of nationals. The awards ceremony is a foil to the members-only, dark, and near-silent ritual patching ceremony that took place just a few hours earlier in the same clubhouse space; it is filled with light and noise and is open to husbands and support members. Whereas the conferral of patches is decided upon by national officers and recommendations from sponsors, the award recipients are selected by all voting members in an example of direct democracy in the club. The most coveted of the awards, Sister of the Year, is described in the Sponsorship Manual:

> The Sister who has gone above and beyond the call of Sisterhood. She's always there, whether it be late night phone calls, or a smile, when no one seems to have one. She reminds you how to laugh when you have forgotten how to. She supports her Sisters in all she says and does. She is not only beside her [S]isters; she is behind them 110%. In 1995, this award was voted to be changed to the "WINONA AWARD" to honor "Shirley 'Winona' Armstrong."[1] She displays the true meaning of Sisterhood on a daily basis.
>
> The honor and status conferred to a single recipient each year functions as a mechanism for measuring righteousness and highlights the kinds of

commitment and sacrifices members make as obedient, allegiant subjects to the national president, Sandy, and to the RSMC. The awards ceremony is a performative place in which individuals are set apart from other members for their contributions and are publicly recognized and celebrated for achieving excellence, or what bikers refer to as *righteousness*. This concept is similar to the ancient Greek term "arete," loosely translated as excellence, and has "always been assigned to the public realm where one could excel, could distinguish oneself from all others" (Arendt [1958] 1998:48–49). To my knowledge, men-only MCs do not engage in this type of recognition ceremony after a patching ritual; they might have a party at the clubhouse or head to a favorite bar or strip club to celebrate the newly patched members. Thus, RSMC provides a fascinating look at the ways in which women engage in formalized processes to publicly award excellence within the RSMC nation.

One year, the national sergeant-at-arms, "Skully," was voted Sister of the Year. At the time, I was sitting next to Sandy at the clubhouse bar, and she joked that "this one [would] really make them cry." Skully's name was read as the winner of the Winona Award, and the otherwise-tough officer broke down into tears as the mistress of ceremonies read dozens of comments submitted to support her nomination, including specific anecdotes of Skully being there for others during a family death, a divorce, cancer treatments, or other personal or familial difficulties. There was nary a dry eye in the clubhouse. Skully was wearing her customary jeans, black leather biker boots, a full-patch T-shirt with her full-patch black leather vest. She is average height with a muscular build, short silvery-gray hair, and dark piercing eyes. Her longtime partner, also a full-patch member of RSMC, was seated with the rest of the more than one hundred people who attended nationals, but as one of Skully's sisters rather than as a romantic partner.

Members must be willing and able to earn their keep, and they must prove their usefulness to the biker nation. Skully enlisted in the U.S. Marine Corps in 1976, a time when the women's movement and the antiwar movement greatly influenced sex-segregation in the U.S. military. In 1977, the Women Marine Program was disbanded, which eliminated separate command structures for men and women. Skully described strictly enforced protocols for women, such as wearing dresses, girdles, and wigs all the time. "We never saw a rifle or a grenade. Our motto was to free a man to fight. They trained us to do parties so that we could host parties. That's all we knew, and I didn't care because I was going to change the world," she said. Work sections included making coffee and typing. Skully, who was in motor transport, said, "They would never let me drive the trucks. I had to drive the cars, even though I am from a truck-driving-type background. I originally wanted to be a mechanic, but no women were allowed to turn wrenches [*pauses*] because they might work on combat vehicles [*laughs*]."[2] Although the U.S. Marine

Corps policies were officially changing, Skully's experience demonstrates the lag in implementation. In 1976, the first women drill instructors graduated from Drill Instructor School at Parris Island, and all regulations differentiating the sexes were supposed to have a "valid and rational purpose," according to Commandant General Louis H. Wilson Jr. (Stremlow 1986). Skully took great pride in her role in training women in the U.S. Marine Corps and then, upon retirement, joining her local fire service and rising in rank there, training recruits. Decades of pushing women to be their best in male-dominated fields and her willingness to submit to command suited Skully perfectly for her role in RSMC; she posed no threat to Sandy's authority and was extremely well positioned to socialize prospects and members to be righteous sisters.

Other members gain recognition by using their bodies to labor for the nation; they build, paint, tear down, cook, clean, mow the grass, and landscape. Members can distinguish themselves through a variety of mechanisms, such as philanthropic endeavors on behalf of the club, which provide both notoriety and press for the club, and gift giving as a coercive and competitive means through which to demonstrate loyalty. In MCs, there are cash cows who might not be traditional biker types but who support the club monetarily through their purchases, gifts, and donations. Muscle and brute strength play almost no role in female status or righteousness, and although several women, including Skully, bragged about their prowess in shooting and many held weapons permits, beating people up or shooting them was not part of RSMC, or if it was, it was hidden so well that I never saw it or heard about it in a decade of participant observation. The need to go "above and beyond" and stand behind one's sisters "110%" set up literally impossible standards for the Sister of the Year Award, and like many other things in RSMC, it is highly subjective and heavily influenced by the national president.

Throughout this monograph, RSMC has been described as a political entity. Sandy and members of RSMC refer to the club as a nation, which is common across MCs. More simply, the club is a polis. Arendt describes the polis as a place for "the sharing of words and deeds" that has two functions: women members of RSMC can win "immortal fame" and the polis offers "a remedy for the futility of action and speech" through a "kind of organized remembrance" ([1958] 1998:197–198). The polis is not the walled-in physical location; "it is the organization of the people as it arises out of acting and speaking together, and its true space lies between people living for this purpose, no matter where they happen to be, 'Wherever you go, you will be a *polis*'" ([1958] 1998:198). This expansive notion of a realm of action and the possibility therein to distinguish oneself in a way that is not possible outside the polis is apropos. When women become prospects in RSMC, they are looking for ways to distinguish themselves. The pinnacle of this distinction is the Sister of the Year Award, and one of the ways this honor is immortalized is through entering the name in *The Book of Sisters*, as a living archive of biker arete.

In describing the patching ceremony and the symbolic importance of the patches in Chapter 1, I relied on Arendt's notion of power, authority, and strength. In Chapter 3, RSMC is examined as a polis in which individuals are capable of achieving arete—or righteousness, to integrate biker argot—through action and having that righteousness immortalized. Chapter 3 begins by delving into the life histories of two key players who achieved arete, or righteousness: the national president and national sergeant-at-arms. Next, I describe labor within RSMC as a type of pseudo-righteousness for some women. Gifts to one another, to oneself, and to the community through philanthropic efforts are then systematically analyzed as additional spaces of appearances for women to distinguish themselves.

Achieving Arete

Skully became a member of RSMC shortly after I began my participant observation research. It was clear she knew how to operate in a strictly hierarchical system, and her military background clearly positioned her to be a good MC prospect. However, even though she had built a career in two rigorous male-dominated fields, her background and training as a sergeant first class in the U.S. Marines and a lieutenant in the fire service did not catapult her to a position of leadership or advanced standing; she started at square one with no patches and no status in the club. Within five to six years, Skully became national sergeant-at-arms. She described the three-to-five-year RSMC initiation, first distinguishing it from one-percenter clubs in which killing might be part of the initiation, as follows: "It's because we don't go out and kill people. We have to make sure you are going to stick around. They leave as a better human being, not just a woman. We look at it as a lot bigger than us as individuals, and I don't think guys' clubs look at it that way." For gay, lesbian, and queer sisters, the RSMC's cisgender, heterosexual values create the same kind of twoness Skully experienced in the military, and likely in the fire service, in terms of both gender and sexuality. She identifies as a woman, but her presentation is more masculine. This is accepted and even coveted in male-dominated organizations such as the military, the fire service, and motorcycle clubs, and Skully took it as an indicator of success when a fire service trainee said he didn't think of her as *a woman*. Although Skully and her partner have been together as long as they have been in RSMC, their lesbian love must be hidden. A deep admiration and respect for each other could be seen when they were at large club gatherings at nationals, but they did not display any intimacy or even casual affection like hugging or kissing, both of which were totally acceptable for heterosexual couples. Skully slept in the

"Big House" with the other national officers while her partner stayed elsewhere. When I traveled to several cities and stayed in hotels with Skully, her partner did not attend, and her same-sex relationship was club business and therefore strictly off-limits.

Skully's utility to the club was clear from the beginning, and when I asked Sandy about the value of military veterans, such as Skully, she said: "A lot of military women are joining clubs because they are used to the camaraderie, and they are not catty. They are so awesome, these women that are coming in, and because they don't have service anymore, they are ready to commit to something. Most of them are officers, which I find even more amazing." I asked about their leadership potential. She quickly said, "Hell yeah, oh hell yeah. I know they know their shit. Very quiet and timid, but don't fuck with them. One of the sister's husbands bought her a pink gun, and one of the sisters was showing her how easy it was to take it away from her because it had no handle and how easy it was to shoot. This was in my living room." In those moments, Sandy's one-percenter background came through: she associated leadership with the kind of bravado that characterizes the one-percenters, and gun play in her living room was a perfect scenario to display one's utility to the club.

In addition to being supremely qualified for a leadership position within RSMC, Skully's loyalty to Sandy and the club was unquestioned. She knew how to patiently work her way up the ranks and wait for the opportunity to be called into service as national sergeant-at-arms. Her new space of appearances was a matriarchal polis, and the requirements for excellence were clear, and Skully's reward for her years of service and dedication was the Sister of the Year Award, a public recognition of her value to the club. A sense of meritocracy pervades initiation—if recruits follow the steps, it is suggested, they too, can achieve arete—but the Skullys are set apart, even tracked for leadership, early on.

The founder and national president of the RSMC, Sandy, is completely different from Skully. Skully is college educated with multiple certifications, whereas Sandy completed her general equivalency diploma (GED) in her twenties. Sandy was a teenage bride, an emancipated minor, married to a one-percenter; Skully's personal background from her twenties to her forties remained private, but her life partner was a member of RSMC for many years. Sandy typically wore Bermuda shorts, flip-flops, and a loose-fitting feminine top with long, wavy blond hair, whereas Skully's "uniform" was black boots, jeans, and a full-patch club T-shirt. They are different in background, training, and appearance; however, both are bikers, and their attitude and service to the nation align them and create a special bond. Sandy's background gives her political legitimacy in the ways described in Chapter 1, and it enabled her to single-handedly move Righteous Sisterhood from a riding club to a motorcycle club. In the motorcycle world, she is a singular powerhouse of almost mythical proportions because of her personal history, longevity, and accomplishments within the strict confines of the one-percenter world, her realm of action, as well as within the nation she built and has led for decades. For Sandy, club life is about "being strong, knowing who you are, honor, and respect." Club life as an ol' lady negated a realm of action for Sandy; as she described in our initial interview, she stayed silent and jumped into the pool when told to do so by male one-percenters. As the national president of RSMC, on the other hand, she leads a nation of approximately one hundred women in at least three countries and runs a small business. Her movement from a one-percenter woman to a biker woman uniquely positions her to lead RSMC.

Sandy's legitimacy also comes from her commitment to God and family, two of the club's core values. She was a single mom for ten years after she became a widow, and she became a mother to her second husband's daughter and filled that role for the past two decades. The commitment to God was interspersed with frequent diatribes on orbs, spirits, fairies, crystals, and other mystical things. Her belief in a personal God contradicts an omniscient God. She stated, "God knew he fucked up. That's why he gave me another chance." The "fuckup" was her first husband's violent death, and the second chance was her second husband. This view of a God who makes mistakes and consciously corrects by creating new opportunities for individual humans is a conception of a monotheistic God and a rationalization of the one-percenter lifestyle. Sandy's spirituality came through as she described the unique qualities of the national clubhouse and the sisters who came to the property as being able to imbue their energy fields and create colored orbs. One summer, she showed me dozens of photographs of different balls of light (orbs) at the clubhouse and insisted that I go outside at night to see them for myself. I was encouraged to touch her residential home before leaving to give it some of my energy and to do other ritualistic practices consistent with New Age belief systems. Crystals and other gemstones were sold in the RSMC gift shop. Praying to a monotheistic male God before dinner and looking for colored orbs were both consistent with the spirituality and belief systems in RSMC.

Sandy's commitment and loyalty to her three daughters and her husband are central to her arete. One of her daughters lives out of state with her husband and children and purposefully lives outside biker life. I met her once in ten years. Sandy's other two daughters live in her residential home and on the nearby ten-acre clubhouse grounds. Sandy became a mother to her second husband's daughter, "Em," when the little girl was a toddler. Em was a student (junior high, high school, and college) during my period of observation and lived at home. One of Sandy's daughters, Stormy, a single mom with two daughters, lived in the same rural area, but after a natural disaster, Stormy and her daughters moved "on property." They were local fixtures who spent significant amounts of time with some of the sisters.

When members "marry" into RSMC by becoming full-patch members, the ideal mother and motherhood are intimately tied with this matriarchal nation and its founder and sole national president. Sandy's role as a mother to three daughters and a grandmother to five grandchildren, and particularly her decade as a widow with two teenage daughters, adds to her power and mystique. Her backstory creates a unique space for Sandy as founding mother and national president to play a maternal role in the nation. The kind of labor involved with birthing RSMC is viewed with reverence, mystique, and a sense of impossibility. The question of succession becomes more complex when Sandy's own narrative and unwritten policies all but preclude the most qualified person, Skully, from serving as national president. The awards system, which includes three sets of patches and annual awards such as the Sister of the Year Award, is coupled with huge responsibilities and the demands of a motorcycle club, which include time, money, obedience, and labor. The quest for righteousness within RSMC is fueled by loyalty to the nation and to its founding mother. Sandy and Skully have achieved arete through two distinct paths and are immortalized through various honors and accolades, codified in *The Book of Sisters*. Their arete is also cemented by their physical contributions to the club, their labor, performed in public. For Arendt, the public realm is the sine qua non for human excellence, and RSMC created this public.

The Public Space of Appearances

One of the standout features of RSMC is the sheer amount of labor and work that goes into all facets of club life, particularly the clubhouse. As stated earlier, in 2010, Sandy's personal home doubled as the clubhouse. When my then husband, my three-year-old son, and I arrived, we were greeted by a large German shepherd and several dachshunds all barking ferociously. A righteous sister ushered us inside Sandy's home and then left us near the living room, which adjoined the kitchen. The latter was abuzz with sewing machines, which I later learned were part of an embroidery business owned and operated by Sandy, which produced items for RSMC as well as other MCs. Without any introduction, Sandy beckoned me to follow her outside, where we sat on the steps. The flurry of activity was also outside as other women were unloading a trailer full of plants and planting them in her yard. As we spoke, she occasionally covered her eyes to show that she was not seeing the "surprise" birthday gifts. After nearly two hours, she led me into her office and said with a hint of a smile, "Not many people get to come in here, you know." The small office was filled with framed newspaper clippings, photographs, and other RSMC artifacts. Her large desk was only matched by a large leather executive-style chair. A small chair faced the desk, and since her patches were hanging on the back, I stood by the chair as she explained what several of the artifacts on the walls and on her desk were. She nodded and removed her colors, signaling her appreciation and acknowledgment that I knew not to touch her patches. Her office felt like a museum with pieces of RSMC's history on the walls, on her desk, and scattered around the tastefully decorated office. Her office was a space of appearances that showcased her righteousness.

Later, I went to retrieve my son, who was playing in Sandy's saltwater pool with her three-year-old granddaughter. He knocked over a poolside decoration, and it broke. My son was startled and looked like he was ready to cry, so I picked him up while several members of RSMC swooped in and picked up the pieces. As I reflect on this incident a decade later, what stands out is the breakable items near a swimming pool with young kids. In some ways, this is illustrative of RSMC. Certain "knowledge items" and "action items" are like glass near a swimming pool in that they inevitably will be broken. Sandy placed the glass poolside and remains unquestioned while the sisterhood cleans up the mess.

In 2012, Sandy's residential home burned down, and she and her family moved to a rental home nearby, while she and her sisters rebuilt her home. It was clear that it had been a hive of sorts from RSMC's earliest days in the 1980s and 1990s, with women doing all kinds of things inside and outside the home like what I observed at her birthday party in 2010. It was also the "Home" of nationals, or the annual meeting in which all members got together for one week. Throughout the years, I was regaled with stories of dozens of women camping out in the front yard and using the garden hose as an outdoor shower. A deep nostalgia for the "good ol' days" and "roughing it" in tents pervaded FOG and other longtime members, and it was one of the many reasons that so many members, longtime and new, worked to rebuild her home after the fire. Sandy invited me over for lunch at the rental house in the summer of 2012. As we ate the iceberg lettuce salad she had prepared for lunch, she told me what had happened to her home. The hot water heater exploded and nearly burned the house to the ground, and nothing was recovered. Without emotion, she stated, "No one was injured, but the cat, the dumb one, was missing." Colorful fliers were posted in her old neighborhood, but the cat didn't resurface. Her husband, daughter, motorcycle, and dogs were all okay. The flatness with which she described losing all her material possessions surprised me and contradicted the sentiment she had conveyed in 2010 when I was in her office, but it represents larger contradictions and tensions.

The anthropologist Daniel Wolf asserted that the "hedonist biker psychology," whereby bikers live a free and unconditioned life, is much more symbolic than an accurate description of their lifestyle; like many lower-working-class men, "most have jobs to go to when Monday morning comes" ([1991] 2000:57). Righteous sisters like Sandy reject material possessions outside their motorcycle and patches. Her response regarding the total loss of what were precious artifacts illustrate her views of work, money, and material possessions, and though contradicted somewhat by the physical rebuild, this attitude and lack of attachment to material things reverberates across bikers as part of a larger freedom ethic. To be without material possessions is to be free—houses can be rebuilt, furniture can be bought anew, and even if her patches burned, she could do the embroidery herself to make a new set of patches. More than that of most of the RSMC members, Sandy's unique position in the one-percenter world often seemed at odds with the all-female MC she founded and led, at least in its contemporary and quite materialist formation.

Her rebuilt home was extravagant and included many upgrades from her previous home, and Sandy credited the massive interior and exterior renovation to the sisterhood, saying hundreds of hours were put in by a variety of women near and far. This was one of the biggest spaces of appearances in which members of RSMC could distinguish themselves with physical labor, denoting their dedication to the nation, its Home, and its national president. Sisters came Home on weekends, from a few miles or several hours away, and worked collectively to rebuild Sandy's residential home while simultaneously bonding over shared construction projects in what they fondly referred to as "Sister Time."

The fire catalyzed Sandy and other members of leadership to expand and secure a Home for the growing nation outside of Sandy's residential home. In 2012, the RSMC National Clubhouse was established as a limited liability corporation (LLC), and that LLC leases the building to RSMC Estates, which leases it to RSMC. Sandy serves as the property manager but said she does not pay herself a salary. The original owners of the home and surrounding ten acres still reside there for half of the year, and "Mom" is a member of RSMC and FOG. The same kind of transformation that occurred at Sandy's home, which doubled as a clubhouse for the first twenty-five plus years of RSMC, occurred nearby at what would become the new national headquarters. Over the course of a few years, sisters transformed ten acres of unkempt swampland and an old house into a luscious green lawn teeming with plants and flowers, a new fifty-thousand-square-foot clubhouse outfitted with a bar, pool tables, seating for up to one hundred people, and a screened lanai for eating and gathering. In 2019, there were six housing units including cabins for rental or purchase, places to park one's RV, a wide expanse to pitch tents, a communal bathroom and shower facility with four toilets and four showers and sinks, several sheds to house lawn equipment and tools, a chicken coop, and a massive pond with a rocked-in waterfall.

In 2014, Sandy invited me to purchase shares in one of the "cabins," which were outdoor sheds, and I bought shares for $1,500. This provided me with a space in the cabin for as long as I remained in good standing. Our cabin had two sets of bunk beds, a queen-size bed, two loft spaces, a small front porch, and two windows. Each large outdoor cabin was customized by the group of women who used it. One summer, I helped to install a laminate floor, insulation, and plywood walls inside our cabin with a few of the cabinmates and a nonbiker friend. Each cabin on the row had its own distinctive identity and occupancy based on geographic location or other identifiers, such as the "couples cabin," which was occupied by three married heterosexual couples. Officers stayed in the "Big House," a rambler-style home that was gut-renovated by the women when it became part of RSMC Estates. Near the clubhouse, the Big House was a three-bedroom, one-bathroom home with a large dining room table, an open kitchen, and a large sunken family room with a huge leather sectional, a full bar, and a pool table. Sliding doors from the kitchen led to a large lanai with a saltwater pool. As additional "cabins" were constructed in a line toward the rear end of the property, the "Big House" took on new meaning with its plantation-style building occupied by white women. Mom and her husband went to the Midwest each summer to be with their family, and Sandy invited me, among others, to stay in the "Big House" in the summer.

From demolition to drywall, painting, and landscaping, sisters did the vast majority of the work, and their labor was documented in RSMC photo albums and on the walls of the new clubhouse. Sisters who worked the most were given praise, public recognition, and a sense of belonging and purpose as they created what would become "Home" to the nation of one hundred women. A few men participated in the heavy construction and renovation over the years and were similarly rewarded for their righteousness at the annual awards ceremony. The national president's brother was awarded the Big Brother Award, sometimes referred to as the Den Daddy Award, for his help with the heaviest construction. A contractor and heavy machine operator, he was a regular fixture for a few years but was very introverted. Not wanting the public recognition, he didn't attend the awards ceremony, so a dozen women found him working on a far corner of the property and presented him with the award as others clapped and cheered. A few of the sisters' husbands would also come on the weekends and assist with specific projects depending on their professional training, whether it was plumbing, carpentry, painting, or electrical. Most seemed to revel in the attention from the Big Brother Award, and Sandy's husband was notorious for campaigning for himself to be nominated, and indeed, he won the award several times.

Sandy acted as foreperson and directed the work. Sisters who lived closest to the national headquarters did the majority of the physical labor and would continue to do so as it required a tremendous amount of upkeep. At various points, some lived "on property" and seemed to have an arrangement to work off their rent by taking care of the massive lawn or doing other things around the property. A few would come with an RV or trailer to spend the winters at national headquarters and work on various projects for extended periods of time. Other members took their vacation time to go Home and work on the property. Sandy was never on the sidelines watching—she worked alongside her sisters and was a literal property manager, doing much of the work herself. Her role as visionary allowed for a continuously evolving Home. When one project would end, one could almost see the wheels turning as her blue eyes took in everything around her, and another idea would lead to another project, thus creating new spaces of appearances for women to become righteous sisters, allowing them to further commit themselves to the nation, its members, and the quest for immortality.

Sometimes the new projects involved animal rescues; there was a giant potbellied pig at Home. A huge animal lover, Sandy had a special pen built for it and mostly took charge of its care; a sister owned the pig and needed a place for it, and Sandy agreed to take it. After several raccoon rescues, including a baby, a special cage was built on the property. Stormy, Sandy's daughter, was also an animal lover, and toward the end of my participant observation, Stormy and I went to Home Depot one night during summer 2019. We had a hot tip that the store had thrown out a lot of plants. We drove over as it was getting dark, near the time the store would close, and the summer sky opened, and rain came down in sheets. She looked at me as we pulled up alongside the dumpsters, she in her SUV and I in my rental car, and we both jumped out and started loading the plants into the back of her SUV while the rain pelted us. We were laughing above the roar of the rain, our clothes soaked, and quickly filled her entire SUV with the discarded plants and flowers, trying not to spill the wet dirt, and then we filled my rental car. We unloaded the plants near her home on the back end of the property, and Stormy's dog discovered three newborn animals. We couldn't tell what they were—squirrels, mice—but they had no hair, their eyes were closed, and they looked very, very ill. Stormy and I discussed what to do, and as she set about making an emergency setup for them, I went to the store and found eyedroppers for feeding. She stayed up all night long, dispensing a few drops of milk every two to three hours. One died that night, but she continued to nurse the other two back to health over the next several days. That story became another escapade that spread quickly among RSMC. My son played with her daughter when they were three years old, and I watched her girls grow up over the years, playing with them, talking to them, and checking in with Stormy.

Through the escapades, I experienced the space of appearances, mostly with Sandy's family of origin. I helped her youngest daughter prepare for college, served as the designated adult watching her youngest granddaughter during public events, and talked to Sandy about things like diet and exercise. This was possible, in part, because of the length of my tenure with RSMC and the week or more I spent at national headquarters each summer, when few RSMC members were around. It was also because, as an outsider who was not seeking membership, I was not competing for righteousness and Sandy's favor, and I was familiar with biker subculture.

Although I completely stood out visually as the only woman not wearing a leather vest, I was most comfortable working alongside other women. Doing so allowed me to get to know women, and I preferred to stay busy, but for other women who were hoping to get one of their patches conferred, it turned out to be a competitive space of appearances. One year at nationals, I was picking weeds with a full-patch member from Canada whom I didn't know very well, and I was really enjoying the conversation. I enjoy being outdoors and gardening, and for a New Yorker with no personal green space (still), it was cathartic to go down there and work with my hands, and I appreciated the accommodations Sandy provided in the Big House, so puttering around outside was also a way to repay Sandy for her hospitality. A member named "Chatty" got very angry and complained to other members, saying I was trying to "show everyone up" by picking some weeds around the pool. It became a "club issue" because Chatty made a snide comment in front of several sisters, which violated the "no gossip" rule, so it escalated to Sandy, who was then put in a position to resolve it. Sandy spoke privately to me and reassured me that I had not done anything wrong and that Chatty did not understand that I had spent weeks at the clubhouse over the summers doing similar work. The incident was not mentioned again to me that nationals, but it highlighted my insider-outsider status. I was not a member, but some of the rules applied to me. Chatty did not get her top rocker that year, and she was out of the club within one year for "talking too much."

"Sister Time" could involve very heavy labor under a hot sun, but it also included things like communal dinners, motorcycle rides, and fundraisers. One weekend, "T-Shirt Tammy"[3] and I, at the behest of Sandy's brother, painted the lower half of the clubhouse. Sandy was away with her youngest daughter on a college tour, so we painted without her knowledge or approval. T-Shirt Tammy was a full-patch member who lived on the property in a trailer. She mowed the grass in exchange for having a piece of land and electricity. She worked at a local chain home improvement store, and her motorcycle was her only form of transportation. To my knowledge, she had never been married and had no children, and she seemed very happy to be a member of RSMC and to put countless hours into maintaining the ten-acre property and contributing to whatever new projects started. T-Shirt Tammy generally went with the flow, so when Sandy's brother suggested we "surprise her," she agreed. We spent most of the day kneeling down to tape and then paint around a large oak molding that divided the approximately 2,500-square-foot clubhouse in half and another two-inch molding around the bottom, and then we rolled it out. Sandy nodded her approval when she returned, and I heard her tell other sisters how crazy we were to do that without her approval. She then followed it up with praise. My utility to Sandy was not my painting or gardening skills, but I was in the space of appearances whether I chose to be or not. T-Shirt Tammy, on the other hand, achieved a kind of righteousness through her physical labor at national headquarters. T-Shirt Tammy would not be a chapter president or national officer, and both she and Sandy were aware of the club-imposed structural limitations.

Members came "Home" for a weekend or week and did as much work as they could around the "property," both terms used to describe the new ten-acre compound that housed the Big House, the clubhouse, six cabins, and the Little House. The vast majority of members lived out of state, and several lived in Canada or the United Kingdom. A few women became snowbirds and flew south for several months, during which they assisted with all maintenance while living in their own personal RV. A handful of women, the composition of which changed over time, were locals and did the lion's share of the work alongside Sandy. They referred to themselves as "fairies" for many years because it seemed almost magical that the massive property and everything on it was always in pristine condition when everyone else showed up at nationals each year. Over time, some fairies became "Bad Ass Fairies," who were predominantly weekend warriors—those who came somewhat regularly to work—and a handful became "Bad Ass Mother Fucking Fairies," or BAMFFs. The BAMFFs included Sandy, T-Shirt Tammy, and a few other sisters who either lived on the property all or part of the year or lived close enough to spend significant amounts of time and hard labor there. The BAMFFs made T-shirts to recognize their status, and each year at nationals after the name stuck, the BAMFFs were publicly recognized and stood up as the entire nation applauded their efforts to keep the national headquarters in pristine condition year-round. T-Shirt Tammy, the longest-running BAMFF, was proud of the title and the accolades at nationals each year.

Thus, the spaces of appearances for women like T-Shirt Tammy were open for words, action, and one's own shot at immortality within RSMC. Working alongside the national president and other national officers (the vice president at the time was also a BAMFF) provided the club with an egalitarian feeling in which status nearly disappeared during the many renovation projects. This space provided fertile fields for Sister Time and camaraderie. While they hammered plywood into the cabin walls, there were stories, pranks, laughter, and adventures leading to new stories to be shared. The physicality of the labor coupled with the fun atmosphere created a deep investment for these members in the national headquarters and a collective sense of ownership and pride. There was also an exuberant sense of a particular kind of female empowerment, particularly when projects included large machinery, power tools, or a full trailer of materials from Home Depot. The outward manifestations of the countless hours of labor, including a swamp area that was converted into a waterfall, were admired each year when civilians and other motorcycle clubs were invited to the clubhouse for an annual party during nationals. This widened the space of appearances to male motorcycle clubs and elevated Sandy's position within the COC, deepening her righteousness in the larger, and notoriously misogynistic, world of MCs and raising the status of RSMC as a "real club."

Sandy's remodeled residential home remained a very special place to many of the members, both old and new. One of the requirements for all prospects is to have "cave time with Boss (Sandy)." The cave is a small windowless spare room just off the dining room, and it has two sets of pocket doors and a small bed. I stayed in the cave a few times and slept like a rock. Once, I saw a raccoon paw underneath my bed (a rescue that was not yet old enough to transition to the cage at the clubhouse), and Sandy cajoled it out before I went to sleep and closed the pocket doors for the evening. Cave time is a way for Sandy to vet prospects, but it also functions as a way for new members to get to know her when she is not as busy. Many sisters speak about meaningful time they spent in the cave with "Boss." One sister said she came Home after her father died and felt healing energy. Another sister described her blood levels being off and said Sandy provided both "knowledge and healing" after noticing what was going on with her physical health. Many prospects are scared. One said, "I was scared to death—like the Cowardly Lion going to see the Wizard of Oz." Sandy said, "The cave heals deep pains, and there is soul-baring around the table." This type of New Age healing and mysticism pervades both her home and the national clubhouse. Both are primary spaces of appearance for Sandy.

Each year, at the close of nationals, national officers remind all sisters to ride by Sandy's house on their way out and to give energy back to the house by touching it, saying, "There are fields of energy that need to be regenerated by sisters." Some of the members were perceived as being more in touch with energy fields, orbs, and the mystic arts, and this was viewed as a special source of power and intelligence, much as Sandy's healing power contributed to her righteousness and words and deeds in the realm of action.

During nationals, one of the full-patch holders supervises each of the chore duties. Earlier, the massive duties entailed in preparing meals three times a day was described, but similar were the cleaning crews who worked on the toilets and showers near the cabins, the clubhouse toilets, and the dozens of trash receptacles around the grounds. Sandy is neat—her home is clean; her truck is clean; her bike is clean. The ten acres of land, the Big House, and the clubhouse are always impeccably clean. At first, I thought the newest initiates would be given some of the "worst" jobs, such as guarding bikes on the night shift (i.e., from two o'clock to five o'clock in the morning), cleaning clubhouse bathrooms, and taking out the trash, but just as the BAMFFs consisted of top-ranking women, I noticed a similar division of labor at nationals. In 2019, I flew around the property on a golf cart with two national officers, emptying trash cans and ashtrays while accompanying them on garbage duty. We had a blast—hitting small sand dune speed bumps, taking sharp turns, telling jokes, and discussing pranks to pull—to the extent that someone commented that we were having *too much* fun on trash duty. Sisterhood is created through joint labor, but it can also be a source of jealousy.

In RSMC, the primary function of having women work together in teams to complete different tasks in and around the clubhouse and expansive club property is to beautify the space that is considered communal property and "Home" to even the newest members of the club. All members contribute to the upkeep of the property, and the most righteous sisters, such as Sandy and Skully, could be frequently seen dumping trash, picking up a piece of garbage, or pulling a weed when no one else was looking. This communal model of shared responsibility, regardless of status, during nationals takes place one of fifty-two weeks in a year. Members who cannot contribute labor and time during the offseason, or the fifty-one weeks a year that the national headquarters are not populated with one hundred club members, are encouraged to submit monetary donations to the fairy fund, which can be utilized for any number of supplies, fairy food (lunch for the BAMFFs), and general upkeep, such as gas for the lawn mower and electricity. The many secondary functions, described herein, are primarily to increase the sense of belonging in the sisterhood and to create a space of appearances for every member, lending a kind of equality to RSMC that is not evidenced in other MCs.

When it comes to work, as in what one does for a living, Sandy's views are very much in line with traditional bikers. She said, "Work doesn't define who you are. How many people really live for their job?" As someone who really loves my career, I must have inadvertently raised my eyebrow when Sandy was talking about the ridiculousness of living for one's work, leading her to assert with incredulity, "You work to get a paycheck. That's it. Does anyone actually live to work?" She described two scenarios—one in which she was unexpectedly laid off and another in which a sister lost her job—and the moral of both stories was to consider what you *need* and to find a way to put your energy into what you enjoy doing. To end the conversation, she said, "Life changes. You move on and you evolve." For several of the women in RSMC—including Skully and several other members who were in technically trained service professions like fire management, rescue, and nursing—their occupations did seem to be a huge part of their identity. There were a few educators in RSMC, including a college administrator, and many of the women were college educated and had white-collar jobs. Many members of RSMC were retired or widowed and able to devote the time and service required in an MC. In Wolf's conclusion of *The Rebels*, he wrote, "The source of opposition lies in the fact that an outlaw MC is a reaction against the superego of technocracy—the Protestant ethic: the principle that one's work is one's life. Outlaw bikers desire to go beyond a purely rationalized sense of self and society. The core motivation for the outlaw biker is to achieve a sense of personal self that transcends the ordinary, and to live an existence that occasionally breaks the shackles that chain one to the mundane" ([1991] 2000: 348). This is one area in which Sandy's forty-plus years in the one-percenter world seep through. Like the outlaw bikers in Wolf's ethnography, Sandy's "sense of personal self" is purely transcendent and absolutely defies the conventions of womanhood. She exudes a kind of power and charismatic authority that is unique among MCs, male and female, and also in other organizations and in many ways turns on its head the kind of feminism in which a woman seeks validation and status through work. Sandy's life as a young widow and single mother of two with a high school education positioned her to a life of low-wage work and struggle, much as her own single mother with two children lived in the Midwest a generation earlier. The kind of misogyny she observed as an ol' lady in a one-percenter MC and her secondary status as a woman and nonclub member, while not mundane, surely led to a shackled existence. Sandy's existence is exceptional in the way Wolf describes because she has created a life for herself in which her limited educational and economic future are buttressed by her position in the MC and her relationships with dozens of other MCs, thus securing her economic future while also consolidating power, status, and righteousness. She is her own boss, and dozens of women from all walks of life call her "Boss" and demonstrate their willingness to serve her nation in order to establish themselves as righteous sisters.

The contradictions inherent in providing unpaid labor and work to the club and unquestionable loyalty to Sandy were put to the test one nationals, the ultimate space of appearances for members of the RSMC. One member turned off from the pack on a group ride, and several others followed her back to the clubhouse at national headquarters. Sandy was furious because sisters broke off on their own, disrupting not only the pack but also Sandy's leadership and command of the pack and of the nation. This incident was publicly aired at the business meeting the following day. Sandy briefly described what had happened and then said, "You should follow me into the fires of fucking hell. 'I need my private time'—never has happened. Riding with your sisters is the most important thing in the world. I would run out of gas and push my bike before turning off from my sister. I tear up when I'm in the pack. I feel this big [*gestures with her arms*]. Then there are times when I am running the pack and it's my fucking pack." The silence was deafening. In that moment, Sandy sounded like a one-percenter, the national president of a motorcycle club demanding that her sister-wives follow her into the "gates of fucking hell" and reasserting her supreme authority with "it's my fucking pack." Simultaneously, she publicly eschewed the regimented, bureaucratic schedule that dominated life at national headquarters during nationals. It seemed every woman in the room was afraid to breathe, let alone speak, but within moments a full-patch member named Candy stood up and admitted that she had turned off and explained that she had been on kitchen duty and thought she had to begin preparing dinner. Her eyes were filled with tears, but her voice was steady and clear, and she met Sandy's gaze as dozens of women stared at her. Sandy replied a bit too quickly, which made me wonder whether the entire scene was staged as a mechanism to publicly sanction the senior member in front of the nation. A brief soliloquy followed: "We all run 110 miles an hour, get drunk, piss our pants—it's happened—and prank each other. The bottom line is sisterhood, being together and having fun. Taking what you need to take. Put pressure to keep things rolling, but the bottom line is sisterhood. Plan your vacation and give yourself that last day with your sisters. I am sorry that somehow it got twisted that dinner was more important than sisterhood." By ending with an apologetic phrase, Sandy softened the moment even though she was not apologizing.

The incident was surprising to me for several reasons. First, Sandy rarely rode her motorcycle at nationals, and unplanned rides were even rarer. Second, the pressure for the kitchen crew to have food ready at the appointed times was massive. Thus, the biker ideal of freedom on the road was rarely enacted among the women, and I inferred that Candy's military background coupled with her being a mom superseded any biker identity. The bigger problem seemed to be that sisters followed Candy, not Sandy, so the very public lesson Sandy was imparting was one of a single authority figure. It also highlighted the contradictions in the growing, bureaucratized club, in which order and a schedule were paramount but Sandy's whim to pass the road to national headquarters was to be understood by all as an indication that they would keep riding. The kind of loyalty and obedience Sandy demanded is exactly that of a one-percenter MC; however, the highly regimented schedule and food preparation duties would not have been potential detractors in one-percenter clubs. Thus, the combined routinization and bureaucratization of RSMC complicates the traditional "ride or die" mentality found among bikers.

In every weeklong nationals I attended, the only organized ride was the spirit ride, and the route was mapped ahead of time, with national road captains leading and guiding. Sandy often rode in one of the chase cars rather than on her motorcycle at the front of the pack. There are contingency plans for everything in RSMC; if a sister goes down on her motorcycle in a pack ride, there is a specified protocol for who peels off to stay with her. This seemingly unplanned ride during nationals was unusual, and Candy's choice seemed rational; however, it was framed as a threat to the national president's control of and authority over the nation—an affront to her leadership and to the nation as a whole—and was publicly sanctioned in front of all members. Women on kitchen duty can be replaced, but the decision made by Candy (and those who followed her) resulted in Sandy reaffirming what it means to be righteous or pseudo-righteous—"follow me into the fires of fucking hell!"

Gifts and the Space of Appearances

Scant attention is paid to gifts in books and articles written about other MCs, but anthropologist Daniel Wolf included a brief section on gift giving based on the perspective of one who patched into an MC:

> A special form of gift giving that is highly symbolic in nature is the exchange of outlaw-biker paraphernalia.... Bikers in general, and club members in particular, adorn their leathers and colours (jean jacket and club emblem) with pins, badges, and pendants that are emblematic of the biker subculture. These pendants and badges are a personal statement by the individual that he is a biker. The exchange or giving of a badge or pin symbolizes the mutual sharing of that biker status and conveys a sense of in-group comradeship. (Wolf [1991] 2000:69)

"Pins and badges are often kept by members as keepsakes of their personal history as club members," according to Wolf ([1991] 2000:70). This section takes Wolf's analysis a step further and connects it to gift giving within the social structure, or polis, and the ways in which gifts, both given and received, constitute yet another area in which women can strive for righteousness within the realm of action. The origin story of a gift, The Yellow Socks, connects back to the Sister of the Year Award and to words and deeds that lead to immortality within RSMC. The Yellow Socks are part of a ritual gift-giving activity for all members that is a key space of appearances. Gifts to outside organizations through philanthropic activities are additional performative spaces within which sisters can distinguish themselves as righteous.

The highly coveted Sister of the Year Award was renamed after Winona, who is an original member and a member of FOG. Standing barely five feet tall, Winona wore her long gray hair in braids or a single ponytail and spoke proudly about her Native American heritage and her lineage with the Frog Clan. On several occasions, she took me for walks around the ten-acre national headquarter grounds to show me various plants, flowers, and trees; on these walks, we held hands. Winona exuded warmness and unconditional love, and she was an incredible storyteller. One of these times, we went to her camper, and I typed as she spoke and was able to record the long version of "The Story of the Yellow Socks:"

"Patty" had a horrible motorcycle crash coming to nationals. She busted herself up. One leg was really bad. Hospital. She was T-boned after a man ran a stop sign. My personal sister, my natural sister, she knew a lot about things that helped people. She was visiting from Alabama at the time. "I have a sister that went down on her bike. I want to send her something to make her really feel better." She suggested the color of yellow. The sunshine, the corn, the warmth, and the Mother Earth. That was a happy, good-feeling color, but they have to be on the feet. That's it. We'll do it. "Send her a couple of pairs of yellow socks or slippers. It will help her be grounded, and every time she looks down, she will remember all the [righteous] sisters who are praying for her and thinking of her." I sent her several pairs, and they became the first yellow socks.

The next year at nationals, I decided I am going to give all my sisters yellow socks. I would get calls throughout the year, and I would be sending socks from my home. So after this I gave everyone socks at nationals. Yellow socks help connect us with the sisterhood. Yellow socks are not just for feet. They get pulled out for noses and teary eyes. The socks are used to hold you.

I tell people they are hard to find, so I spent my life looking for yellow socks. About ten years ago, Costco came to town. I chose men's socks in white because they will fit all of our feet and we have sisters who are big-footed and regular socks would not fit. We evolved from the yellow socks to white that I take home and dye and put in a Ziploc with names and a piece of candy. The pens. You might have seen them. When we see the yellow pens, we know where they came from. My yellow socks don't necessarily come from me. I want people to see the yellow socks, not people. Not that I gifted them. Think of their sisters.

I had a terrible time this year. Now I am up to ten dozen. No Nonsense. She hasn't been out there very long, I guess. It's a brand. I can dye them pretty good. I sure as hell hope they don't throw them in with their whites.

Patty was our beginning. She is still alive, I assume, but she is no longer with us [RSMC].

This Herculean effort to dye by hand a hundred pairs of yellow socks each year remains one of the primary origin stories of RSMC. "The Story of the Yellow Socks" is so powerful because a woman nearly died after a motorcycle crash and her sisters were there for her. It doesn't matter that Winona has no contact with Patty. Yellow socks are imbued with healing power and energy and are historicized as part of the folklore of the MC, which is perpetuated annually with gift-giving, storytelling, and the Winona Award. I have a pair of yellow socks for each of my years at nationals as a visual reminder of Winona and the ideal of sisterhood. Obtaining and wearing the socks was a highly accessible ritual, and even the newest member felt a sense of belonging after this ritual.

Each year members of RSMC work to distinguish themselves through RSMC Christmas, the "Secret Sister" gift exchange, and Sandy's annual birthday celebration (described earlier). These events provide opportunities for recognition and excellence through potlatches, or ceremonies that confer honor, prestige, and status. While no woman can compete with the yellow socks—a gift that is small, deeply symbolic, useful for bikers who wear through socks quickly, and historic—there is a lot of thought and effort put into the potlatches. Marcel Mauss's influential *The Gift: The Form and Reason for Exchange in Archaic Societies* describes the two essential elements of potlatch: "the honour, prestige, and mana conferred by wealth; and the absolute obligation to reciprocate these gifts under pain of losing that mana, that authority—the talisman and source of wealth that is authority itself" ([1954] 2002:11). The honor and prestige conferred is evidenced by Winona—the epitome of a righteous sister—and the award named after her. These gift-giving rituals also pave the way for reciprocation through myriad gift-giving opportunities among members, to the national president, and through service to the nation through one's labor, monetary contributions, and specialized knowledge.

The rituals surrounding RSMC Christmas include creating some kind of stocking-type vessel with one's name on it, which will hold the gifts. Once the ceremony begins, on Friday night after the all-day business meeting and patching ceremony, each sister walks around to each of the fifty to seventy-five placeholders for members in attendance and offers her trinket. At the end of the ceremony, each woman gathers her gifts, and after thanking as many sisters as she can, she returns the items to her sleeping quarters for safekeeping.

Many of the gifts given at RSMC Christmas are of types that Wolf describes, but the ritual and ceremonial aspects surrounding gift giving in the club and the emphasis placed on its importance are unique characteristics of RSMC and are analogous to those of the groups Mauss described as "suffused with rituals and myths . . . [retaining] a ceremonial character that is both obligatory and effective" ([1954] 2002:92). Gifts ranged from handmade coasters to pens with the club's name on them, handmade bracelets or earrings, and items that could be attached to one's biker vest, all in club colors. Beaded items, makeup, CDs with RSMC's favorite songs, and other crafty items were gifted and received. Since some of the sisters ride their motorcycles long distances, the expectation was that the gifts would be small, but it always seemed like a lot of stuff, and the space of appearances was very public. As membership grew from a dozen women in the 1990s and early 2000s to approximately one hundred women, the challenges were noted by forever sisters and FOG. One forever sister said, "It used to be you only needed twenty to twenty-five things, so you were running around during Bike Week looking for twenty-five-cent gifts, and then there got to be so many people." For many of the long-standing members, there is a mixture of wistfulness for the way things used to be coupled with an acknowledgment that things have changed and a clear recognition that this is no longer a five-dollar affair. Given the financial constraints of some members and the growing number of women in the club, some chapters decided to make their RSMC Christmas gifts as a chapter to cut costs and reduce the number of knickknacks one had to pack home.

A woman's social class is not secret among club members—some women have multiple motorcycles costing tens of thousands of dollars each, big homes, and new vehicles—and although most women dress the same throughout the week, as if wearing a private school uniform, class differences cannot be hidden. Winona was a retired senior citizen who lived frugally in the South, and both the monetary value of the socks and the time it took to manually dye and package them individually only ascribed additional value to the talisman. Most of the gifts come with small name tags attached so that the recipient knows who gave each small gift, and they also provide a mechanism for comparison writ large, a way for newcomers to become known, for the most creative sisters to show off their talents, and for the wealthier sisters to show off their wealth.

Mauss described the structural hierarchies between chiefs and vassals and vassals and tenants and wrote, "To give is to show one's superiority, to be more, to be higher in rank, *magister*. To accept without giving in return, or without giving more back, is to become client and servant, to become small, to fall lower (*minister*)" ([1954] 2002:95). The practices surrounding gifts in RSMC are notable not only for the status conferred but also for the consistency with which they occur. Mauss describes the constant "'give-and-take'" in the American Northwest tribal groups as well as in Melanesia and notes that "time is needed in order to perform any counter-service" ([1954] 2002:45–46). Sandy received enormous amounts of gifts on her birthday, which was my first port of entry. Sandy did not take part in reciprocal RSMC Christmas, but she was the object of gift giving on her birthday. Her counter-service was one of hospitality and time through "cave time," endless phone calls in which she doubled as a therapist and national president, and her righteousness. Like a chieftain or shaman, she was endowed with exceptional qualities such as "healing powers" that extended to her residential home and national headquarters. Competition for Sandy's love, acceptance, and attention are at the core of sisterhood, and the public arena or polis that creates a very specific "space of appearance" elevates her power. For those in Sandy's inner circle, the price is unwavering loyalty.

I attended several subsequent birthday parties, and the gifts for "Boss" were thoughtful and some were quite extravagant. Several sisters rode their motorcycles or drove several hundred miles to spend Sandy's birthday weekend with her. There was a competitive vibe and playful vibe among the righteous sisters. A few of the BAMFFs, typically wage earners, brought modest birthday gifts. Who found the best, most unique, or funniest birthday present? All in attendance watched her reactions closely to see which one she liked the best, but Sandy seemed to appreciate all of them equally. When I asked her about the wrangling, extravagance, and sheer volume of her birthday gifts, she smiled and shook her head. She said, "They shouldn't spend that much on me. That's crazy. [Name] remembered my favorite flower, a daisy." This response is telling because Sandy's role is analogous to other charismatic leaders who are adorned with gifts. She must not play favorites. She makes it a point to recognize the "least" among them who came with daisies. Sandy not only acquiesces to the annual ritual; she facilitates it welcoming a dozen righteous sisters "Home" for her birthday weekend. At the annual business meeting, time was afforded for the Secret Sister exchange, where members guessed their secret sister from the previous year as they drew a new name for the upcoming year. Most of the time, members could not guess their secret sister, the woman who sent them small and large gifts sporadically or regularly throughout the previous year, so the reveal often entailed a short public speech in which tales were told of the lengths to which a secret sister went to conceal her identity. At the end, it became clear that some of the secret sisters were no longer in RSMC or did not attend nationals (a national officer kept a master list of pairings). Secret Sister involves a great deal of planning as some sisters live outside the United States, making it more challenging to conceal their identity on shipped presents although Amazon and other shipping services seem to assist with anonymity. Some women circumvented that by tag-teaming and sending gifts to someone else's secret sister to throw them off the trail. The issue of extravagance came up at nationals, and Sandy described how original members used to mail gum wrappers or empty beer cans to other sisters—the purpose was to let a sister know that you were thinking about them. She said this has been lost in recent years, where the emphasis has been on costly and extravagant gifts, and also pointed out that the change leaves many members feeling "less than" if they cannot reciprocate.

Several aspects of RSMC's internal economy also provide additional spaces of appearance. At the clubhouse bar,[4] RSMC tokens, which can be purchased for one dollar each, are exchanged for bottled water, soda, and alcoholic beverages outside of mealtimes during nationals and during all RSMC parties. With bottled water and soda costing one token and beer and other alcoholic drinks ranging from two to five tokens, it is an easy way for members to gift one another with a drink or a round of drinks at the clubhouse bar and a way for RSMC to make money as the cost of a bottle of water purchased in bulk is twenty-five cents. Furthermore, everyone pays—or almost everyone pays. This contrasted my experience with men-only MCs, in which some national officers did not pay or started "tabs" so they could "settle up" later at a great discount. Sandy is the only person I never saw with tokens—she does not drink alcohol. She carried around a large plastic to-go cup with a straw and ice water or sweet tea, which was garnered from the Big House kitchen and continually refreshed by the close circle of women who attended to her needs and had access to the Big House. Other women were not allowed to bring their own beverages into the clubhouse, and one year a new rule stated that women must purchase their alcohol from the clubhouse bar and not bring their own to nationals.

Each year at the RSMC nationals, there was an award for best shopper—that is, the woman who spent the most in the shop during the year. The total dollar figure ranged from several hundred to several thousand during the years I attended nationals. Members were consistently encouraged by national officers to check out what was new in the store, to gift other members club merchandise, and, for those with one or two rockers, to store full-patch items by paying for them in advance and allowing the store to hold them until they earn their full patch. Associating shopping with a women's club falls into a traditional gender stereotype that I have not observed in men's motorcycle clubs; hence, I see this emphasis on proving club loyalty through purchases as a mechanism for social control. Members were expected to show loyalty first through their wallets and then through their wardrobe. Men bikers usually had a handful of full-patch club T-shirts, and along with their patches, these constituted their club attire. Women, on the other hand, had dozens of club T-shirts and merchandise, all of which were purchased from the RSMC store and constituted essential components of their identity as loyal citizens.

Further, there is an annual auction that takes place on Friday after dinner and before the awards ceremony. Members donate handmade goods, purchased goods, or RSMC merchandise from the RSMC store (also located in the clubhouse) that will be auctioned off, with the proceeds going back to RSMC. This is one of the clearest spaces in which one can observe a moral obligation to donate items and bid and outbid other sisters. Sandy said repeatedly over the years, "The best place to shop is Home [the RSMC store]." A magical quality is sometimes associated with the item up for auction—for example, one year a quilt was made from dozens of T-shirts from past nationals. The item was only available to full-patch sisters and sold for hundreds of dollars. As Mauss pointed out, "Things sold still have a soul" ([1954] 2002: 84), and that soul is monetized for RSMC profit. This is an event in which new or longtime members can distinguish themselves as righteous through their purchasing power in a very public manner. In a single annual club auction, with club members as the sole bidders, thousands of dollars can be added to the club coffers and a burgeoning internal economy.

As a political community, RSMC has formal structures and norms connected to potlatch and gift giving in the form of philanthropy and service to women and children in their communities. Gifts are also symbolic; they are viewed as ways to connect the nation when it is not physically together. There is both "generosity and self-interest that are linked in giving" (Mauss [1954] 2002:87), and this is demonstrated not only in the potlatches and internal giving described herein but also in the philanthropic activities that the club organizes and that are detailed in RSMC's mission statement, which states: "To change members' communities, improve the lives of women and children, and to raise awareness of motorcycling and female motorcyclists. Prospects and members are required to attend, support, and plan philanthropic events or motorcycle awareness events."

In the club history binders, there is no shortage of newspaper clippings that illustrate the various types of philanthropic activities RSMC has engaged in over the years. From charities like Make-A-Wish to more localized efforts, hundreds of philanthropic events have galvanized the status of RSMC in communities across the United States and more recently in Canada and the United Kingdom. The space of appearances here, then, is widened and immortalized. The mission of the club encourages arete, or righteousness, in the public sphere as well as in the insular subcultural world of MCs and in RSMC. Members and chapters (regional groups of RSMC members officially recognized by RSMC) are recognized at nationals for their efforts, and the winning individual or club, determined by funds raised, is given the award for the Most Funds Raised for the Year. The chapters typically engage in friendly competition for this award, but one chapter dominated most (if not all) of the years I attended nationals. The philanthropic activities are measured by things like attendance, the cause, the money raised, publicity, and a loose fun factor as many sisters will travel to support a particular fundraiser, particularly if they are not part of a chapter because of geographic limitations.

A few of RSMC chapter's philanthropic efforts were focused on organizations that provided services to abused children. Several righteous sisters were primary caretakers for one or more of their grandchildren as a result of their sons' or daughters' neglect or abuse. This was not discussed, nor was the members' parenting or their own neglect or abuse of their children. One member told me, "I was property at sixteen." Those five words signaled abuse, both physical and sexual, of a minor, at the hands of a one-percenter MC. Some "claim" girls or women as "property"; they are expected to give their bodies to any and all club members. A nonmember I met early in my doctoral research ran a pit bull rescue, and she said, "My dad was a Hells Angel, and my early years were filled with drugs, alcohol, and guns. By seventeen, I was on my own. It made me stronger. Maybe that's why I love the bully breed so much." A full-patch member said her ex-husband "shook and threw his three-month son, [*their*] three-month-old son, across the room; [she] grabbed [her] daughter and the baby and walked out the door." A deep, abiding, maternal care for children pervaded RSMC, and all of the RSMC Kidz (as they are referred to) call members "Aunt [club nickname]" as a term of respect and familiarity, and while corporal punishment was widely accepted as "good parenting" among RSMC members, child abuse was a cause all women rallied around.

Although domestic violence was a thread that ran deeply through RSMC, it was not openly discussed. One-percenter women (women who were married to or partnered with one-percenters before joining RSMC) constituted a small number of RSMC members, and several had violent pasts. Of one, Sandy said, "You have to fight to get out. You just have to fight. One sister came from a one-percenter relationship. He kept threatening to kill her. I would go by the house just to look in the windows and make sure she was okay. She joined up with us but can't completely get away. She is still looking to cater to a man, bring him food, wait on him, etc." Referring to her dog, one former full-patch member said to me, "I had a man beat me, and I have a bum leg, so I figured we [*nodding to her dog*] would get along just fine." The dog, a pit bull she had rescued, had an injured leg and was a staple at nationals, spending most of the time in the cabin to avoid too much chaos with other dogs that were on the property.

In 2019, the chapter that won the Most Funds Raised for the Year Award was successful not only because of the large sum of money raised but also because of the large biker turnout and the positive publicity from local press. The chapter also collected new stuffed animals for first responders to provide to children at the scene of a domestic violence or child abuse emergency call; this collection was at the behest of local first responders and was hugely popular with the general public. Other MCs do Toys for Tots Runs (rides), which provide similar photo opportunities of bikers with stuffed animals, and in spite of their outer appearance, the image of a burly biker holding a teddy bear softens the public perception of bikers. Biker turnout was measured and quantified in evaluations of RSMC chapter philanthropic initiatives: How many sisters showed up? How many members from other three-piece patch clubs supported the event? How many members of riding clubs (RCs) attended? These philanthropic events provided an additional avenue to obtain excellence—by the approval of other MCs—and also a way to showcase the organizational capacity of RSMC. The events were planned up to a year in advance. At the national business meeting, each RSMC chapter would report every event it planned for the upcoming year, including dates. These were logged into the minutes, and members were expected to plan to attend any and all events within one hundred miles of their home.

Another event that stood out to me was titled "A Walk in Her Shoes," in which funds were raised for breast cancer awareness through a bikers' walk in high heels, or "her shoes." Bikers don't wear heels, as a general rule, and the gendered performative aspect is likely what raised the most money. Both male and female bikers untied their black leather motorcycle boots to parade in high heels on a platform stage to raise money. Chapters promoted their events heavily through social media and word of mouth and were expected to document every aspect of the event and report back to nationals and to the nation at the annual business meeting. The annual report of this event was boisterous and caused raucous laughter among those who attended as well as those who wished they attended, elevating the chapter's status in the polis.

Sisters who attended these philanthropic events had another anchor experience that allowed both veteran and new members to share stories and jokes and to bond. Since RSMC members were spread out across thousands of miles, from Alaska to the United Kingdom, this also created some in-groups within the club in addition to chapters, which are intentional in-groups. Some members were more mobile than others because of retirement or their type of employment, financial circumstances, or familial circumstances. These members strengthened their ties to other members and to the club by attending several philanthropic events throughout the year, and this had the dual function of also raising their status as devoted members of the nation—patriots of sorts—and their righteousness. The philanthropic events grew in scale, organization, and output as RSMC grew in size and geographic reach.

Before Righteous Sisterhood became a motorcycle club, these events were small, local, and relatively informal. They included some type of run, an organized ride, or showcase of cycling skills. A poker run, popular among many different types of groups, includes several predetermined spots where bikers get a playing card, and then riders compare their cards at the end to see who has the best poker hand. Evidence of these early events filled albums and three-ring binders with the club's history, and FOG members told me about them. The lines between rides, Sister Time, and philanthropy were blurred in some cases, and the stories that were told of these events in the late 1980s and 1990s were filled with shenanigans. One member described how her chapter would ride one hundred miles and meet up at a Harley-Davidson dealership with another chapter who had also ridden one hundred miles. The dealership's owner, a woman, provided hot dogs and "would have them waiting when [they] arrived." Looking at old photographs, the member said, "Back then we all rode Sportsters. Now we all have bigger bikes. We rode those Sportsters all around." She continued: "Back then, we used to ride as a big group, but it got too big, and we thought it was too dangerous. Instead of a big group ride, we would have a smaller run. Poker ride. [*Looks at a photo.*] Close to one hundred bikes at this gas station." She continued to page through an old photo album as I listened and took notes. Looking at one page of photos, she shared this story: "Ah, I remember this [*names the run and location*]. We had a radio station that was having a contest; for every bra we collected, they would pay one dollar to breast cancer. So we had this poker run, and we told people to bring new and old bras, and I think we were going tie them together across the river, but they ended up putting a limit on it because we had so many. Here they are hanging in the tree. And this is all our chapter." Like many other veteran members, her trip down memory lane became increasingly wistful. She continued, "Gosh, we must have been in our [*pauses*] I think I was probably thirty, and 'T' was twenty-five back then. We rode to the [location]. I think that was probably our first children's run. We probably had fifteen people, and it got bigger and bigger. T and I and two other girls started our chapter, then T went on to become national vice president." In these cases, riding and fundraising were linked together as a way for chapter members to bond and to make themselves known in their communities, many of which are thousands of miles away from national headquarters.

Winona, another forever sister and FOG, talked about the various antics the women engaged in while on weekend runs. She told the following story:

> What was that state we went into and got chased out of? [*Pauses.*] I got chased by the hotel owner with a hammer. At that particular event, it was getting very cold, and it was a midsummer. There was a little house that we all went to ... but there were like so many of us, and there were people who needed to get back home, and there were people coming in slow from [the Southeast] like me. I believe it was the city of [city name], and we went on a ride and were up in the mountains.

It was a Jesse James home. One of these bad-people towns, and it was catered to him. We went second shift, and we filled a room without it being cleaned or anything. I had a really nice Harley hood [hooded sweatshirt] with a zippy and hung it in the closet, and then we went about the town and did our thing. Our girls were leaving, and I found a place by the side of the road, and I was waving and saying goodbye to my sisters in a very Winona way, and there were a lot of motorcycles doing their vroom-vroom thing, and he actually had a hammer in his hand, and I did the jump, jump thing. There was a story in *Easy Rider* [biker magazine] that was exaggerated. "Four foot ten, get chased out of town."

These women, many of them now FOG, maintain their righteousness through the photographic evidence, which comprises crucial pieces of RSMC's story and immortality as well as examples of righteousness for prospects and patched members alike.

A few philanthropic efforts directly benefitted Sandy's children and grandchildren. A scholarship fund for RSMC Kidz was developed around the time Sandy's youngest daughter was nearing the end of her high school years. Her daughter had been active in the Kidz group and was college bound, so the collection for the fund took place at the national business meeting and was done table by table by chapter, with the amounts raised read aloud at the end of the collection, which increased the pressure on each group to raise the most money. Standard contributions per member were twenty-five to fifty dollars, resulting in a few thousand dollars raised in that twenty-minute time period. The amounts promised by each member were documented, and if one could not pay that day, the expectation was that a check would be sent in a timely fashion. This kind of high-pressure collection, where someone was standing at each table with a clipboard, ready to repeat and write down the amount as the rest of RSMC waited and listened, created internal competition, yet another space of appearances, and a chance to show one's righteousness through word and deed in the polis. During my first few years, it was done individually, which really increased the pressure, especially among those who were assumed to be better off financially and more capable of donating fifty or one hundred dollars. The chapters circumvented this by creating a pool in subsequent years, where only the chapter president would report the total and each member was responsible for contributing the amount they promised. At one point, I was asked to create a scholarship application and agreed to do so, but when I asked who would be applying, the national president's youngest daughter was the only one eligible, so it seemed to be a formality with the appearance of equity but with a predetermined winner. Another large fundraiser was held for the national president's middle daughter,

Stormy, who lost her home to a natural disaster and did not get federal relief to rebuild or move. Because she was a single mother with two children, RSMC raised large amounts of money to build the Little House, a small, prefabricated home, at national headquarters. Stormy and her daughters thus became permanent fixtures, residing at national headquarters year-round.

Each year at nationals, there is one all-day party dubbed an "open house" that is open to the public and advertised widely to other MCs and bikers, and there was frequently a rodeo theme with motorcycle barrel races (in which bikes pushed barrels fifty yards or so), motorcycle obstacle courses to showcase skills, relay races in which passengers picked up objects strewn across the ten-acre property, and the most popular, motorcycle "sledding," in which someone would lie on the ground on something resembling a sled and get pulled behind a motorcycle, racing other contestants. The sledders ended up with scrapes, burns, and other physical markers of the gladiator-style games, but it was a highly performative space with status and prestige attached to all who participated. A mistress of ceremonies would announce everything into a microphone, adding to the carnival-like space of appearances for individuals to demonstrate their loyalty to the nation and their excellence as individual riders. Proceeds from the event went to RSMC and any specific fundraising efforts, such as Little House and other major renovations.

Gifts and philanthropic efforts were primary ways for members of RSMC to achieve righteousness and to prove their loyalty to the club and its members. As detailed in the previous section, most of these were extremely public, resulting in a polis-wide space of appearances for women to demonstrate, through word and deed, their righteousness, or arete. From being the "best" secret sister to donating the most valuable event to the RSMC auction, planning and executing the "best" fundraiser, and putting one's body on a sled behind a speeding motorcycle at the RSMC rodeo, sisterhood entails a great deal of gifting in myriad ways.

Conclusion

As a Jewish refugee, Arendt's fundamental insight was to champion a political structure that would create equality of public voice. Relying heavily on the Greeks and their direct democracy, Arendt looked to the polis as a means to publicly participate in democracy through speech and action. This space, or space of appearances, also allows individuals to be judged on their words and deeds. The public realm "must transcend the life-span of mortal men," and Arendt claims that "there is no clearer testimony to the loss of the public realm in the modern age than the almost complete loss of authentic concern with immortality" ([1958] 1998:55). As evidenced in this chapter, members of RSMC seek to "make the extraordinary an ordinary occurrence," such as taking out trash and whizzing around on a golf cart making jokes and pulling pranks, and to "offer a remedy for the futility of action and speech" by offering women the chance to be righteous sisters and to be included in *The Book of Sisters*, immortalizing their contributions to RSMC ([1958] 1998:197). The founding mother and national president, Sandy, effectively uses the space of appearance to encourage arete, which is described as an impossible standard ("behind them [her sisters] 110%") to create myriad opportunities for women to distinguish themselves and achieve the ultimate accolade, Sister of the Year. In Chapter 4, the highly secretive ritual of exit from RSMC is uncovered.

4

From Righteous Sister to Civil Death

A Beginning and an Ending

In the summer of 2014, my then seven-year-old son and I were driving south from our apartment in New York City to central Florida where his dad lived. I had just completed my first year as an assistant professor of sociology and was working within a complex web of institutional bureaucracy to obtain approval to study human subjects. As the national president of RSMC, Sandy approved the study for the nation, and it seemed ironic that I had to jump through hoops to protect them from me given the incredible difficulty of gaining entrée into motorcycle clubs. However, it was important to me that all of the women knew I was there to do research and write and that my research was not just approved from the top. The nation's elaborate system of communication and weekly check-ins complemented the informed consent process I went through with each woman I talked to over the years. As I was planning the road trip, Sandy offered to let me stay at her place and also to connect me with members of the club along the 1,100-mile journey. She sent a group email to several members, writing, "Sarah is doing a story/paper on [RSMC] and I suggested that she stop in and say hello to some of you along her way down to the club house. Where she will be staying with me. I thought she might like to stop in [lists several states]." The brief email continued: "She is coming from Brooklyn NY with her son. She is also helping us try to get a grant. I/we have worked with her before so she is ok. Please get back with her ASAP and talk with her. also keep me posted please." The email, sent at 6:00 A.M., resulted in offers for us to stay with all five recipients by 6:00 P.M.

This email, my first introduction to several key players in RSMC, did a few things. First, Sandy vouched for me by saying that I was staying with her, that I was a mom traveling with my son, that I had something to give back to the club (I offered to help Sandy identify funding sources for her idea to open "Home" as a retreat space), and that I was "ok." Second, Sandy tapped some of her most trusted full-patch members, "'Bama," Skully, "Gravel," TEO,[1] and "Curly," who she knew would respond immediately to offer hospitality and would also be well positioned to observe me. I met a dozen other women, including "Whisperer," "Marjorie," and "Twig," to name a few. When I met these women, I was convinced they would be members of RSMC for life, similar to the members of the men-only MC I observed from 2005 to 2010;[2] however, from 2014 to 2019, there would be a significant turnover of members, including some of the most trusted full-patch members who were asked to host me.

This initial road trip allowed me intimate views of women outside of national headquarters, and early in my research process, I was able to build rapport with members that lasted for the duration of my research. The rapport was strengthened by my own circumstances; I was a single mom with an adorable young son on a cross-country road trip, and the women were eager to give us some southern hospitality, and several were grandparents, so they were happy to have a little boy in their homes. Our first stop was in North Carolina. Our host, Gravel, a military veteran and longtime RSMC member, was gracious and diligently took us around to meet other women from her chapter and to visit a few historical sites near her home. Her voice, raspy from decades of smoking cigarettes, was only matched by her incredible stature, giving off the physical manifestation of a biker—jeans, black boots, biker T-shirt, long hair, and a tough posture—that matched her quiet and guarded demeanor.

Our second stop was in South Carolina. TEO and Twig met us off the interstate at a truck stop. After a quick welcome, we followed them deep into the South Carolina woods for approximately twenty minutes to Twig's new small prefabricated home. My son jumped out of our vehicle and immediately started playing with her three dogs, two chihuahuas and a corgi, and then wanted to play catch and frisbee before finally settling on riding his bike around the yard. Twig and TEO stood by watching and laughing as we chatted. TEO stood just over five feet tall, and she had short blond hair, glasses, and a thick build, and she almost always had a cigarette in her hand or mouth. She said she was a delegate for the state of South Carolina and spoke at length about corruption in politics and about "knowing who is going to win before anyone votes." She stated she was strongly against Barack Obama, who was then president, and pro-military. Given all of her experiences with the local magistrate, TEO said, "I should have been a lawyer," although what followed did not sound particularly lawyerly. She said she had a parking ticket and ended up with a $750 contempt of court bail and then TEO filed a grievance against the "redneck magistrate" that fined her. She won but lost her title as senior magistrate. The owner-operator of an automobile repair company, TEO presented herself as a shrewd businesswoman when describing another case, in which she asked the judge, "Can you read?" and ended up winning the case. She had three daughters, one of whom was in the military, and several grandchildren, and she told me her husband was on the waiting list to receive a liver transplant, which quickly led her to her problem with the United States "giving money or medicine to people in other countries"; she insisted that we need to "take care of our own." Although I never expressly asked any member about their views on contemporary politics, over the years many expressed the sort of ultraconservative ideas that became more obvious after the 2016 and 2020 elections, particularly in southern states and during the COVID-19 pandemic.

Twig was very thin, smoked incessantly, and had long mousy brown hair. When I met her in 2014, she was fifty-four years old and on 70 percent veteran's disability. Originally from North Carolina, she had been living at national headquarters in a travel trailer until she moved to South Carolina. Twig told me that she had paroxysmal exercise-induced dyskinesia (PED),[3] which can be a precursor to Parkinson's disease, and that the available treatments were not funded. The disease caused regular, painful spasms in her legs, which she attributed to her military service. Twig said her father's dying wishes were "don't get married again, no more children, and never go to New York." I didn't learn or hear anything about Twig's ex-husband or children, and I did not inquire further about New York. As someone who lived in New York City for the majority of my adult life, I did not want politics or geography to be a barrier to developing rapport, and over the years, I would find out that dozens of members of RSMC grew up in New York and moved south. Gravel was from the Bronx but spent most of her adult life in the American South. Twig found out she and TEO were blood cousins after she joined RSMC, and they seemed very close; however, Twig presented as a very solitary person and alluded several times to trauma she had experienced.

Dinner that evening was a huge southern feast, and Twig invited two other sisters and their husbands, all of whom traveled long distances after a day of work to meet my son and me. Marjorie did not look like a biker. Originally from Nebraska, she had a very midwestern look and attitude, and I was initially shocked when I met her because she looked like an all-American Betty Crocker. In contrast to the well-established and often accurate stereotypes about bikers, women bikers came from a variety of backgrounds. While many shared key characteristics—time in the military or similar organizations, a history of social neglect and abuse, an indifferent educational background, political and social conservatism—such similarities only highlighted the many differences that I saw among the habits, attitudes, and backgrounds of these women. Marjorie was a fantastic cook and was in charge of the kitchen during several nationals. She didn't look the part of the biker, but she rode more miles than many women in RSMC, both with her husband, who also loved to ride, and with other women in RSMC, especially Whisperer, who was her closest friend. Marjorie had a governmental office job, was educated, and was happily married to "Paulie," who did many things to improve national headquarters, specifically painting and construction. Together, they had grown children and grandchildren. Marjorie was one of the few women who didn't smoke, and until she got the RSMC center patch tattooed on her forearm in 2016, she could have been on a Ladies of Harley poster targeting middle-class, middle-aged white women.

Whisperer was known for her ability to connect with animals, and she told me her dream was to become a veterinarian or vet technician, but she had suffered some debilitating back injuries that prevented her from doing many things she wanted to do. She also smoked heavily, and her voice was hardly above a low whisper. Her hair, which almost reached her buttocks, was long and black, and her eyes were light blue. Whisperer's presence was exceptionally calming and steady. Whisperer was married to Bill, who was much loved by all of the members of RSMC, and both were originally from Long Island, New York. He was a dedicated big brother and won the Big Brother Award at least once. A United States Postal Service mail carrier by day, Bill loved to ride his Harley-Davidson and take photographs outside of his job, and one of his roles in RSMC was as official club photographer.[4] Whisperer and Bill had a blended family, each with kids from different marriages, and both frequently talked about how much they preferred South Carolina to New York. Their daughter, a teenager during most of my observation, was involved with RSMC Kidz and spent a week with several of us during Kidz Week.

Marjorie was awarded her full patch in 2016, one of only two women that year, which proved to be an indication of the tumultuous year for RSMC membership. Twig was also patched at nationals in 2016, and both wept and gave me huge hugs along with every other woman in the room. Twig lived in her trailer at national headquarters, and as a result, I saw her more frequently and observed her physical pain, financial struggles, and loneliness. As discussed in Chapter 3, the internal mechanics of the RSMC remained private from me despite my closeness with these women, and from my insider-outsider standpoint, decisions regarding patching were made with an eye toward group management, keeping members from becoming too complacent about their place in the MC, and keeping them guessing. Some, like Twig, relied heavily on Sandy for emotional and financial security, using Home, or national headquarters, as their actual home whereas others, like Whisperer, Marjorie, and their husbands, gave a lot to the club in terms of time, skills, and physical labor.

Thus, it came as a total shock to me (and seemingly the rest of the nation) when Twig was exiled with another member during nationals in 2016. Summarily removed from the club, the cabin, the text tree and individual phone contacts, and the social media networks, they were no longer allowed to communicate with anyone in the club or wear any full-patch RSMC apparel. The other member, "Nurse Nan," a Canadian nurse, was extremely tall. Like Gravel, she looked like a biker and only wore jeans, black boots, biker T-shirts, and her patches, and her silver hair was always pulled back in a ponytail. Nan presented as masculine/butch, but like all members, she used female pronouns, and no discussion of her sexuality was ever brought up around me. She had been in the cabin since it was formed in 2014, but I don't recall her being at nationals until 2016. Since she was so quiet and somewhat guarded, it came as a surprise when one night she stumbled into our cabin in the middle of the night, obviously intoxicated, knocking over a soda can, which spilled, and waking up her bunkmate and dog, who slept below her. My cabin space was in the loft, so I peered down and saw a bit of the chaos in the darkness as Nurse Nan tried to unbuckle her biker belt and take off her boots. Within moments, I could hear her snoring in the top bunk slightly below me. I heard some murmurs and whispers the next day, and members noticeably did not talk in front of me; this was "club business," without a doubt, and was to be kept from me. In my field notes, I wrote, "Physically escorted out of the cabin. Wheeling her suitcase across the yard with a cane in the dark. I offered to help and someone else said, 'No, we got this.' Then I said, '[Nan], are you sure?' and the patch holder said, 'No, we got this.'" At that time, I didn't know she was being exiled in front of me. Her bunk was empty, and all her things were gone. I later overheard that Twig was also gone and noticed her absence from the next meal.

Both women, and their belongings, vanished. I knew that their patches would be confiscated along with any full-patch T-shirts and other apparel. If they were tattooed with the club logo, that would have to be covered with another tattoo or removed. This was the domain of the sergeant-at-arms and other national officers, and related conversations and procedures occurred behind closed doors. Since Twig lived on the property, in an area fondly dubbed "the Trailer Park," her exile was more complicated, especially given the timing and the express desire to keep it out of view. Twig was not only exiled from the club but also evicted, with a broken-down trailer, no money, and nowhere to go. Nurse Nan, whose flight back to Canada was not for several days, was also evicted from her purchased space in the cabin and was not refunded whatever money she had paid in at that time. She had to either stay in a hotel room or camp out at the airport until her flight departed for western Canada, and I am guessing she had to find her own way to the airport (ninety minutes away).

Just like that, Twig and Nurse Nan were gone, the bonds of sisterhood broken, and their space of appearances in RSMC shattered. Since these exiles occurred in the polis, the greatest space of appearances, they provided a unique window for me as an ethnographer because they laid bare the mechanics of exile in a way that would have been impossible for me to see had they not occurred literally underneath my bunk and in the space outside my cabin. Sisterhood, then, was tenuous. Just as one could obtain righteousness in the polis, one could experience inferiority and public shaming by way of a public exile, with one's membership as a sister summarily stripped along with all copyrighted RSMC gear.

The immortal fame provided by *The Book of Sisters* with the first entry at the patching ceremony (Chapter 1) was sharply contrasted with how quickly club life moved on, almost as if these women were never there. Our annual cabin meeting was held in the cabin as usual, and as an original owner, I attended. Nan's empty bunk was a visceral reminder of what transpired. There was a stern reminder not to leave open cans in the cabin and a cursory statement that we had cabin shares (Nan's) for sale, followed by a brief reminder that shares were not refundable if cabin members left RSMC on bad terms. Each year, the cabin leader, "Blondie" and then "Blue," typically rented a space or two, so that was discussed, as were the names of any potential new cabinmates and a reminder of how the process worked—new members had to be unanimously voted in by all cabin members, including me. Nan had not paid off her bunk shares, unlike me and several others who had paid in full, which soured her abrupt exile even more. The member who left the open soda can was scolded, and all cabinmates were reminded not to have soda or food in the cabin. There was tension, and it was clear that those in the know were not going to share any details of what had happened with Nurse Nan or what I later came to find out had happened with Twig. The cardinal rule of no gossip was frequently broken in small ways, but throughout the five years I observed, there were some things that were so seriously taboo, particularly exiles and sexual orientation, that no one spoke about them to me or around me except the national president, who only told me what she wanted me to know.

The national business meeting was similarly tense, but the national president opened by proclaiming, "We fucking rock," followed by roaring applause. Although it was always an all-day meeting with several-hour morning and afternoon sessions, the seven-hour meeting was particularly grueling and took its toll on everyone as the day wore on. There were reminders that everyone should unfriend and then block exiled sisters from social media and that absolutely no contact was allowed with members who were out. Information about Nurse Nan and Twig would have gone through the text tree, described in Chapter 3, with something like "Nan and Twig are out. No contact." Skully provided the report: 90 percent of members responded within one hour, and three members never texted back.[5] This was viewed as a breach of protocol as the 90 percent response rate was not 100 percent and "excuses" such as "I don't have cell phone service" were not accepted.

Sandy said, "Don't take that shit personal." The "shit" was what Nurse Nan and Twig had done to get exiled, and taking it "personal" would mean absorbing it as a negation of the bonds of sisterhood formed in RSMC. Given that the double exile occurred during nationals, the one week a year that is devoted to strengthening sisterhood and the nation, this statement reflected Sandy the biker, the ol' lady of a one-percenter, not the maternal national president who spoke of orbs and energy fields and invited women for "cave time." She continued: "It's none of your business," referring to what they had done or what had happened. Alluding to the golden rule of "no gossip," she said, "The only thing that is going to bring us to our knees is ourselves." Before moving on to the next item on the agenda, she stated, "When they're out, they're out. You can't buy these patches." "Out is out" refers to the kind of exile or out on bad terms discussed in the example of Twig, Nurse Nan, and, before that, Curly. Sandy was reminding members of the sacrifices they had made to earn the patches through a lengthy initiation process, and for the dozens of members who were not yet full patch, there was also a double message: the patches have to be earned, and they can be taken away. The meeting remained fairly tense. Toward the end, Sandy said, "We are still in session. I never have to do this [*pauses to reprimand*] and I've had to do it twice." She looked at Skully, who said, "Sorry, Boss." Several times during the meeting, Skully worked to maintain order, hissing, "Shhhh, Boss is talking," but seven hours into the meeting, everyone was drained, including Skully. Sandy seemed to recognize this and shifted the tone by saying, "I have Skully [*looks over*] sending me porn at 5 A.M." All of the women laughed, the ice was broken, and the meeting was adjourned. I laughed because I wondered what kind of porn a lesbian would send a straight woman at 5 A.M., but this was a moot point among the sisterhood because of the club's heteronormativity.

The public exiles in 2016 and the subsequent national business meeting, patching ceremony, and awards ceremony stand out to me as exemplifying the club's tricky negotiation of fervent, quasi-feminist sisterhood and belonging and the mechanisms of social control and exile that make the sisterhood precarious. It was not until July 2018 that Sandy provided some insight into the exiles and the way they fit into the broader issues RSMC viewed as potential threats to sisterhood and to the nation. In a one-on-one interview, Sandy told me, "Twig started dating one of the sisters. So did 'Sunny.' They just brought her [Sunny] into FOG." Sandy then alluded to FOG being disbanded because of the complications resulting from women sucking up to members of FOG. The status of FOG remained unclear, although I suspected it just went underground again. In my field notes from 2016, I noted that I tried to talk to Sunny during a break at the national business meeting, but I didn't realize then that she was crying behind large, dark sunglasses. She was not wearing patches or sitting with FOG, and surprisingly her response to me was generous, given the circumstances, saying quietly, "Not right now." Twig was dating a support member, according to Sandy. This rupture, then, was a threat because of the power dynamic; she viewed members of FOG as trusted elders and advisers, and if members of FOG were open to dating newcomers, she worried it could result in potential leaks of club business, threatening the hierarchy and the trust entailed to members with twenty-plus years in RSMC. With respect to Nan and Twig, Sandy said, "It caused [Skully] to do more of an in-depth interview and go further with the backgrounds. Turns out [Nan] had both body parts—what's that called? She was a high priestess in the Wiccan cult. The other [intersex] you probably wouldn't have found out, but she [Skully] didn't do the research." In typical bluntness, Sandy said, "She was a hermaphrodite hunting other Sisters." Although it was never clarified to me *whom* Nan was "hunting," whether it was Twig or another sister—and if it was indeed Twig, it seemed arbitrary and even cruel, given Twig's dependence on national headquarters for permanent residence, that she would be exiled and evicted rather than protected. The threat was existential for Sandy, even two years later when I interviewed her, and she explained it through a reference to the orbs and fairies she believed protected Home and its sisters. She stated, "That was the first night [Skully] saw all the fairies and the orbs. You can see them going under the fence. The dachshunds followed them. [Skully] lost her mind and got [another national officer] to watch it. You can see them plain as day going around and between the sisters and with the dogs." Beyond the mysticism was the very real homophobia and transphobia and the function of expulsion: it brought the nation closer together and reaffirmed heterosexual and cisgender norms and values. After the expulsions of Nan and Twig, which were described for years to come as major incidents, a formal policy change was instituted that excluded lesbian women from RSMC while "grandfathering in" any existing members, such as Skully and her partner.

Ethnographers' predominant focus is usually on entrée rather than exit, particularly in difficult communities to study such as exclusive subcultures with lengthy initial rituals. As other sociologists and ethnographers have noted, the study of exit is undertheorized (Ebaugh 1988), and exits themselves are "ignored or invisible" and "represent the negative spaces of our life" (Lawrence-Lightfoot 2011:6). Ethnographers' exits are usually omitted, almost as if the participant observer, who spent months or years building rapport, vanishes into thin air, only to resurface with a completed manuscript.[6] One notable exception is Jim Wafer's "After the Field," in which he describes how the postfield experience "may suggest new lines of approach to the postliminal or 'return' phase of rites of passage ... the person coming back from the sacred space is necessarily transformed, and returns to a 'profane' reality that has also changed" (1996:260–261). Feminist ethnographic texts have focused on power and inequality in the field and on issues such as friendship, detachment, objectivity, and insider-outsider research, to name a few; however, the issue of an ethical exit is not part of the topical organization or discussion in most texts. In *Translated Woman* (1993) and *The Vulnerable Observer* (1996), the anthropologist Ruth Behar struggles to leave her field site in Mexico and only does so after being told the house she rented is no longer available since her visits were growing shorter each year (1993:263); then she returns to her home in Michigan and writes a book.

Up until Chapter 4, this book has been almost entirely about how the nation operates—from the meaning of the patches (Chapter 1) to the highly structured initiation process (Chapter 2) and the ways in which women seek righteousness within the space of appearances in RSMC (Chapter 3). The historical account of women in the "outlaw" MC world (Introduction) provided context to situate the uniqueness of RSMC but also to draw parallels to the external constraints as well as the reductive practices carried over from other MCs. Adding to these preexisting challenges, exit within RSMC was regarded as club business, and while I could spend months or even years gaining rapport with a member, that relationship could be terminated very quickly, as demonstrated in the opening road trip and subsequent exits and exiles.

Like many ethnographers, the possibility that I would be exiled was always present, and inquiring too deeply into club business would be more than sufficient to warrant my own swift expulsion. As it turned out, I was summarily exiled in July 2019, an event I describe later in this chapter. As my participation deepened, the expectations that I adhere to club norms—including deleting exiled women from my phone and receiving some updates from Skully regarding who was out—grew; however, I was not part of the private weekly communications, nor was I added to any text trees. As a researcher, I found the thought of contacting former members directly very appealing; however, I did not want to jeopardize the trust and rapport with Sandy and the club that took so long to build. These are not things Sandy wanted documented in a book about RSMC. Given that I was not a member, I was not held to most of the rules; however, because I had spent more time with RSMC and some of the exiled sisters were ones I knew well, the national president made it expressly clear that I was to delete them, literally and symbolically, and that the no-contact rule applied to me.

Methodologically, then, my research for Chapter 4 differs from the previous sections because I did not conduct interviews with exiled or exited members of RSMC; however, two sisters who exited voluntarily for personal reasons related to their families and caretaking responsibilities returned and became members again. This provided a great opportunity to see what it's like for exited members to return Home. Another way to understand exit is through the deaths of two members in 2020 and the public postings surrounding the deaths of righteous sisters. My own experience of exile provides the clearest observable experience and elucidates the arbitrary and abrupt decisions made by the national president and the possible rationale.

In this final chapter, then, I focus on exit and exile as unique rites of passage and draw upon existing ethnographic accounts of the role of exit to create a framework within which to understand these processes in RSMC. Then, through additional stories of exit and exile in RSMC and a few stories of exile and exit from male one-percenters and bikers observed during my doctoral research (2005–2012), I illustrate the framework with observable data. While exits are not unique to nations or to groups and ethnographers have been told their research was finished before they thought it might have been, the complex relationships among sisters and the dominant hierarchy complicate the ideal of righteous sisterhood. The contradictions between the (literal) manual on how to obtain and maintain righteousness and the lived reality of the dozens of sisters who were exiled over five years highlight the types of abrupt exile of trusted advisers we saw so clearly during the Trump administration (2017–2021) and can examine in other types of exclusive groups.

"She's Dead to Me"

In ancient Greece, losing one's citizenship rights, or voice in the polis, was the greatest of all punishments. Leaving one unable to achieve excellence through speech and action in the realm of action described by Arendt, civil death was a terrible punishment meted out in ancient Greece and included not only suffrage but other legal rights, such as the ability to file lawsuits and own property. Similarly, for women who obtained righteousness in RSMC, banishment and being cut off from one's sisters and one's nation is the greatest of all sanctions. Twig's and Nan's stories show two sisters, one full patch and one close to full patch,[7] whose seemingly arbitrary and unilateral exile was imposed after years of service to the club and close bonds with their sisters. In Chapter 1, I noted the sacredness of the patch as well as the fact that patches are trademarked club property that are collected (without refund) if a member ceases to be a member. Those who leave by choice can have some contact with members of RSMC, but with the exception of one member whose biological sister left the club, it was clear that members did not maintain contact with ex-members.

The national president relayed the story of one former RSMC national officer who was exiled and tried to attend a party of a one-percenter MC. According to Sandy's contact, a one-percenter with whom she was very close, the ex-sister was turned away at the door, and he said to her, "I thought you were dead." The civil death referred to is thus not only within a former member's own nation; it extends to other MCs across the United States and potentially in Europe and Canada as RSMC grows and expands its reach. Sandy told this story with her characteristic dry sense of humor and a sense of pride that *the guys* had her back. In this case, it is also important to note that this national officer was uncharacteristically young, likely in her thirties, and attractive, which only bolstered Sandy's confidence regarding loyalty between the nations. Thus, the loss of the space of appearances is not limited to RSMC.

After exile, the events that structured members' lives such as nationals (e.g., the group ride, patching ceremony, auction, and awards ceremony), fundraisers, the spirit ride, and the weekly Sister Time chats vanish. Some of these women are on the margins. Twig, for example, struggled economically, suffered from a debilitating disease, and leaned heavily on RSMC for economic, social, and emotional support. For Victor Turner, this marginality, or the "interstices of structure, in liminality," is where "communitas breaks in" ([1969] 1995:128), and it is contrasted to social structure. Unlike the "failures" Turner described that cannot reconcile "tribal communitas" and "tribal structure," RSMC has done both for nearly forty years; however, ex-members proved to be as important as prospects (new members) in maintaining both the former, what I've termed sisterhood, and the latter, which has been described as the RS nation.

"She's dead to me" can be theorized within Robert Merton's work on statuses, particularly the observation that one's history of past statuses can inform future statuses ([1949] [1957] 1968), which led to more specific work around "role exit," a term coined by Zena Smith Blau (1972). In Chapter 3, the choices of philanthropic endeavors were strongly influenced by women's past statuses, including as a formerly abused partner and child or as a one-percenter woman who became a member of RSMC. Ex-nun and sociologist Helen Rose Fuchs Ebaugh theorized role exit, elucidating a four-stage process. In *Becoming an Ex*, Ebaugh defines the process of role exit as "the process of disengagement from a role that is central to one's self-identity and the reestablishment of an identity in a new role that takes into account one's ex-role" (1988:1), saying it is *not* simply the reverse of socialization or initiation because of the "hangover identity" that lingers. Sandy's hangover identity as a one-percenter woman greatly influenced the way she "ruled" her nation and also enabled her to network with one-percenters in neighboring MCs. Sociologists studying aging initially looked at disengagement, describing it as "an inevitable mutual withdrawal... resulting in decreased interaction between the aging person and others in the social system he belongs to" (Cumming and Henry 1961:14). The disengagement and hangover identities I observed, particularly for Skully and Sandy, help to better understand the quest and attainment of righteousness; however, I was not able to observe or interview ex-sisters.

The social and political aspects of RSMC have been described, but as with many social institutions, including families, education, and economic, religious, and political organizations, leaving the club is as much a part of institutional life as entering into it. Ex-sisters are cut off not only from the immediate family but from the nation, so sisterhood does not accurately describe the exit. Furthermore, when an ex-sister is cut off from the entire nation of sisters, she still retains the national citizenship of her country, losing only her biker nation, its members, and the material culture. Therefore, I propose that exit from RSMC is more akin to a civil death. Although these women are not stateless in a literal sense, they are effectively cut off from citizenship and the citizenry, their sisters.

In *Becoming Un-Orthodox*, Linda Davidman, a Hasidic defector, examines those who leave the ultra-Orthodox world of Hasidism and pays explicit attention to religion as embodied practices and to the body itself as the "medium of identity changes" (2015:200). Davidman, like Ebaugh, builds a framework of role exit, within a larger religious and cultural context of Orthodox Judaism, paying explicit attention to heteronormative gender role norms as central to embodied practices. For righteous sisters, wearing patches (and all of the rituals described in Chapter 1 for caring for one's colors), getting a visible tattoo of the club's logo, and riding in the pack are all embodied practices. If one were to examine a photograph of one hundred members of RSMC, they would look very similar, with almost identical clothing, stances and postures, and even expressions. In this way, righteous sisters, nuns, and Hasidic women share a similarity among themselves in terms of their outward identities. Without the vest and club patches, one no longer belongs to the nation, and the ritualistic acts related to wearing and caring for those symbols of the nation are removed as one's identity changes from sister and biker to motorcyclist. Ebaugh and Davidman interview voluntary defectors and weave their own ex- and defection stories throughout their monographs. *Righteous Sisterhood* deepens this schematic by examining involuntary exile in addition to voluntary exit and by weaving in my own story of ethnographic exile.

Ebaugh outlined nine variables, and of these, two concepts she adopted from Barney Glaser and Anselm Strauss ([1971] 2010) are particularly useful in constructing a framework for compulsory exit: degree of control and reversibility. These terms are fitting for one's exile or exit from RSMC because expulsion from the group has such severe consequences in these women's lives that it represents a civil death from the realm of action and a separation from their identity as a righteous sister as well as from the sisterhood itself. For sisters who exit, there is a brief window in which time is afforded for closure. For sisters who are exiled, it is a closed awareness context, and contrary to Glaser and Strauss, there is no opportunity for control over the process. Twig and Nurse Nan had little, if any, control over their role exit, and since they were out on bad terms, the decision to expel them is not reversible and they cannot become righteous sisters again.

During participant observation (2005–2010) of a similarly sized all-men MC during my doctoral research, I observed several exits, mostly through deaths, and two exiles. That MC was founded in the mid-1970s and was a decade older than RSMC, but it had the same power structure, in which the founding national president was the *only* national president. Sandy described bringing in three or four new members each year with one or two leaving RSMC, but her estimation sharply contradicted the figures on the national business meeting minutes and my cross-referencing. The range of new members in 2015, 2016, 2018, and 2019 was six to twenty-seven new members per year, and the range of "lost" members was fifteen to thirty-three per year. These membership counts, however, were not consistent, in part because two key positions, the national secretary, who wrote and kept the minutes, and the membership director, who provided the figures, changed, and the ways in which numbers were reported also changed.[8] Compared to other MCs, RSMC had higher turnover rates. Davey confirmed that in many all-male MCs, the minimum commitment is ten years. Few are out on bad terms, or exiled, leaving death as the most common way out.

The RSMC leadership considers ex-sisters as the greatest threat to group cohesion, whereas all-men MCs consider women (particularly wives or long-term partners and the mothers of their children) as the greatest threat to the group.[9] The incident described in Chapter 4, however, shows that sexuality and same-sex relationships within RSMC constitute a perceived threat to the stability of the club and the sanctity of club business. Although Twig and Nan provided observable exiles, Sunny's sanctions included being removed from FOG and losing her patches for a year, which highlighted a much deeper threat to the sisterhood and one that is analogous to the fears described in studies of other subcultural groups where homosexuality is taboo, leaving the "threat" to come from women who were not allowed in as members. While the newly patched Twig and never-patched Nurse Nan were expendable, Sunny, a member of twenty-plus years, could not be expelled so quickly or easily. Rather, her sanctions were severe but were kept quiet—I did not know she was kicked out of FOG or had her patches removed in 2016 until *Sandy told me* in 2018. Sandy curated all of the narratives. The public focus stayed on Nurse Nan and Twig, while Sunny suffered in near silence, weeping behind big sunglasses, seemingly relieved at not being exiled herself and willing to undergo the year-long punishment to be allowed back into the sisterhood.

Ruthless as Sandy could be, she was adept at reading the room, and tonal shifts occurred nearly in the same breath. Referring to Twig and Nurse Nan (or any members who had left on bad terms), she said, "Good fucking riddance." But referring to "Apples" and "Janet," two women who left the club voluntarily and returned to become members again, she said, "Their lives have changed, and they need time. They'll be Home. Apples and Janet came Home." Since I knew Apples fairly well, I inferred that her reasons were related to her move from New York to the Midwest, where she took over primary caretaking duties for her aging parents. Janet and I spoke on a few occasions, and I assumed that her role as a teacher and a mother and wife led her to take a leave of absence from RSMC until she later retired from her profession and returned to RSMC. In both cases, their "years," or time in, were returned to them which meant they did not have to come back as prospects. The national president was speaking to both those who were angry at the ex-sisters and those who were sad at the loss of the ex-sisters. The reminder that their presence was not erased also served to calm the fears of those who might contemplate their own exit or exile. All women who join RSMC have a line in *The Book of Sisters*, which is an integral part of the initiation process described in Chapter 2 as well as a space of appearance and immortality in Chapter 3; it is referred to as "the Bible," signaling its sacred role. Similarly, ex-sisters are not removed from framed photograph collages on clubhouse walls or photo albums that are shelved in the clubhouse or in the Big House. Sisters who die as members of the club are commemorated in the spirit ride, but ex-sisters are not.

RSMC functions as a closed context, and the national president calls the shots. Sandy has the final say on all matters of club practices, particularly with respect to exits, exiles, and the communication surrounding both types of departures. To avoid splintering and gossip among the ranks with each new expulsion or exit, Sandy created some spaces for communication and some inside rituals. About the right to know the circumstances of exile or exit, Sandy said, "They have a right to know if they call Home. The sponsor will give them what they know, but if the sponsor cannot give them a bottom line [they can call me]. If they had a connection with the [out] sister . . . I always call them. 'You have six hours to call and say goodbye, and then the door is closed.' Mostly you get back 'No.' I always give them an opportunity to say goodbye. Otherwise that is just mean." The process is extraordinary for its tight control over these ruptures to sisterhood and solidarity. The rituals that take place, including nationwide notification, the amount of time allotted for goodbyes, and the ultimate ritual—the opportunity for those who were hurt the most by the ex-sisters to *burn their patches* as a mode of cleansing and catharsis. Although I never observed a patch-burning ceremony, the centrality and sacredness of the patch as a symbol of the nation positions this act as extreme, even for an MC. The physical evidence of a member's sisterhood and membership in the nation is destroyed, and the cremation of the patches, imbued with so much meaning for the owner, marks that rite of passage and exile, that civil death.

Family members of RSMC are also expected to adhere to the rules pertaining to ex-sisters. Women who were sisters and "aunts" to members' children and grandchildren one day were excommunicated the next. Sandy's daughter Stormy, who grew up around the club, was very close to Curly, and one time she yelled at her mom in front of me, accusing her of taking away the best sisters when they do something she doesn't like; her complaint may have been valid, but her mother remained unmoved. The exited women also lost a large extended family that included sisters' partners, children, and grandchildren. Another form of cutting off ex-sisters includes notifying all of the MCs that a particular woman is out of RSMC, removing any privileges or protection associated with her club membership. Sandy said, "When they out someone, the [one-percenter MC], they send me a photo, but they usually turn outed [RSMC] members away at the gate." She continued with a dilemma posed when a sister's "old man" was a regular fixture at RSMC activities and fundraisers; when the sister became "dead to them," they asked, "How are we supposed to let her old man in without her?" The biker world is relatively small, so the possibilities for ex-sisters remain limited by Sandy's outsize influence within the biker world and specifically within the regional Coalition of Clubs (COC).

In spite of the rigorous yearslong initiation process that is conveyed to applicants, some women are admitted but don't last very long. "There are the ones who are out before they've even gotten in. Six hours is the record. We just started laughing and counting," Sandy said with a chuckle, recalling a sister who joined and was expelled within the space of a single day. While ex-sisters provided some fodder for inside jokes, they were also a major source of consternation not just because of their potential to undermine solidarity within RSMC but also because of their potential to pose external threats by starting or joining a rival group, seeking damages for cabin shares, or sharing club business with outsiders. She stated that once the "underground" (the group that was responsible for the alleged coup) was "dug out," they started a new MC and "terrorized the girls who were in California." She explained, "It's like when you quit a job, you need that interaction. It's not just something you do; it's a way of life." This is exactly the type of "hangover identity" Ebaugh described. Indeed, although patches and trademarked items are confiscated as part of the exit protocol for *any* woman who leaves RSMC, it is not that easy to remove the RS identity and bodily practices.

Becoming a righteous sister takes years, but it can be obliterated in the blink of an eye. Although many factors seem to be at play, the final decision rests with the national president. Nurse Nan, Twig, and Sunny all seemed to participate in the same transgression—dating other sisters—and Sunny's posed the biggest threat to the nation because of her position on FOG; however, Sunny's sanction was a yearlong punishment, whereas Twig and Nurse Nan were banished. The Sponsorship Manual is clear: "If a member leaves, she has chosen to walk away from us. We have no reason to talk to her anymore. Our attention should focus on the Sisters still with us, not the former member who turned her back on us." Although it is possible to maintain contact with the former member, as long as club business is not discussed, few sisters kept in contact with ex(ited) sisters. The ruptures were deep. Speaking to the nation, Sandy said, "It can shake the nation, but it shouldn't. If your heart is hurting, call me." Ex-sisters provided yet another way for the national president to assume a maternal counselor role to the nation, and the way she framed banishment it assumes the emotion will not be anger or resentment toward her or the nation for expelling its members. Rather than appearing as a cold, calculating leader of the nation who eliminates threats with expulsion and exile, Sandy is able to leverage the exiles as a way to strengthen the nation by solidifying the in-group by framing the exiled members as "threats" who could "harm the nation" and reifying the common "friend-enemy" distinction found across the MC subculture. Banishment is an issue of "national security" with no space for dissent.

Life Changes

New personal factors, such as a new role as caregiver for one's parents or grandchildren, constitute one of the reasons sisters chose to leave RSMC. Given the aging population of club members, health issues were a primary reason members stepped back and sometimes exited. Glaser and Strauss ([1971] 2010) describe this within reversibility, and these kinds of life circumstances make sense considering that RSMC is not a one-percenter MC, in which the expectations of membership are to forgo all other statuses, including that of husband or partner, father, son, and employee, to name a few. Sandy described "life changes" as the number one reason sisters exit, and she was sympathetic to life changes, saying, "You have to make some decisions in your life. You were a member in good standing and enjoyed the camaraderie. You finally got strong enough to leave him, and your life is changing. Do you still want the responsibility to be a sister when you are making all of these major life moves? Eighty-five percent choose to stay, but they call, and they can step back and lighten up on phone calls home. Some just muddle through." We see the emphasis on women who "finally got strong enough to leave him," signaling an abusive relationship, which was referenced in a different direct quote in Chapter 2, in which Sandy said, "You can come from a bad background, and some stay with us a short period of time, and others stay with us for good. God sends them our way, and we help them along. They say, 'I've been raped, or I've done this.'" The national president seemed quite aware that the bond of sisterhood is not forever for *most* members and that her role, and the role of RSMC, can be a therapeutic one that guides them through a particularly difficult phase of life. This is a unique feature. While women are expected to give back to the club, there is a definitive give-and-take described here, and the kind of service RSMC provides to members can be transitory, it can be paused, or it can end. Like many things that appear binary, the question of in or out is not actually a binary. There are intricacies that are largely determined by the national president and her close allies who collectively serve relatively short terms as national officers. The ability to step back, an option provided by Sandy at her discretion, offers a middle option for women who cannot meet all of the membership requirements described in Chapter 2, and it is available to both full members and support members. Stepping back is a temporary leave rather than an exit, and since it is not an exit, it was easier for me to observe and document.

Several women had pretty serious health issues, and one year I had a chance to converse with "Chaser," one such chronic sufferer who was an RSMC support member. Chaser was petite, standing five foot two or so with silvery hair and a raspy voice, and she often had a cigarette in her hand or near her mouth. Chaser talked about being a military police officer, an investigator, a law instructor, and a drill sergeant. She said, "I was the only female drill instructor in the two companies that I was in. There were two other drill instructors in other companies. In military law, I was the only female too." Then she laughed. She said she "grew up in the army," going in at eighteen and retiring at thirty-eight years of age. Chaser said she had a broken neck but didn't know it when she retired. She said, "I have metal pins in my neck and cervical spine. That's what got me started with heavy metal," and she waited for me to laugh before laughing boisterously at her own joke. The injury occurred two years before she retired when she was training with pugil sticks and was "getting the best of [her] opponent, a big tall guy." She said, "Guys were all around the ring jeering him and came up behind me and got me in the back of my neck. I was knocked out." Chaser described going to the doctor after she retired and finding out the numbness and "shocks down [her] hands" were a result of the way her vertebrae healed—closing up on the nerves in her arms. That was the first of many surgeries, and she had two vertebrae and two discs removed.

Chaser started riding with her husband, who was a member of an MC, when she was thirty years old. Initially, she rode on the back, but she said, "I preferred to ride my own." She was a bartender at the COC, which is where she met "'Bama" in 2006. Chaser said, "I saw her patch, and I told her, 'I'm interested in your club.'" The following year, Chaser saw 'Bama at the COC again. Chaser said, "I told her that I looked at the website and I researched as best as I could and really wanted to join, so she handed me a card. 'Call me sometime.' And I called her *all* the time." Twig, who was sitting with us, chimed in. "That's how she got her nickname ["Chaser" is a pseudonym]— she calls all the time." Chaser said, "After twenty years with just guys, I was looking for some women to ride with, women to hang out with. You go out looking for girlfriends, you are not going to find them." Reflecting on her first nationals in 2009, Chaser said, "I had people on me like white on rice.... My husband supported me all the way. He's actually a little jealous. We are so organized, and his club was all arguments and fighting. It's not that it's a rule: everybody is just so happy to see each other."

I did not see Chaser too much over the years. At the spirit ride at the 2015 nationals, I was her passenger on her three-wheeled motorcycle and got to know her, but health and financial issues precluded her from attending other nationals during my period of observation. Although I don't know whether Chaser began as a prospect in 2008, when she joined and became a full-patch member and then moved into the role of support sister, Chaser's medical issues, including a critical motorcycle accident in 2010 in which she almost lost her leg, created physical roadblocks to her participation. As a result of the accident, she had a massive scar down her leg, walked with a severe limp, and had a metal plate in her ankle, a new knee, and a new hip. Three-wheeled motorcycles, or trikes, are not allowed in the front of the pack, and because Chaser rode one after her accident, likely because of weakness on her left side and the inability to balance an eight-hundred-pound Harley-Davidson with a "bad leg," she was forced to ride at the back of the group. Although support sisters ride behind sisters anyway, trikes rode behind both. Although disabled members of RSMC were welcomed into the sisterhood, putting disabled sisters in the back, regardless of status, is another example of adopting the troublesome tenets of the larger MC world. Chaser did not complain, and I only knew her as a trike rider, but Blondie, a longtime full-patch holder, organizer of my cabin, and member of the national chapter, hated both her trike and riding in the back to the point that she likely stopped riding before her health prevented her from doing so.

Chaser was loved through and through and was one of the favorites at nationals. Since her chapter affiliation was with the most active chapter in RSMC, her participation was likely robust at the local level, which did not require extensive travel or funds, and I saw her pictured in the annual fundraisers hosted by her chapter affiliate. For people like Chaser, the requirement to attend nationals was lifted, and this is indeed the gray area of "stepping back" Sandy described. Because of her age, physical constraints, and time in (2008–present), Chaser was a valuable member of the club. She told me that whenever she met a new member, she would say, "Your first nationals is like someone handing you a newborn baby. The amount of love you feel is so overwhelming." That sisterly love is conveyed both nonverbally with big hugs and verbally; "Love you, Sis" is a frequent greeting and goodbye. When I didn't see Chaser at a few subsequent nationals, other women told me "life" was the reason she could not attend. Sisters did not readily share personal information about other sisters. The journey was tough on her body, even if she was riding in a truck with a motorcycle trailer behind it, and it was costly. Chaser is an example of a righteous sister whose membership in RSMC was flexible enough to work around her significant physical challenges as well as some financial challenges. For the nation, there is an emphasis on taking care of the elderly and the infirm, and there were several members who had canes or other mobility devices, and while the ableist predilection has been discussed, the flip side is a softness for longtime members who age within the club. In this regard, RSMC provides a unique place for women to age with dignity and respect off their motorcycles and retain their righteousness, even as they are relegated to the back of the pack if they have to transition from the two-wheeled Harleys they have ridden for decades to three-wheeled motorcycles.

Because I was not privy to the text tree or regular inside communication about who was exiled or exited, the national business meeting provided an inside glimpse into the numbers of women who were lost each year. Most of the dozen or two dozen members were quietly exited. In one case, a full-patch member I met in 2014 left the club before 2015 nationals. She spoke briefly about the tension between her and her husband as a result of her membership in RSMC and the time demanded of her. This member lived fairly close to national headquarters, and her obligations to the club were far greater than those of other members who lived far away. When I interviewed Sandy's husband, "DJ," a former one-percenter and longtime MC member, he said, "There are some that [*pauses*] I don't know. The women that want to join—I've seen them come and go. Their husbands don't like it. They go away, you know? They actually got their full patch, and then they quit." While men are not discussed or perceived to be a threat to this all-female biker nation, DJ had additional insights from the male perspective on the role of sisters' husbands. He continued: "Some guys show up for nationals, so they come, the other guys are there, the husbands, the boyfriends. I'm friendly and try to talk to them. 'Let's go for a ride!' And they just sit there the entire weekend. What the hell, man? It's Bike Week." At any given nationals, the ratio of women to men is probably ten to one.

DJ's own story, which he readily told, included two exits from MCs. His first was a medical exit, and his second was retirement. His role as "big brother" in RSMC fit him. He said, "I love it. I don't have to do anything or be anywhere. I can go anywhere I want without having to worry about getting in with a patch on. I still have the fun of being a big brother. I really like that. I mean, you can see all the plaques I've got, so they must love me [*laughs*]." Each year at nationals, he was found behind turntables volunteering as DJ for the club's final night. DJ's own exit from an MC provides a fascinating look at the kind of "hangover identity" Ebaugh described in *Becoming an Ex* as well as the importance of men in facilitating their partner's participation and longevity in RSMC.

Other women chose to leave RSMC because of different kinds of family obligations. Women with young children appeared to come and go more rapidly, and in general few of these women joined and stayed. Distance also proved to be an issue for some members. Some chose to move closer to national headquarters, and some chose to leave. Many members were also at the stage in life in which adult children moved back home for financial assistance or relied on their parents, members of the club, for full-time childcare; simultaneously, their parents were aging and often required substantial care. The "sandwich generation" (Miller 1981) has since been expanded, particularly during the COVID-19 pandemic, which increased the responsibilities for many women with aging parents and adult children. Particularly among the younger members with children of their own, parenting style was heavily scrutinized. Each year, an annual event for members and their families was put together, and one year, there was a Kidz Camp at national headquarters in addition to the annual family event, which changed location each year and was hosted by an RSMC chapter. These events, designed to bring sisters, their partners, and their children and grandchildren together, also functioned as a microscope to examine sisters' parenting styles and also to critique parenting and kids' behavior. One member broke down in tears at Kidz Camp after being criticized for her adolescent daughter's behavior, and she exited the club shortly thereafter. Respect was a core value heavily emphasized during these events, and a lack thereof reflected back on the parent or the grandparent, albeit unevenly.

Sandy's youngest daughter was held up as a model for others, and she led many of the club activities for teenagers. "Paula" and I spent a great deal of time together and talked at length on several occasions, and one time she alluded to the pressure and said:

> I feel you need to hold your head high and not do anything stupid but not just because my mom is the president but because I wouldn't want to be seen like that in the first place, but you are holding the whole club on your back. It's not just something you can fool around with when you're hanging out. I did get in trouble a couple times. [The national vice president] was very unhappy with it.

As a teenager, Paula did not smoke or drink, and had a very different adolescence than her two older sisters. She lived a sheltered life at home with her parents into her twenties. Paula did not drive or work until she was nearly finished with high school, and she never showed any interest in motorcycling. It is unlikely her rare bouts of getting in trouble at club events created any blowback for Sandy; however, the pressure this young woman felt of "holding the whole club on your back," to just hang out, illustrates the incredible responsibility she took on as the national president's daughter.

Most of the national officers had grown children who were uninvolved with the club. In some cases, members who held national positions, were the primary caretakers of one or more of their grandchildren. As described in Chapter 3, there was a common denial of responsibility for the behavior of their own grandchildren and a collective blame, or at least headshaking, with respect to the absent parent, who in many cases was their own child. Blondie and 'Bama were two longtime members of high rank and status who had granddaughters who raised some eyebrows at Kidz Camp. Blondie's granddaughter was a teenager, and 'Bama's granddaughter was just seven or eight years old at the time. Holding an insider-outsider position throughout the research, I breathed a sigh of relief that I did not bring my son to Kidz Camp (he was invited) because there was a high level of scrutiny. Most of the members who assisted with Kidz Camp were not trained to work with children or adolescents, and although the planned activities were fun and the kids had a spacious ten-acre property (national headquarters) and were allowed to use the saltwater pool at the Big House (strictly off-limits to regular members during nationals), the pressure on being a *righteous mom* proved to be too much for at least one member, who quit RSMC shortly thereafter.

For this particular member and dozens of others, the national president viewed this type of exit as natural and even expected, which took me a long time to grasp. Striving for a clarifying metaphor, she said, "If the shoe doesn't fit, it doesn't mean it's a bad shoe." Although I think Sandy was referring to women as the shoe and the club as the foot, the metaphor actually works well for this situation. Many women try on RSMC, and some wear it around the store or take it home for a while. Some even wear the shoes outside before realizing they are not a good fit. The somewhat open attitude about exit, in general, is a unique feature. Sometimes, a sister purchases a pair of shoes, wears them for a few years, and then returns them, only to buy them again. For Apples and Janet, the club was a good fit when they were young, but as caretaking and career responsibilities increased, they needed and were allowed to step back. In Apples's case, what she initially thought would be a temporary relocation from the Northeast to the Midwest to care for her parents turned into a decades-long relocation. Janet told me that she and her daughter were members of RSMC for a while and that she came back to RSMC after retiring as a teacher.

Apples and Janet were members of RSMC in the "early days," before it became a three-piece-patch MC and when the number of members was two dozen or fewer. Both returned in their fifties and sixties after exiting sometime in their thirties (a guesstimate), signaling a shift in their life cycle that provided them with additional time, money, and a desire for the camaraderie and sisterhood they experienced as younger women. By the time Apples returned, she had advanced degrees and a high-status position in higher education. My guess, based on things she told me over the years as measured against my age and experience, is that Apples was in her early fifties when she returned around 2015, but unlike many bikers, she looked much younger than her age. Apples was tall, blond, and thin, with exceptionally large breasts, and she was one of the few bikers in RSMC who had arrived as a young woman with experience in one-percenter MCs as "property." Her relationship to Sandy was unique among all the members, which likely shaped her reentry. Janet's reentry was a bit less ceremonial and emotional than Apples's but functioned in an important way as the messaging was clear—if you leave on good terms, you can always come Home.

Exit, in RSMC, can be a temporary stepping back, or it can be permanent, with the same basic consequences as exile, and there is also space for a return. Like the prodigal son, Apples was welcomed with open arms by Sandy. Most of the exits were small, hardly notable, with a dozen women leaving each year, some of whom attended one nationals and then left RSMC. These exits do not pose a huge threat to the nation, and the narrative surrounding them firmly places the impetus for exit on the individuals, although my suspicion is that many of these were forced or strongly suggested exits. This is an area of inquiry ripe for future research—if a researcher can circumnavigate the many roadblocks posed by club business.

Biker funerals are a final way for sisters to exit the club, and this type of exit is treated with reverence, provided the member is in good standing, and is commemorated each year with the annual spirit ride described in Chapter 2.

Other commemorative rituals take place and further solidify the bonds of sisterhood and elevate the space of appearances even in death through ritual rides, a virtual memorial page, and visible reminders of those lost, such as special patches created for their vests.

Until Death Do Us Part

Although I went to several male MC biker funerals, including one for a chapter president, I did not attend any funerals for righteous sisters. A virtual memorial club website showed one woman whose death corresponded with my period of research; I never met her, and any ritual aspects were outside my observation. In July 2021, nearing the completion of this book, I visited the virtual memorial and was stunned to see two new faces that I knew well. Blondie and Blue died in late 2000 and early 2021, respectively. My throat got tight, and I felt tears immediately come to my eyes. These two hit me hard. Both were cabinmates and women I spent significant amounts of time with from 2014 to 2019, and they were some of the most *righteous* of sisters.

Blondie had serious health issues for the last several years, and she was not able to stay for the full week of nationals by the end of my period of observation. As she aged into her late seventies, she was stick thin, tan, blond, and covered in wrinkles from years of chain-smoking and the sun. A native midwesterner, wife, ex-wife, career veteran, mom, stepmom, and grandmother, Blondie was gruff. In July 2014, she walked up to me and asked with incredulity, "So what do you know about one-percenters?" With her, I needed to establish myself as a woman with knowledge of the biker world. Whether I was a good ethnographer or writer was not her concern. My response satisfied her for the time being. She lived close to the national headquarters, so I saw her more than most members from 2014 to 2019. Blondie was not happy when Sandy invited me to purchase shares in the first cabin to be built for club members, but as cabin leader, Blondie resigned herself to having me in her cabin. In January 2015, I assisted with the construction of our cabin as we built out walls and began to make the cabin-shed into a home for eight to ten women. Like a drill sergeant, Blondie observed the work being done, made several complaints, and issued orders. Since I paid off my shares fairly quickly and worked on the cabin, I earned some favor with Blondie. By 2018, she had to plug in her CPAP machine each night, which whirred below my bunk, and by 2019, she no longer stayed overnight in the cabin. A heavy lifelong smoker, Blondie moved with style and swagger, even with her oxygen tank. When she gave up the trike (mostly because she hated riding in the back of the pack), one could hear her coming as the motor of her American sports car roared down the block and as she strode out of the brightly colored car.

Blondie was deeply loved by RSMC, but she also seemed to be one of those women who got into trouble for voicing her many opinions and never backing down, telltale biker behavior. One time Blondie said to me, "Things have changed. They are charging for everything now." She also told me about a "girl" who was briefly a member of RSMC and had really taken center stage during one nationals but subsequently was out. Blondie was troubled by the fact that she had been used as "bait" with a one-percenter MC and then "discarded." Her terminology was strong, but I understood her to mean Sandy wanted to forge connections or obtain information, so she used this young member to seduce one or more one-percenters. She was exiled shortly thereafter for reasons unknown. At the time, I was driving and Blondie was talking. Knowing my intention to write a book, she clearly wanted me to know what was going on and to include it in the larger story of the club, and we were far from the clubhouse and other sisters. Very few single women in their twenties or thirties joined RSMC in the 2000s, and this particular young woman, a single mom, struck me at the time as someone who would do anything to belong. During the annual rodeo in which outside people were invited to national headquarters, she participated in the "sledding" behind a motorcycle on grass so many times her arms and legs were full of burns, and she drank, flirted, and did her best to make her presence known. As Blondie told the story from my passenger seat, she shook her head repeatedly, disgusted. To the devoted and longtime member of the club, using a sister as "bait" was off-limits, and her retribution, in addition to speaking out about it to Sandy was to share it with me. The already-contradictory picture of RSMC became increasingly so; many of the exits and exiles seemed fairly arbitrary, but this one reeked of a manipulative setup at the expense of a young woman who desperately wanted to belong. However she justified these perceived wrongdoings, Blondie stepped back but did not exit RSMC until her own death in late 2020.

Blondie's last communication with me was to tell me that I was "out" in July 2019. She texted early one morning asking me to call her. Our conversation lasted no more than five minutes, and her tone was resigned. She broke the rules and reached out to me—more than likely, there was no six-hour window for me since I was not a member—because she wanted to give me a heads-up. She was also fishing for information regarding what had happened, which I honestly did not know, and as I threw out a few ideas, Blondie became more resigned. If I had to guess, I imagine Blondie would be one of the few, if any, women who might have spoken up and wanted information from Sandy about my expulsion, if not enough to put herself in too much trouble with her national president, to whom she was loyal.

There was a short online tribute to Blondie on RSMC's website and a three-sentence obituary I found with an online search; the latter said nothing about the club. The obituary did not tell me anything I did not already know about Blondie, and there was only one comment on it, by ex-sister Twig, which made me wonder if Blondie was more out than in when she died, so I started to explore RSMC's social media pages, which are public. There was no announcement of Blondie's passing, which confirmed my suspicion that relations between Blondie and the club were strained. Blondie's health had been deteriorating rapidly, and although she was a lifelong smoker, she took great care to protect her health—for example, by shortening her time at nationals. She would have been particularly vulnerable to COVID-19 and likely would have skipped nationals in March 2020 to protect herself. Still, the lack of *sisterhood* surrounding Blondie's death was surprising.

In sharp contrast to Blondie's meager online tributes, Blue's death was heavily memorialized on club social media pages, a private memorial page that was full of tributes by members of RSMC, and her short tribute on the club's website. A British woman with gorgeous silver hair, light blue eyes, and flawless skin, Blue was extraordinarily intelligent, well spoken, and extremely capable as a rider. During a trip I took to London to present at a conference, she attended with me as an eager and inquisitive guest. When we heard a colleague give a presentation on the noise a motorcycle emits with loud pipes, which the presenter attributed to female power, Blue said, "I would be really mad if someone told me I couldn't make noise. I think I would feel like they are trying to silence me." All of Blue's Harley-Davidsons were big bikes, and while her bikes were not obnoxiously loud, they did emit a healthy roar. She rode me to Canterbury, which was my request based on bookish curiosity, in spite of the fact that it was a weekend and Blue knew there would be significant traffic as it was a route to coastal destinations and getaway spots for Brits. We white-lined the entire way there, probably ninety minutes of hard and fast riding, weaving in and out of traffic. Sitting behind her, I had a thrilling ride and felt completely safe as her competence and skill outweighed any danger. When we arrived, she made me promise not to tell "Boss" (Sandy) about the white-lining, and I assured her I would not. Because Blue can no longer get into trouble, I am choosing to include this story here. Another British member of RSMC, who was newer to the club, rode with us and struggled to keep up. I had the distinct impression it would *not* have been her choice of how to spend a weekend; however, there is an expectation of hospitality, and I am sure that the "pairs rule" was firmly in place and that our trip was reported to the national road captain and the national president. When we arrived in Canterbury, we walked around and ate outdoors at a delicious Moroccan restaurant. We took a few photographs, got back on the bikes, rode back to a motorcycle showroom and tavern in London, and met up with some of my colleagues from the conference. Blue enjoyed one beer, and even when she was not riding, she did not drink a lot, likely because of her role on the security team. Unlike many of the members of RSMC, she did not smoke and appeared to be incredibly healthy.

Blue said that when she came into the club, everyone told her I was a writer and that I was "okay with Sandy." She kept her distance; she said, "I didn't want to say something I would regret later," and then laughed. I asked a few questions about what it was like to be a woman MC member in England. She said, "The one-percenter clubs in England won't allow any other clubs to wear back patches. Only boob patches are allowed." So at her home in England, Blue cannot wear her patches. I found this fascinating because her outward identity as a sister was relegated to the two trips Home each year. Unlike many of the other women, who rode together and wore their patches throughout the United States, Blue could not. Although she said England was less dangerous because there are few guns, she described some instances of one-percenters taunting other clubs by riding outside "their area," but most drove in cars or avoided wearing their patches altogether.

Standing at least five foot ten, Blue was a physically towering presence; she stood tall, and she stood out vocally with her soft voice and British accent. She moved through the RSMC ranks quickly and served under the national sergeant-at-arms with Skully. Blue occasionally talked about her job, and on the basis of snippets she told me over time, I imagined it to be in information technology and in some type of male-dominated corporate environment. When she took over for Blondie as the leader of our cabin, I could tell by the way she ran business meetings with formal agendas, minutes, voting procedures, and email communications that her white-collar experience brought a valued skill set to the club, which was likely why she became cabin leader. She was educated and earned a good living, as evidenced by the Harley-Davidson she kept at Home for when she was in the United States and the one she picked me up on in England as well as by her ability to travel several times a year to national headquarters. She was as comfortable with a roomful of academics from all over the world as she was with a roomful of bikers. This kind of authenticity and confidence was likely tested in the club, and I wondered how women like Blue and Apples navigated the terrain when they didn't agree with something. Dissent was not allowed, and women with power were inevitably put into difficult situations with other members and even with me. My last communication with Blue was regarding my cabin shares. In 2020, from her personal email (not her RSMC email), she wrote, with characteristic professionalism and an uncharacteristic, detached businesslike tone:

Hi Sarah,
Attached is a copy of the Shareholders Agreement that you signed with us.

I understand that you ended your relationship with us. At this time we are not sure what we are doing with your share.
With respect,
"Blue"

The agreement was in no way binding or legal since the "property" itself was not a legal unit available to be sold, and of course, Blue knew this and also knew that if I ended "the relationship," I would be entitled to a refund of my shares according to the same agreement. Blue died ten months later and by all of the available evidence was a loyal sister "until death do us part," as she promised when she "married" into the club. Blondie had a decade more time in than Blue. Although I do not know her cause of death either, I assume both knew they were close to death.[10] Blondie was in her seventies and had been sick for many years, struggling to breathe without her oxygen during the day and her CPAP at night, and toward the end of her life, her disposition seemed to create space to be critical of RSMC. She was the only member to call me directly after receiving notification that I was out. These forms of dissent, though subtle and likely not unique acts of defiance, probably led to her own exit. Although she is commemorated on the club's website, it was shocking that there was no mention of her on any of the public social media sites, in sharp contrast to the posts, photos, hundreds of likes, and dozens of shares for Blue, who died three months later. Blue was in her fifties, had fewer than ten years in the club, and continued to be careful of what she said and to whom, highly valuing her position and relationship with the national president. Her outside life looked very different from her life in the club—diverse friends, evening gowns, white wine in long-stemmed glasses in middle- and upper-middle-class English apartments and homes, and likely a high-powered white-collar job—but she chose to live both lives and reconcile the two until the end. Both lives provide glimpses into righteous sisterhood and reveal the complexities and inconsistencies of sisterhood and the space of appearances, even in death as a space of appearance and immortality. These final exits, particularly Blondie's, shed light on my own exit and subsequent exile, which occurred in July 2019.

Ex-Ethnographer

For anthropologist and ethnographer Daniel Wolf, his exit from the Rebels MC was anticlimactic and is described in one paragraph, the last in his 349-page book. As noted earlier, Wolf became a member of the Rebels, carrying out "formal data-gathering procedures" for one and a half years after the club approved his study ([1991] 2000:349). He wrote:

> As my role as an ethnographer became more evident, my role as a biker became more contrived and I began to be excluded from the brotherhood. Once again, there were no formal decisions or announcements; my contact with members simply became less frequent and less intense. As an ethnographer, my relationship to the club lost its substance and meaning, and I lost touch with the innermost core of Rebel reality; I simply faded away. What I shared with these men led me to believe that I would at least maintain ties of friendship after I completed the ethnography, the enduring emotion would be one of comradeship. I was wrong. I would be like so many of the ex-members who simply drifted away, never to be seen or spoken of again. (Wolf [1991] 2000:349)

Wolf entered as a biker and then became a friend of the club and then a patched member of the Rebels MC and received permission from the club to conduct his research as a personal favor. Once the friend-turned-brother turned ethnographer, the Rebels began to cut him loose. This fading away was not mutual—it seems clear that Wolf did not anticipate it or understand it—and although he does not delve any further into his own role exit, it is clear that his exile "never to be seen or spoken of again" and the end of the friendship ties were painful. For anthropologist Ruth Behar, the decision was made for her as well in *Translated Woman* (1993), and it was abrupt and similarly done unceremoniously. These ethnographers were informed that their period of study was closed by those they were studying. For Wolf, it was a Canadian motorcycle club; for Behar, it was the people whose home she had been renting in Mexico during her field research.

In my case, my exit was closed and likely determined single-handedly by Sandy. Like Wolf, this occurred when "*my* role as an ethnographer became more evident [emphasis added]." Since my formal status still bordered on an insider-outsider dynamic, in which I had access to things no other outsiders had access to but was not affiliated with RSMC in any official capacity, I was expendable. On several occasions, Sandy said, "You will never know what it's about without joining," yet she provided informed consent and facilitated my ongoing ethnographic research of the club knowing that I would not become a member. Without Sandy's approval, this book would never have been written, or even begun, because I would not have had access to her or to any women in the club; there would have been no invitations to nationals or other club activities. I was not searching for a phenomenological understanding of what it was like to *be* a righteous sister; therefore, I did not need a motorcycle, nor did I need to become a member. I wanted to understand how women bikers became *righteous sisters* and how power and politics operated within the club and among a complex global web of one-percenter MCs and other MCs. The basic things Sandy reiterated to me, such as the golden rule of "no gossip" and "marriage," were not to be taken at face value as she said these things as a way of shaping the book into the story she wanted to be told about her nation. I avoided bias, or as my writing group called it, "the cult of Sandy," through reflexive techniques, time away from research for writing (2019–2021), and the careful readers in my writing group. This is not to suggest there is no bias, but I strove and strive to be transparent and to situate myself as the Writer.

Like Wolf, I was deeply embedded in an MC for a substantial period of time (2014–2019), but my involvement deepened over time, in sharp contrast to what Wolf described as, "I simply faded away" ([1991] 2000:349). I was formally "outed," or exiled. My civic death, in July 2019, likely was sent through the text tree and read something like this: "Sarah, The Writer, is out. No contact. Any questions, call Home." As described in the preceding section, Blondie reached out to me and asked, "What did you *do*?" Good question—what *did I do*?

In late 2018, I published my first article about motorcycling and women based on original archival research on women's clubs that were present during the Hollister motorcycle rally, or "riot," in 1947. My piece troubled the dominant narrative of biking groups being exclusively about men and provided an alternative history of this critical moment in biker history that reinscribed the women present and corrected some of the still-dominant assumptions about biker culture using archival records from local newspapers and town records at Hollister. That article piqued some interest and led to a small amount of recognition, mostly by my home institution, the City University of New York (CUNY), which shared my research interests on social media. One of the offshoots from the article was an interview with Abi Ishola on *Urban U*, a program on CUNY TV. It was filmed in February and aired in July 2019. In March 2019, I found out that I was a recipient of the prestigious ACLS/Mellon Fellowship shortly after attending RSMC's nationals. In May, I attended the National Coalition of Motorcyclists (NCOM) Conference for the first time with Sandy and several other national officers. The weekend provided a fascinating insider's look at one-percenter MCs, Black MCs, MCs, and riding clubs, but it was difficult to get any one-on-one time with Sandy; Skully, the national sergeant-at-arms, and other RSMC members did not leave her side, and Sandy was there to be seen and to network. As the end of the weekend approached, Sandy demanded to see "what [I'd] been writing about RSMC." The conversation had a different tone than the dozens of similar conversations we had had in the past regarding the book. The unexpected impatience seemed at odds with the recent developments, especially the ACLS/Mellon Fellowship and the recent interest in women and motorcycling that followed my Hollister article. Through conference presentations in which I copresented with members of RSMC,[11] conversations, and the article, she was peripherally engaged in my academic writing; however, I had not sent her anything of the manuscript I had begun to draft in 2016. My prologue provided a broad outline of the major points and book sections, so I emailed it to Sandy immediately after leaving NCOM on May 13, 2019. Days later, on May 15, ACLS submitted its press release about the inaugural group of 2019 ACLS/Mellon Community College Faculty Fellows. The same day, I texted Skully and suggested I should disconnect from any RSMC social media, and she replied, "Sounds like a good idea . . . have you spoke with [Sandy] about this yet?" I had not. I quickly unfriended and unliked anything related to RSMC on social media, and since I had not tagged any member, checked in, or posted about any club event, I felt fairly confident I could keep the identity of RSMC, and its members, concealed. The vast majority of women wanted me to write about *them*, but some members did not publicly tout their club membership because of the negative connotations of MCs and the types of security clearance a few women had with their jobs. On May 16, my institution, Hostos Community College, put out a press release. As I predicted, there was a significant amount of attention since I was the recipient of the first cohort of national ACLS/Mellon Community College Faculty Fellows. On May 29, I received the following email from Sandy:

> I hate the fact u feel the need to say a few things
> like gay officers . . . whats the point to that
> about sisters of color . . . no reason for that
> and the way you head into things . . . not sure why.

I immediately emailed her to set up a time to talk and tried to call. Late the same evening, with no response, I wrote:

> The short answer is that I'm a sociologist and an ethnographer so writing about gender, sexuality, class, and race are core elements of any scientific study of a human group (definition of sociology). It's objective, not what I feel. The point is to describe the group and then situate it within the larger subculture and society.

There was no further communication for several weeks, and while this would be totally unacceptable for a member, I was not a member. My work life and personal life were quite busy, and I thought that it would be better to speak with her in person. At NCOM she had suggested I have my "cave time" with her that summer, and I had already sent her some dates for late August. As described in Chapter 3, cave time was a requirement for membership, and although I previously stayed in the cave, Sandy's "suggestion" implied a tightening of the reins that likely coincided with outside recognition of my research and writing, and perhaps with a realization that it might be out of her immediate control. On June 4, 2019, I texted a handful of women the following:

> Hi Sisters,
> I don't have too many people's numbers but just wanted to let those closest to me know I removed all Sisters and family members from Facebook to protect everyone's privacy.
> I was awarded a Mellon Fellowship for the book and the press release is all about the topic (a women's MC). It came out suddenly, so I quickly texted [Skully] and she also thought it was a good idea to play it safe.
> Hopefully I'll be on Sister Time soon. Love y'all!
> Sarah

The responses—"Congratulations! Can't wait to see how this evolves! Love you!" ('Bama), "Congratulations" (T-Shirt Tammy), and "That's fantastic and congratulations my friend can't wait to read the book" (Diesel)—quickly followed. In 2018, I had requested access to Sister Time, RSMC's closed chat room, and Sandy conceded to let me in, but it was not a request that had been granted easily or quickly. There were some issues connecting with 'Bama, the information technologist of RSMC, and then some more time passed before the tech issues were sorted out. Like the exit interviews and club finances, the private chat space and regular communications seemed intentionally off-limits for me, in spite of the go-ahead from Sandy. Those texts would be the last communication I would have with any members of RSMC outside Blondie, Apples, and Sandy the following month.

The *Urban U* interview was set to air in July 2019, and I knew it would be widely available on social media. Although the four minute and fifty seconds of produced reel centered on my archival research in Hollister, Abi Ishola described the recently awarded fellowship and stated that the research project "largely focuses on a women's motorcycle club . . . who operate anonymously due to the stigma many patched members face" (Hoiland 2019). When I viewed the interview for the first time, postproduction, I knew "operate anonymously" and "stigma" would be problematic in Sandy's eyes, although I did not anticipate how crucial those three words would become. About the research and RSMC, I said, "They have negotiated respect, and I would say that among many of these [*pause*] hard-core bikers, they *are* considered righteous sisters" (Hoiland 2019). I texted the clip to Sandy on July 9 and spoke to her within a few days, and although she expressed disdain for the three words, she also said these things happen and made a comment about the media twisting words. She didn't sound surprised when I told her my request to approve the final product before it was aired was denied. I was somewhat relieved, as it appeared to blow over, but I found out via Blondie on July 11 that I was exiled. In my notes, I wrote, "[She] called me to tell me about the order and shared a bunch of other recent power plays. In spite of the fact that she [Sandy] liked the documentary, she told the women I was putting things on social media without permission." The interview, which Sandy knew about in advance, was shared by several entities other than me. The RSMC was not named (even by pseudonym), nor was it the topic of the interview, so saying I put "things" on social media was deceptive at best and outright libel at worst. Sandy and I spoke on July 14, and while she acknowledged that I was out, it seemed temporary. The text tree and official communication constitute Sandy's space of appearances—and one in which she has the ultimate authority. On one hand, a public shaming to put me in my place and to reassert her control seemed reasonable. On the other hand, the no-contact decree initiated a series of events that would be nearly impossible to reverse.

On July 15, Apples, with whom I developed a great friendship over the years, texted me and told me that she had offered to broker the negotiations between Sandy and me. She opted to text rather than talk because of discomfort from oral surgery she had had earlier that day. She was a perfect intermediary—she knew the national president for twenty-five years and me for nearly ten—and she was familiar with the proverbial "club business" as well as with what an academic book entails. She had exited the club and come back. I had deep admiration and respect for Apples, and I valued her friendship and her insight. Like me, she was one of the few people who straddled academic and biker worlds. Although I did not "need" Sandy or her blessing at that point—I had five years of participant observation research, more than enough to write the kind of book I wanted to write—I did not want to sever ties or be exiled. First, and foremost, I did not want to take the stories and then use them for my own personal and professional gain, leaving little if anything in return other than the book. I always planned to share with the club a portion of any material success and the excitement of a published book. Second, I did not share things on social media and had taken swift and immediate actions to protect members from any ties or connections that could compromise their anonymity as participants in the research. Third, I was not certain if there would be other types of retaliation from Sandy. There was the potential for physical threats and intimidation and potential libel or even copyright claims. Although I knew I had not done anything ethically questionable, my experience has taught me that is not always enough, and fighting accusations can be exceptionally time consuming and costly, particularly when the stakes are low. For all of these reasons, I was eager to communicate with Apples and optimistic that she would be an effective intermediary.

As I tried to go over the points of contention—race and sexual orientation—with Apples, I continued to learn more about RSMC. With respect to the "women of color" I referred to in the original prologue I had sent to Sandy, Apples asked, "*Who are* they," and then said, "I can't think of any." I listed three names off the top of my head, and she responded, "They don't see themselves as women of color. Do they?" I mentioned tattoos and direct references to Native American lineage, for example, but for each case, Apples had a rebuttal that played down any direct associations with their ethnicity. With respect to the third name, "Whiskey," someone who appeared to be biracial, Apples wrote, "She doesn't identify as anything but white." I had never interviewed Whiskey. She was a longtime member of RSMC and a biker. My most notable encounter with her was when she escorted me out of the business meeting in 2014 because she didn't believe the national president had approved my participation and attendance. In 2019, I had a few conversations with Whiskey and got to know her a bit, but she still was the most closed-off, private person in RSMC, and although it seemed clear to me that she was biracial, I had never asked. I wanted to respect her desire to be private, so I never asked to interview her. Given the overtly racist nature of some of the members and national officers and the observable lack of women of color in the group, it was not a subject I was comfortable broaching with white members or the few women of color. "Diversity" within the club took the form of accents—British, Canadian, and New York—and similarly regional diversity. Given the racist history of MCs in the United States and also the advent of highly segregated one-percenter clubs, some of which I witnessed at NCOM with a Black one-percenter MC and the Banditos one-percenter MC, the history and context of the issue made it quite taboo, on par with questions about sexuality. Apples closed the subject abruptly by texting, "I've had African American and Hispanic Sisters before. It isn't a big deal." Having spent hours looking through RSMC photo albums, this did not match what I saw in the albums and observed between 2010 and 2019, but Apples made it clear that there would not be any further discussion.

The topic of sexual orientation was so taboo in the club that it was never discussed outside a few brief conversations with Sandy; it was not casually discussed among sisters and it was not part of the formal interviews I conducted with at least two lesbian women. Apples wrote: "The sexual orientation, I agree, is trickier. I don't know what she [Sandy] is wanting but I believe you can hash it out with her. Just stay close. Don't make her think you've come in and taken what you want and then left her/us. That is a big trigger. She needs to know you are committed to the truth." In retrospect, reading

Apples' statements years later, she was manipulating me. Apples, a doctoral student and higher education administrator, knew that I didn't need Sandy's permission to write the book. She also knew that I had spent years building trust and rapport by working alongside Sandy and the sisters and lending my time and talents to RSMC, so her choice of words "taken what you want and then left her/us," "trigger," and "committed to the truth" are things that she knew would influence me to go back to Sandy. Apples wrote, "Let her know how much you care" and "This project is precious to us both." By "us," Apples is referring to herself and Sandy. The proverbial long midwestern goodbye continued over text with "Thank you, and good night. Love you." The conversation continued for a while, and she added, "I have permission to speak to you but no one else does" and "She [Sandy] and I trust each other implicitly." The hour-long text conversation would be the last time I would speak to Apples.

On the basis of what Apples and I identified as potential issues and solutions, I drafted a memorandum of understanding (MOU) that outlined a plan for communication and transparency but asserted authorial control over the content. I sent Sandy the MOU on July 17, and we spoke on July 19. She rejected the MOU outright and said, "You still don't get it." At one point, she said, "Talking to you is like kicking a dead fucking horse." The idiom, albeit modified from its original, described how I felt as well. One of the demands was that I remove the word "feminism" from the book and replace it with "fierce." She also demanded I remove any references to sexual orientation, gender, and race and ethnicity. During the phone call, I made it clear that the research was mine—she consented, as did each of the women in RSMC—and that I could write the book with or without her approval. I could hear hesitation on her end; I do not think she anticipated this or realized that she could not control the data I had already collected or that I would write a book.

Getting out of RSMC, for me, meant standing up for myself, asserting control over my prose, and honoring the women I met, both the righteous sisters who are still in RSMC and the ex–righteous sisters, by writing honestly and without Sandy's interference. Although my dream of cocreating *Righteous Sisterhood* evaporated, when we ended the call and the period of officially being an ex-ethnographer began, I never felt freer.

Epilogue

Since my exile in the summer of 2019, a few members of RSMC have reached out to me, risking violation of the no-contact rule Sandy imposed. I observed something very similar when Dave left his MC after more than a decade of membership. A few of his closest friends continued to stay in touch, violating the rules of exile and directly defying the national president, but the brotherhood quickly eviscerated. From our first meeting until our last phone call, Sandy took great pains to show me and explain to me how different RSMC was from other clubs, and I *wanted* to see RSMC as a feminist response to a male-dominated subculture—a space of empowerment, camaraderie, philanthropy, and personal growth. Sandy's bravado made sense and still makes sense because RSMC was doing something that had not been done in the biker world, and she deserves credit for starting and leading her nation of righteous sisters for decades. The potential for RSMC to create and sustain a global sisterhood of righteous bikers who eschew the troublesome tenets of the one-percenters and MCs and to form a space of appearances for women to become righteous sisters is there, but it is stymied by the club's adoption of some of the most troublesome tenets of the outlaw MCs and, more recently, the politicized rhetoric of far-right motorcyclists and clubs. This research builds upon the larger literature of incredibly diverse women's groups, such as sororities, racist groups, and the Red Hatters. In *Righteous Sisterhood*, I problematize race, gender, and sexual orientation, which accelerated if not finalized my own forced exit.

When I first met Sandy at her family home in 2010, she said, "The whole world has changed, Silly Rabbit; they don't rob trains anymore." She was referring to my skepticism regarding her description of her biker birthday party as "family friendly," but these statements encompass her wider worldview about the changing nature of the biker world. Coming from the founder and only national president of a three-piece-patch all-women's MC, her bravado makes sense. Her arete has been almost totally unquestioned within RSMC (minus what she called the "coup attempt"), and she experiences respect in segments of the one-percenter world that are reserved for male righteous bikers. Her transformation from being a teen bride and a woman who jumped in the pool when a one-percenter said "Jump" to being at the helm of RSMC for decades undergirds this truth in her own life. *Her* whole world has changed. Not only has RSMC been a space of appearances for herself but the promise of righteousness and sisterhood has been there for the hundreds of women who have prospered. This kind of political community beckons women who ride motorcycles to join by powerfully leveraging the human need for belonging and for power. For Arendt, "Power corresponds to the human ability not just to act but to act in concert" (1970:44) and without the group, there is no power. For many sisters in RSMC, riding together as a pack and coordinating activities around motorcycle safety or child abuse provides a deep sense of power and purpose that they did not get through their jobs, through their families, or as woman motorcyclists. This is particularly true for the aging sisters and those who were not likely to exercise power in other areas of their life, from work to home and their communities, without RSMC. Sandy is acutely aware that she has no power without her nation, and the COVID-19 pandemic provides yet another space of appearances for her to prove her righteousness.

In 2024, it feels like the whole world *has* changed. Unsurprisingly, RSMC nationals took place in March 2020, despite the growing alarm at the rapid spread of COVID-19, lockdowns, and travel restrictions, and again in 2021, amid the onset of the omicron variant and after the controversial August 2020 Sturgis Motorcycle Rally. Although I was not privy to any of the conversations surrounding the pandemic, this decision was heavily political and polarizing, and if RSMC is a microcosm with which to understand politics, gender, race, and class in the United States, particularly as the club functions as a space of appearances for middle-aged and senior white women, the decision to host large, in-person gatherings with international attendees positions RSMC politically in a way that it was not positioned before the pandemic.

The yearning for *righteous sisterhood* and the creation of the "righteous sister" as a descriptive and analytical category addresses this "new world," claiming a word that has been solely associated with masculine excellence in the biker world. Early in my fieldwork, it was rare to hear members talk about politics or religion at RSMC events, but as the national culture and political climate continued to divide the United States, this changed, and by 2019 these references had become ubiquitous. Righteousness, rather than something to describe "real" sisters, seemed to reflect larger political movements outside RSMC. The club's acceptance, or even tolerance, by the larger increasingly politicized misogynist biker subculture is predicated on sticking to the party line as demonstrated at NCOM with "freedom" at stake. I have described how helmets, and the freedom *not* to wear one, motorcycle profiling, and a one-percenter club's legal battle to wear their patches were heavily politicized issues that were centrally important at NCOM in 2019. Since then, U.S. bikers have been at the center of several controversies.

There are a few well-known motorcycle rallies that occur annually in the United States. Laconia is known for being the oldest (the first was in 1916), and Sturgis and Daytona are known for being the largest (both typically have over five hundred thousand attendees). Like the 1947 Hollister Gypsy Tour, these motorcycle rallies are massive commercial enterprises. Sturgis, South Dakota, is a town with seven thousand people and is just under four square miles. In 2022, the tax revenue from the ten-day Sturgis Motorcycle Rally was $1.54 million (South Dakota Department of Revenue 2022). These rallies serve as spaces of appearances for MCs that plan annual gatherings or "runs" to coincide with them. Local and state politicians support the rallies because of the tremendous amount of revenue generated. The 2020 Sturgis Motorcycle Rally ("Sturgis") became the subject of intense scrutiny because it was the largest public gathering to take place since the start of the COVID-19 pandemic, and it was called a "superspreader event." Dave Dahvel, Drew McNichols, and Joseph Sabia conducted the first study on the public health impacts of Sturgis and estimated that there were 115,283 to 266,796 new cases nationally because of Sturgis, with a cost of $3.8–$8.7 billion, mostly incurred outside of the small town (2021:801–802). While righteous bikers have eschewed the increasingly commercialized rallies, especially after many bars and restaurants implemented "no colors [patches]" rules, Sturgis and other large biker rallies speak to a larger freedom ethic and refusal to be regulated that permeates bikers and motorcyclists and is increasingly consolidated along political party lines.

The widely publicized criticism of the "Sturgis superspreader" did not deter RSMC leadership from having nationals again in March 2021 nor did the death of Blondie in December 2020, who was immune-compromised prior to the COVID-19 pandemic. At nationals in 2019, Blondie expressed her concerns to me about her susceptibility to infection and the increased risk for her to be around so many people. It appeared likely that she continued to pull away from RSMC until her death. The close sleeping and eating quarters provided optimal conditions for COVID-19 to spread among an aging population who were lifelong smokers or had preexisting conditions that made them vulnerable. The populist, libertarian, and conservative political leanings of Sandy and other RSMC national officers call into question the larger ethos of RSMC and sisterhood. This decision likely forced difficult choices for members, particularly prospects who were desperate for a space of appearances and full membership in the polis but also for veteran members who had to show their support for Sandy's decisions and leadership and who are likely older and more susceptible to airborne viruses. These choices align RSMC with a particular kind of national fervor, but they also ingratiate RSMC with extreme causes and clubs.

In 2023, RSMC aligned itself with a new philanthropic project connected to Operation Underground Railroad (OUR), an anti-trafficking group founded by Tim Ballard. Publicly available content includes two TikTok videos featuring RSMC kids—the first has different members of RSMC asking kids, "Do you know what human trafficking is?" and the kids all say no or shake their heads. The second TikTok has the kids educating the public about different types of child trafficking by holding sheets of paper that depict child labor or child marriage and wearing T-shirts that say "God's Children Are Not For Sale." Both videos feature OUR at the end with OUR hashtags. Another TikTok video features a "simulated preparedness exercise" in which a white woman is walking out of a hotel with a dog on a leash and a young Black girl. The girl flashes some signs behind her back with her free hand, and a group of righteous sisters intercepts the girl, who is then seen smiling on the front of a motorcycle with a white woman biker behind her. Ballard worked as a special agent for the Department of Homeland Security for over a decade, and when he was told to "come home" before two investigations were completed, he quit. The conservative talk show host Glenn Beck funded Ballard's unsanctioned work on sex trafficking and has been a longtime supporter of OUR. One of these investigations is the focus of the 2023 *Sound of Freedom*, an indie film that has been heavily criticized and heavily praised, resulting in $217 million at the box office.[1] The film has been heavily praised by leading conservatives, including the former president Donald Trump, who hosted a private screening that Ballard and the actor who plays Ballard, Jim Caviezel, attended. Although Caviezel has denied having ties to the conspiracy theory QAnon, he has repeatedly used "adrenochroming," a QAnon term "for the falsehood that traffickers torture children and drain their blood to harvest an elixir of youth," which the film's director, Alejandro Monteverde, says "did hurt [his] work" on this film (Cain 2023). While philanthropic activities by "elites and outlaws" can be a way to cover up for various forms of violence and illegal activities (Kuldova 2018), more research is needed to uncover the ways in which groups like RSMC can be political conduits for philanthropic enterprises that have extreme political and religious ties. Likely, RSMC views OUR as a way to "save" children by raising awareness and perhaps even by involving themselves in "rescues," but given the organization's fervent support by the Far Right, they are aligning themselves politically through philanthropy in a way that has not been part of their decades-long history. Bikers for Trump are a single-patch riding club that has garnered national and international headlines for their unabashed support of Donald Trump. The group's founder, Chris Cox, anticipated that five thousand bikers would attend Donald Trump's January 2017 inauguration and told Fox News, "In the event we are needed, we certainly will form a wall of meat" to protect the president against the expected protesters (Calfas 2017). Cox's estimate, like Donald Trump's predictions of crowd size, were exaggerated. Nonetheless, these bikers have been repeatedly encouraged by the then-sitting Donald Trump to provide security. The January 6, 2021 insurrection inside the Capitol unleashed a torrent of investigations. Donald Trump's unwavering support for what he referred to as the "J-6 hostages," or the men who have been imprisoned for their criminal acts and some who are awaiting trial, has promoted "outlaw" activities. Citing three separate sources, a January 2024 Supreme Court *amici curiae* brief describes the danger to U.S. democracy posed by Bikers for Trump, among other groups, in the following extended passage:

> The vigilante group Bikers for Trump, provided volunteer security to multiple Trump rallies, and Trump's head of security reportedly embraced Chris Cox, its leader, and conferred with him during a 2016 rally when a reporter was present. As with the Bolivarian Circles in Venezuela, these groups are willing to engage in acts of lawless violence out of personal loyalty to Trump. Cox, the leader of Bikers for Trump, explained at the 2016 Republican National Convention in Cleveland, "I'm anticipating we'll be doing a victory dance," but, "if the Republican Party tries to pull off any backroom deals [to prevent Trump's nomination] . . . our role will change." (Supreme Court of the United States 2024:16–17)

The U.S. Supreme Court ruled in March 2024 that the Colorado Supreme Court erred in excluding Donald J. Trump from the 2024 presidential primary ballot. In a case with dozens of *amici curiae* briefs, this brief and its emphasis on history, law, and a comparative lens, compellingly argues that our democracy is fragile. Indeed. On July 13, 2024 former president Trump was shot in the ear in a failed assassination attempt. On July 21, 2024, President Joseph Biden dropped out of the 2024 presidential election and endorsed his vice president, Kamala Harris, to run for president. These events will likely embolden vigilante groups who spew racist and misogynist venom and call it "freedom."

Bikers will continue to pepper headlines and capture popular culture's imagination through television and film. The 2023 film *The Bikeriders* focuses on MC life in 1960s through the perspective of Kathy (Jodie Comer), who unsurprisingly falls for Benny (Austin Butler), the baddest and most disarmingly good looking of the bikers in the Vandals MC and the second-in-command to the founder and president, Johnny (Tom Hardy). The Vandals MC experienced growing pains from a societal transformation after the Vietnam War to conflicts between members to conflicts between members and their wives and families. Similarly, RSMC is in the midst of its own set of growing pains as it considers succession of leadership, chapter expansion, leveraging social media and the internet while maintaining control over information, collaborating with other MCs and one-percenters on special projects, and attending events like NCOM that are still exclusively male-centric. No longer classic closed societies, contemporary MCs are performing on national and international stages, and the opportunities for disrepute, arete, and immortality are magnified.

Notes

INTRODUCTION

1. This is one of two real nicknames that is used.
2. "MC" refers to a three-piece patch club. Typically, MC members wear an MC cube, or a patch that denotes they are part of an MC. The argot of MCs uses "club" interchangeably to refer to this particular type of club—an MC—so I use the words interchangeably.
3. "Outlaw" denotes an MC that has strict membership requirements and rigid hierarchies and that sometimes, but not always, participates in illegal activities as a club. Many bikers refer to themselves as "outlaws" but do not use "outlaw motorcycle club (OMC)" to describe their clubs. The Outlaws Motorcycle Club is a specific kind of club in which "Outlaws" is part of the trademarked name.
4. Many bikers refer to their long-term partners as their "ol' ladies," which is both familiar and respectful. In this MC, someone's "ol' lady" was afforded respect.
5. The unemployment rate in our county was 11–15.5 percent in June 2009, according to the Florida Agency for Workforce Innovation, Labor Market Statistics Center.
6. Righteous Sisterhood Motorcycle Club (RSMC) is a pseudonym intended to both describe the women members, the righteous sisters, and reinforce that it is a motorcycle club. To protect the group's confidentiality, no identifiers are used.
7. This term refers to a specific type of MC biker, many of whom wear a one-percenter (1%er) patch. A more thorough description follows, but a one-percenter puts the MC above everything and is both revered and feared among bikers.
8. For a detailed gendered analysis of how the media portrayed women bikers and motorcyclists at the 1947 Hollister Gypsy Tour, see my article in the *International Journal of Motorcycle Studies* (2018).
9. The Hells Angels Motorcycle Club was founded in 1948, and its name is trademarked. It is a one-percenter club with chapters worldwide.

10. *The Rebels: A Brotherhood of Outlaw Bikers* ([1991] 2000), by anthropologist Daniel Wolf; *Born to Be Wild: The Rise of the American Motorcyclist* (2015), by historian Randy D. McBee; *The Brotherhoods: Inside the Outlaw Motorcycle Clubs* ([2002] 2003), by sociologist Arthur Veno; and *The Mammoth Book of Bikers* (2007), edited by sociologist Arthur Veno.

11. Ferrar's ([1996] 2001) *Hear Me Roar: Women, Motorcycles, and the Rapture of the Road* chronicles the history of women motorcyclists and Ferrar's journey into motorcycling.

12. I have provided an extended discussion of this term elsewhere (Hoiland 2018), but briefly, William L. Dulaney's "A Brief History of Outlaw Motorcycle Clubs" (2005) defines it as such, and because he is a noted expert on OMCs, the article has carried significant weight.

CHAPTER 1

1. RCs do not break their patches into three parts, and they typically have less rigorous membership requirements.

2. The ideal is purposely concealed to protect the RSMC's confidentiality.

3. No reference to protect the confidentiality of the female MC as it is named in the quote.

4. For more information, see the project's website, available at https://www.motorcycleprofilingproject.com/.

CHAPTER 2

1. See Thompson [1966] 1999; Ginsberg 1973; and Wolfe 1968.

2. Veno writes about bikers in the Australian context.

3. The percentage of motorcycle owners fifty or more years old increased from 8.1 percent to 25.1 percent from 1985 to 2003 (Morris 2012).

4. The distinction between motorcycle clubs (MCs) and outlaw motorcycle clubs (OMCs) is part of Dulaney's historical analyses of motorcycle clubs (Dulaney 2005, 2007). Veno uses OMCs ([2002] 2003).

CHAPTER 3

1. Both the nickname and the full name are pseudonyms.

2. The U.S. ban on women in combat was dropped in 2013, and in 2016 the Defense Department ordered the Marine Corps to open all combat arms career fields to women, although in 2018 less than one hundred women were in these previously male-only jobs (Snow 2018).

3. The pseudonym reflects her side hustle of selling biker T-shirts at large biker events.

4. As with many social clubs and other private organizations, exchanging money for alcoholic drinks is problematic since they don't have a liquor license, so RSMC has a token system with its own token dispenser.

CHAPTER 4

1. The Evil One (TEO) was this member's actual club nickname. Given its generic nature, only club members from that era would be able to connect the nickname with the member, and I am only presenting general facts.

2. During this time in a similarly sized male MC, one died, one was exiled, and one quit on bad terms.

3. PED is characterized by recurrent episodes of involuntary movement disorders usually precipitated by sustained walking or running. See Erro et al. 2014.

4. Photographs were supposed to be turned over to the national officers for review. Each member was asked to download her photographs onto a shared drive. Bill did this each year. There were three official photographers, two members and Bill, who took photographs at nationals. Everyone else was expected to put their phones away and to not take pictures.

5. This was the way it was reported. I am assuming there were approximately seventy women on the text tree and the three who did not text back were included with the slow responders in the 10 percent—likely seven women in total did not text back within the hour, including three who did not text back at all.

6. See Lila Abu-Lughod (1993), *Writing Women's Worlds: Bedouin Stories*; Howard S. Becker (2008), *Tricks of the Trade: How to Think about Your Research While You're Doing It*; Robert G. Burgess (2002), *In the Field: An Introduction to Field Research*; J. L. Simmons and J. McCall George (1969), *Issues in Participant Observation: A Text and Reader*; George Marcus (1998), *Ethnography Through Thick and Thin*; Leonard Schatzman and Anselm L. Strauss (1973), *Field Research: Strategies for a Natural Sociology*; John Van Maanen (2011), *Tales of the Field: On Writing Ethnography*; Kamala Visweswaran ([1994] 2003), *Fictions of Feminist Ethnography*; Diane Wolf (1996), *Feminist Dilemmas in Fieldwork*; Margery Wolf (1992), *A Thrice-Told Tale: Feminism, Postmodernism, and Ethnographic Responsibility*.

7. In my field notes, I postulated that Nurse Nan would be one of the members to receive her full patch in 2016 (the same year she was ejected from nationals).

8. Minutes in one year, for example, included a breakdown of support members and full members. The former, described in Chapter 2, are similar to "friends of" in the male MC world and are not striving for patches. They serve the nation by attending events and paying support member fees, and although they are part of the sisterhood, they do not earn patches. In the next / a different year, this breakdown was not detailed, leading to variance of counting practices with each new national secretary.

9. See Veno [2002] 2003:153–155; Wolf [1991] 2000:137–142.

10. Blue's obituary noted that she had specific preferences regarding the celebration of life.

11. These presentations were discussed thoroughly. Because I never used the club's name or any identifiers, having club members, wearing their patches, attend conferences with me would compromise the anonymity of the club, but it was the club's decision to participate, wearing their patches, and to not be listed on the program.

EPILOGUE

1. In a summer of *Barbie* ($612 million) and *Oppenheimer* ($311 million), *Sound of Freedom* ranked sixth among the U.S. box office movies for gross revenue.

References

Abu-Lughod, Lila. 1993. *Writing Women's Worlds: Bedouin Stories*. Berkeley: University of California Press.
Anderson, Benedict. [1983] 2016. *Imagined Communities: Reflections on the Origins and the Spread of Nationalism*. London: Verso Books.
Anderson, Elijah. 1999. *Code of the Street: Decency, Violence, and the Moral Life of the Inner City*. New York: W. W. Norton.
Anti-Defamation League. 2011. *Bigots on Bikes: The Growing Links between White Supremacists and Biker Gangs*. New York: Anti-Defamation League. Available at https://www.adl.org/sites/default/files/documents/assets/pdf/combating-hate/ADL_CR_Bigots_on_Bikes_online.pdf.
Arendt, Hannah. [1958] 1998. *The Human Condition*. Chicago: University of Chicago Press.
———. 1970. *On Violence*. San Diego: Harcourt Brace and Company.
Barbash, Fred, and Meagan Flynn. "The Feds Spent a Decade Trying to Seize the Mongol Club's Notorious Patch. A Judge Ruled They Can't Have It." *Washington Post*, March 1, 2019.
Bauer, L. 2005. "A History of Sisterhood: Women's Secret Societies, Women's Fraternities and Sororities." *Essentials* 1 (1).
Becker, Howard S. 2008. *Tricks of the Trade: How to Think about Your Research While You're Doing It*. Chicago: University of Chicago Press.
Behar, Ruth. 1993. *Translated Woman: Crossing the Border with Esperanza's Story*. Boston: Beacon.
———. 1996. *The Vulnerable Observer: Anthropology That Breaks Your Heart*. Boston: Beacon.
Bernstein, Richard. 2018. *Why Read Hannah Arendt Now*. Cambridge: Polity.
Blau, Zena Smith. 1972. "Role Exit and Identity." Paper presented at the American Sociological Association Meetings, New Orleans.
Blee, Kathleen. [1991] 1992. *Women of the Klan: Racism and Gender in the 1920s*. Berkeley: University of California Press.

———. 2002. *Inside Organized Racism: Women in the Hate Movement*. Berkeley: University of California Press.

Bohemen, Samira, Liesbet Zoonen, and Stef Aupers. 2013. "Negotiating Gender through Fun and Play: Radical Femininity and Fantasy in the Red Hat Society." *Journal of Contemporary Ethnography* 43:582–600. Available at https://doi.org/10.1177/0891241613 505865.

Bosmia, Anand, James Quinn, and Todd Peterson. 2014. "Outlaw Motorcycle Gangs: Aspects of the One-Percenter Culture for Emergency Department Personnel to Consider." *Western Journal of Emergency Medicine: Integrating Emergency Care with Population Health* 15 (4): 523–528.

Burgess, Robert G. 2002. *In the Field: An Introduction to Field Research*. London: Taylor & Francis.

Cain, Sian. 2023. "Sound of Freedom Director Says Jim Caviezel's QAnon Comments 'Hurt My Work.'" *The Guardian*, August 15, 2023. Available at https://www.theguardian.com/film/2023/aug/15/sound-of-freedom-director-alejandro-monteverde-jim-caviezel-qanon-comments.

Calfas, Jennifer. 2017. "Bikers for Trump to Form 'Wall of Meat' against Inauguration Protesters." *The Hill*, January 15, 2017. Available at https://thehill.com/blogs/blog-briefing-room/news/314429-bikers-for-trump-vow-to-form-wall-of-meat-against-inauguration/.

Callais, Mari Ann. 2002. "Sorority Rituals: Rites of Passage and Their Impact on Contemporary Sorority Women." Ph.D. dissertation, Department of Educational Leadership, Research, and Counseling, Louisiana State University. Retrieved from LSU Digital Commons, 2021. Available at https://digitalcommons.lsu.edu/gradschool_dissertations/2121.

Campbell, Ann. 1987. "Self-Definition by Rejection: The Case of Gang Girls." *Social Problems* 34:451–466.

Cohen, Albert K. 1955. *Delinquent Boys: The Culture of the Gang*. Glencoe: Free Press.

Conner, M Shelly. 2009. "First-Wave Feminist Struggles in Black Motorcycle Clubs." *International Journal of Motorcycle Studies* 5 (2).

Cumming, Elaine, and William E. Henry. [1961] 1979. *Growing Old: The Process of Disengagement*. New York: Basic (1961); reprint Arno (1979).

Dahvel, Dave, Drew McNichols, and Joseph J. Sabia. 2021. "The Contagion Externality of a Superspreading Event: The Sturgis Motorcycle Rally and COVID-19." *Southern Economic Journal* 87 (3): 769–807. Available at https://doi.org/10.1002/soej.12475.

Davidman, Linda. 2015. *Becoming Unorthodox: Stories of Ex-Hasidic Jews*. Oxford: Oxford University Press.

Dulaney, William L. 2005. "A Brief History of Outlaw Motorcycle Clubs." *International Journal of Motorcycle Studies* 1 (3).

———. 2007. "A More Complete History of the Outlaw Clubs." In *The Mammoth Book of Bikers*, edited by Arthur Veno, 127–136. Philadelphia: Running.

Ebaugh, Helen Rose Fuchs. 1988. *Becoming an Ex: The Process of Role Exit*. Chicago: University of Chicago Press.

Erro, Roberto, Maria Stamelou, Christos Ganos, Matej Skorvanek, Vladimir Han, Amit Batla, and Kailash P. Bhatia. 2014. "The Clinical Syndrome of Paroxysmal Exercise-Induced Dystonia: Diagnostic Outcomes and an Algorithm." *Movement Disorders* 1 (1): 57–61. Available at https://doi.org/10.1002/mdc3.12007.

Ferrar, Ann. [1996] 2001. *Hear Me Roar: Women, Motorcycles, and the Rapture of the Road*. London: Whitehorse.

Foucault, Michel. [1977] 1995. *Discipline and Punish: The Birth of the Prison*. Translated by Alan Sheridan. New York: Vintage Books.

Freidlander, Judith. 2019. *A Light in Dark Times: The New School for Social Research and Its University in Exile*. New York: Columbia University Press.
Frere-Jones, Sasha. 2019. "The Chaos of Altamont and the Murder of Meredith Hunter." *New Yorker*, March 28, 2019. Available at: https://www.newyorker.com/culture/cultural-comment/the-chaos-of-altamont-and-the-murder-of-meredith-hunter.
Geertz, Clifford. 1973. *The Interpretation of Cultures*. New York: Basic Books.
Gillan, Kathleen R. 2016. "Great Expectations and Post-feminist Accountability: Negotiating Femininity in a Modern Day Sorority." Ph.D. dissertation, Department of Educational Leadership, Policy, and Technology Studies, University of Alabama. Retrieved from ProQuest Dissertations and Theses Database, 10240408.
Ginsberg, Allen. 1973. "First Party at Ken Kesey's with Hell's Angels." In *Kesey's Garage Sale*, by Ken Kesey. New York: Viking Press.
Glaser, Barney G., and Anselm L. Strauss. [1971] 2010. *Status Passage*. E-book. New York: Routledge.
Handler, Lisa. 1995. "In the Fraternal Sisterhood: Sororities and Gender Strategy." *Gender and Society* 9:236–255.
Hoiland, Sarah. 2012. "Wild Women in the World of Outlaw Motorcycle Clubs: Nomadic Subjectivities in the Borderlands." Ph.D. dissertation, Department of Sociology, New School University. Retrieved from ProQuest Dissertations Publishing, 3495824.
———. 2018. "'Impromptu Fiesta' or 'Havoc in Hollister': A Seventy-Year Retrospective." *International Journal of Motorcycle Studies* 14 (3).
———. Interview with Abi Ishola. CUNY TV's *Urban U*. Aired July 4, 2019. Available at https://www.youtube.com/watch?v=eN_I9eNn26o.
Hopper, Columbus B., and Johnny "Big John" Moore. 1983. "Hell on Wheels: The Outlaw Motorcycle Gangs." *Journal of American Culture* 6 (2): 58–64.
———. 1990. "Women in Outlaw Motorcycle Gangs." *Journal of Contemporary Ethnography* 18:363–387.
Hoschild, Arlie Russell. [1989] 2012. *The Second Shift: Working Parents and the Revolution at Home*. With Anne Machung. London: Penguin Books.
Ilyasova, K. Alex. 2006. "Dykes on Bikes and the Regulation of Vulgarity." *International Journal of Motorcycle Studies* 2 (3).
Joans, Barbara. 2001. *Bike Lust: Harleys, Women, and American Society*. Madison: University of Wisconsin Press.
Kaplan, Joel H., and Sheila Stowell. 1995. *Theatre and Fashion: Oscar Wilde to the Suffragettes*. Cambridge: Cambridge University Press.
Kuldova, T. 2018. "When Elites and Outlaws Do Philanthropy: On the Limits of Private Vices for Public Benefit." *Trends in Organized Crime* 21 (3): 295+. Gale Academic One File.
Lawrence-Lightfoot, Sara. 2011. *Exit: The Endings That Set Us Free*. New York: Farrar, Straus and Giroux.
LeBlanc, Lauraine. [1999] 2006. *Pretty in Punk: Girls' Gender Resistance in a Boys' Subculture*. New Brunswick, NJ: Rutgers University Press.
Lynch, Thomas C. 1965. *Hell's Angels Motorcycle Clubs Report*. N.p.: California Department of Justice.
Malone, Sheila. 2013. "Objects Vibrating Disobedience: A Phenomenology of the Motorcycle, an Orientation of a Dyke on a Bike." *International Journal of Motorcycle Studies* 9 (2).
Marcus, George. 1998. *Ethnography Through Thick and Thin*. Princeton: Princeton University Press.

Marcus, Greil. [1977] 2015. "The Apocalypse at Altamont." Greil Marcus website, March 23, 2015. Available at https://greilmarcus.net/2015/03/23/the-apocalypse-at-altamont-1977/.
Mauss, Marcel. [1954] 2002. *The Gift: Forms and Functions of Exchange in Archaic Societies*. Translated by W. D. Halls. London: Routledge.
McBee, Randy D. 2015. *Born to Be Wild: The Rise of the American Motorcyclist*. Chapel Hill: University of North Carolina Press.
McRobbie, Angela, and Jenny Garber. [1977] [1993] 2006. "Girls and Subcultures." In *Resistance through Rituals: Youth Subcultures in Post-war Britain*, edited by Stuart Hall and Tony Jefferson, 208–222. 2nd ed. London: Hutchinson and CCCS Birmingham.
Merton, Robert K. [1949] [1957] 1968. *Social Theory and Social Structure*. Glencoe, IL: Free Press.
Miller, Dorothy A. 1981. "The 'Sandwich' Generation: Adult Children of the Aging." *Social Work* 26 (5): 419–423. Available at https://www.jstor.org/stable/23712207.
Miyake, Esperanza. 2015. "Deleuzian Motorcycle: Towards a Theory of Motorcycles and the Other." *International Journal of Motorcycle Studies* 11 (1).
———. [2018] 2020. *The Gendered Motorcycle: Representations in Society, Media, and Popular Culture*. London: Bloomsbury, I. B. Tauris.
Morris, C. Craig. 2012. "Motorcycle Trends in the United States." United States Department of Transportation. Available at https://www.bts.gov/archive/publications/special_reports_and_issue_briefs/special_report/2009_05_14/entire.
Online Etymology Dictionary. 2024. "Prospect." Accessed July 13, 2024. Available at https://www.etymonline.com/word/prospect.
Oxford English Dictionary. 2023. "Righteous, *Adj., N., Adv., Int.*, Etymology." Oxford University Press. December 2023. Available at https://doi.org/10.1093/OED/7615599762.
Oxford English Dictionary. "Righteous, *Adj.*, Sense 3.a." Oxford University Press. December 2023. Available at https://doi.org/10.1093/OED/1067596274.
Paes de Barros, Deborah. 2004. *Fast Cars and Bad Girls: Nomadic Subjects and Women's Road Stories*. New York: Peter Lang.
Queen, William. 2005. *Under and Alone*. New York: Fawcett Books.
Rogers, Katie. 2016. "Women's March and Bikers for Trump Claim Inaugural Demonstration Spots." *New York Times*, December 12, 2016. Available at https://www.nytimes.com/2016/12/12/us/politics/womens-march-bikers-trump.html.
Salzinger, Leslie. 2003. *Genders in Production: Making Workers in Mexico's Global Factories*. Berkeley: University of California Press.
Schatzman, Leonard, and Strauss, Anselm L. 1973. *Field Research: Strategies for a Natural Sociology*. Englewood Cliffs, NJ: Prentice-Hall.
Schmitt, Carl. [1932] 1966. *The Concept of the Political*. Translated by George Schwab. Chicago: University of Chicago Press.
Simmons, J. L., and J. McCall George. 1969. *Issues in Participant Observation: A Text and Reader*. Reading, MA: Addison-Wesley.
Simms, Shannon. 2018. "Meet New Orleans's All-Female Biker Club." *New York Times*, July 28, 2018. Available at https://www.nytimes.com/2018/07/28/us/meet-new-orleanss-all-female-biker-club.html.
Snow, Shawn. 2018. "Where Are the Female Marines?" *Marine Corps Times*, March 5, 2018. Available at https://www.marinecorpstimes.com/news/2018/03/05/where-are-the-female-marines/.
South Dakota Department of Revenue. 2022. "Sturgis Motorcycle Rally Tax Revenue Finishes at $1.54 Million." August 30, 2022. Available at https://dor.sd.gov/newsroom/2022-sturgis-motorcycle-rally-tax-revenue-finishes-at-1-54-million/.

Stone, Amy L., and Allison Gorga. 2014. "Containing Pariah Femininities: Lesbians in the Sorority Rush Process." *Sexualities* 17 (3). Available at https://doi.org/10.1177/13634 60713516336.

Stremlow, Mary V. 1986. *A History of the Women Marines, 1946–1977.* Washington, DC: History and Museums Division Headquarters, U.S. Marine Corps. Available at https://www.marines.mil/Portals/1/Publications/A%20History%20of%20the%20Women%20 Marines%201946-1977%20PCN%2019000309400_1.pdf.

Supreme Court of the United States. 2024. *Trump v. Anderson, et al.* No. 23-719. "Brief of Experts in Democracy as *Amici Curiae* in Support of Respondents." Submitted January 31, 2024.

Thompson, Hunter S. [1966] 1999. *Hell's Angels: A Strange and Terrible Saga.* New York: Modern Library.

Tucker, Robert C. 1968. "The Theory of Charismatic Leadership." *Daedalus* 97 (3): 731–756. Available at https://www.jstor.org/stable/20023840.

Turk, Diana B. 2004. *Bound by a Mighty Vow: Sisterhood and Women's Fraternities, 1870–1920.* New York: NYU Press.

Turner, Victor. [1969] 1995. *The Ritual Process: Structure and Anti-structure.* New York: Aldine De Gruyter.

van den Eynde, Julie, and Arthur Veno. 2013. "Participatory Action Research with High-Risk Groups: Best Practices for Researchers' Safety and Data Integrity." *Current Issues in Criminal Justice* 25 (1): 491–501. Available at https://doi.org/10.1080/10345329.2013 .12035976.

Van Maanen, John. 2011. *Tales of the Field: On Writing Ethnography*, 2nd ed. Chicago: University of Chicago Press.

Veno, Arthur. [2002] 2003. *The Brotherhoods: Inside the Outlaw Motorcycle Clubs.* Crows Nest, NSW: Allen and Unwin.

Visweswaran, Kamala. [1994] 2003. *Fictions of Feminist Ethnography.* Minneapolis: University of Minnesota Press.

Wafer, Jim. 1996. "After the Field." In *Things as They Are: New Directions in Phenomenological Anthropology*, edited by Michael Jackson, 259–272. Bloomington: Indiana University Press.

Weber, Max. [1968] 1978. *Economy and Society: An Outline of Interpretive Sociology.* Translated by Guenther Roth and Claus Wittich. Berkeley: University of California Press.

Wolf, Daniel R. [1991] 2000. *The Rebels: A Brotherhood of Outlaw Bikers.* Toronto: University of Toronto Press.

Wolf, Diane. 1996. *Feminist Dilemmas in Fieldwork.* Boulder: Westview Press.

Wolf, Margery. 1992. *A Thrice-Told Tale: Feminism, Postmodernism, and Ethnographic Responsibility.* Standford, CA: Stanford University Press.

Wolfe, Tom. 1968. *The Electric Kool-Aid Acid Test.* New York: Picador.

Index

Arendt, Hannah, 18–19; arete, 72; authority, 45; contempt, 42; polis, 73, 99; power, 42, 136; public realm, 77, 99; space of appearances, 9–10, 12; strength, 45. *See also* Authority; Righteousness: space of appearances

Authority, as gendered, 42; obedience, 57; potential threats, 73; as power, 44; types of authority, 86–88; 132; as a women's motorcycle club, 23. *See also* Arendt, Hannah: authority; Mauss, Marcel; Turner, Victor: community as authority

Behar, Ruth, 109, 128

Belonging, citizenship, 48; as ethnographer, 50; as family, 54; as nationalism, 24; rites and rituals, 21, 28, 90; space of appearances, 80, 85; spirit ride, 53; tensions, 25. *See also* Blee, Kathleen; Ceremony: patching; Citizenship; Nationals: spirit ride; Queen, William; Righteousness: as labor; Righteousness: space of appearances; Sisterhood; Thompson, Hunter S.

Bikers, 1, 26, 36; biker women, 16. *See also* Woman biker

Biker studies, 10, 14

Blee, Kathleen, 15, 25, 56

Business, club, control mechanism, 45–46, 108, 113, 115, 122, 132; definition, 13; as part of initiation, 62, 67, 69. *See also* Exile; Initiation: club business; Nationals: business meeting; Sexuality

Ceremony, 27–28; awards, 40–41, 71–72, 93, 96; patching, 14, 20–22, 26–28, 48, 70, 104; Sister of the Year Award, 71–72, 75, 88–90. *See also* Nationals: gift giving; Nationals: spirit ride; Patches: burning

Citizenship, 9–10, 18, 22, 24, 27, 36; biker citizens, 24; civic death, 112–114, 129; docile, 39; dual citizenship, 25, 35–36, 48; loss of citizenship rights, 110; patches, 28, 34, 115; rebirth, 52; repatriation, 114–115; second-class, 29, 31. *See also* Belonging: citizenship; Ceremony: patching; Turner, Victor: liminality

Coalition of Clubs (COC), 22, 25, 41–42

Code-switching, 35–36

Colors. *See* Patches

Disability, 17, 3, 118

Dulaney, William, 5–6, 14–15

Ebaugh, Helen Rose Fuchs, 109, 120; role exit, 111–113

Economy, internal, 33–34, 39, 93–94
Exile, 10; as civil death, 111–116; as ethnographer, 109, 124, 128–134; ex-ethnographer, 134–135; political exile, 18, 110; rituals, 114–115; as social control, 105–108, 110, 113–114, 116, 124. *See also* Patches: burning; Righteous sister: ex-righteous sister
Exit, 3, 10, 70, 110–111, definition, 122; ethnographers' exits, 109–110, 127–128; death, 110, 122–12; life changes, 116, 119–120, 122, 124; men's motorcycle club, 113, 120; religious exit, 112; rituals, 114–115, 123. *See also* Reentry; Righteous sister: ex-righteous sister

Feminine/femininity, 39, 75, patches as, 48, 56; types of, 56. *See also* Gender
Feminism/feminist, 86; anti/ not, 9, 19, 22–24, 48; ethnography, 109; resistance, 15, 135; quasi-feminist, 107
Foucault, Michel, 38, 43

Gender, 56–57, defies, 86; as exclusionary, 22, 56, 74, 138; as intersectional, 6, 11, 135; masculinity, 5, 7, 25, 27, 55, 136; as righteous, 27, 56; patch, 39, 57; performance, 52, 96; as power, 4, 9, 15, 25, 134; presentation, 74, 105; sisterhood, 70; stereotypes, 93; transgression, 10, 54, 56; transphobia, 108. *See also* Feminine/femininity; Patches: as gendered; Power: as gendered; Righteous sister: as a gendered construct
Gossip, 56, 63, 70, 82, 106–107, 114, 129

Hierarchy, 17, 26, 28, 35, 43–45, 108, 110
Hollister Gypsy Motorcycle Tour, 6, 10, 15, 25, 137; Hollister riot, 2, 4, 10, 129

Initiation, *The Book of Sisters*, 74, 77, 114; club business, 62–63; communal meals, 52–53; ethnographer, 4, 13, 50, 65–66, 101–102; jokes, 73; as a liminal stage, 2, 26–27; 39, 43, 64–65, 111, as marriage, 16, 66–70; re-initiation, 114; sponsorship, 18, 27, 61–70; vetting, 59–61, 108. *See also* Business, club: as part of initiation; Ceremony: patching; Gossip; Nationals: spirit ride; Righteousness: initiation; Sisterhood: jokes

Joans, Barbara, 8, 25, 54

LeBlanc, Lauraine, 15, 25, 55
Legitimacy, 23, 42, 75–76
Lynch Report, 5–7

McBee, Randy, 8
Mauss, Marcel, 90–92, 94
Misogyny, in the biker subculture, 4, 24, 26–27, 38, 41, 47, 84, 86, 137; in politics, 140. *See also* Race: racist misogyny
Miyake, Esperanza, 11, 39
Motorcycle club (MC), 2, 35; chapters, 34, 44; origin of, 4, 5; violence, 45; women's motorcycle club, 3, 4, 8, 15–16, 69–70
Motorcycle profiling, 37–38, 40, 47, 54, 137
Motorcycle Profiling Project, 37–38, 40, 47

Nation, biker, 24, 30, 45, 73, 75; creation of, 22–23; elements of, 9; enemies of, 36, 38; expansion, 63; as family, 58; leadership, 87–88, 112, 116, 129; matriarchal, 77, 116; protection, 31, 59, 119; in service of, 86, 90, 96; types of, 23–24, 29, 34, 36. *See also* Righteous Sisterhood Motorcycle Club
National Coalition of Motorcycles (NCOM), 29, 38, 40–41, 47, 129, 137
National president, 2, 4, 9, 28–29, 31, 34, 41, 61; as mother, 116; role of, 44; power, 45, 47–48, 77, 84, 86–88; 92; 111–116, 128, 134. *See also* Authority; Nation: leadership; Nation: matriarchal; Power: as national president
Nationals, 12, 21, 26, 33; auction, 94; business meeting, 14, 45, 87, 106–107; gift giving, 88–92; spirit ride, 49–53, rodeo, 99. *See also* Ceremony: awards; Ceremony: patching

Obama, Barack, 24, 38, 102
Ol' lady, 2, 8, 22, 25, 30, 41, 76, 86, 107
One-percenter, 4, 9, 15–16, 24, 29, 59, 64; Hells Angels, 5–7, 9; Outlaws Motorcycle Club, 14–15, 28–29; patches, 22, 28; respect, 32, 41; violence, 25, 33, 42; women, 6–7, 16–17, 29, 32, 86, 95. *See also* Respect: one-percenter
Outlaw/s, 4, 5, 14–16; women as outlaws, 8, 10, 14; outlaw motorcycle club (OMC), 5, 14–15, 64; outlaw motorcycle gang (OMG), 15

Patches, 2, 10, 23, 28; burning, 115; colors, 10, 32; defending, 7; front patches, 28; as gendered, 39, 57; national identity, 34; patch economies, 33; as power, 48, 59; prohibited, 126; property of, 22, 29–31; punishment, 33, 69, 107, 112–114; respect for, 20, 23, 29, 31–32, 48; RICO, 37; rockers, 23, 27–28, 47, 68–69; rules, 31; as sacred symbols, 17, 21–23, 27, 31; sisterhood, 58; as status symbols, 48; territorial disputes, 27. *See also* Ceremony: patching ceremony; Citizenship: patches; Economies: patches; Feminine/femininity: patches as; One-percenter: patches; Respect: patches

Phenomenology, 10, 12, 19, 128

Politics, conservative, 9–10, 24, 66, 102–103, 138; political communities, 9, 10, 34, 58, 94, 136; political life, 19; politicking, 22; public, 77; US politics, 38

Populism, 9, 22, 24, 38, 138

Power, as gendered, 4, 7, 9, 15, 25, 31; 134; mystical/ healing, 84, 90, 92; as national president, 45, 47–48, 77, 84, 86–88; 92; 111–116, 128, 134; as patches, 48, 59; public displays of, 40, 50, 52; threats/ usurpation, 23, 108. *See also* Arendt, Hannah: power; Authority: as power; Gender: as power; National president: power; Patches: as power

Prospect, 20, 39; definition of, 64. *See also* Initiation

Prospecting, 26–27, 34, 55, 64–67; striker, 64–65. *See also* Initiation

Queen, William, 24, 29–30, 61, 64

Race, 2, 5–6, 10–11; racism, 6, 47–48; racist misogyny, 16; profiling, 37, 47; white masculinity, 55; whiteness, 48; white supremacy, 7; as a taboo topic, 130, 133. *See also* Motorcycle profiling

Rape, 24; Lynch Report, 5; Monterrey rape, 5–7

Reentry, 113–114, 122

Respect, patches, 20, 23, 29, 31–32, 48; respectability/ respectable, 15, 17; righteous, 16, 46, 51; RSMC, 44, 48, 64, 76, 119–120; sisterhood, 35, 95; terms of, 2, 30, 52

Retirement, 3, 35, 46–47, 59, 73, 86, 91, 96, 114, 117, 120

Riding, as a pack, 39, 86–88, 97, 112, 118–119, 123, 136. *See also* Initiation; Nationals: spirit ride

Riding clubs, 23, 25

Righteousness, as big brother, 120; as a club, 26, 64; definition, 9–10, 12, 16–17, 72; examples, 73; gender, 55–57; as immortality, 19, 52, 77, 99–100, 106, 114, 127; as labor, 57, 64, 73–74, 77, 79–86; meaning, 53–54; as political, 137; pseudo-righteousness through riding, 53; space of appearances, 78–79. *See also* Arendt, Hannah: arete; Respect: righteousness; Righteous sister; Sisterhood: jokes

Righteous sister, characteristics of, 9–10, 75, 79, 102–104; as ethnographer, 82–83, 109–110; definition of, 8, 43, 63; examples of, 74–77, 81, 86, 117–119, 136; 123–124, 126; ex-righteous sister, 18, 105–106, 108–113, 116; as a gendered construct, 15–16, 77, 136; motherhood, 120–121; patches, 36; sanctions, 110–114; spiritual connection, 58, 76, 84; transformation, 55, 136. *See also* Ceremony: Awards, Ceremony: Sister of the Year

Righteous sisterhood, club life, 76; competition, 82, 98; contradictions, 110, 127, 135; creation of, 9; FOG, 108; Home, 78–80, 83–84; hospitality, 101–103, 125; labor, 85–86; membership, 113, 119; motivation, 17–18, 57–58; philanthropy, 26, 94–99; purpose, 136; pranks, 57, 70, 84–85, 87, 97–98, 100; Sister Time, 79, 82–84; threat of violence, 29–30, 44

Salzinger, Leslie, 55

Sexuality, 66; exclusion of, 74, 108; heteronormative, 35, 47, 54, 60, 63, 74, 80, 107; homosexuality as taboo, 106, 108, 133. *See also* Sisterhood: threats to

Sisterhood, 9–10, 18, 12, 18, 35; competition, 92; creation of, 48; disillusionment, 124–125, 127; as a gatekeeping mechanism, 16; as a gendered construct, 70, 108; importance of, 86–88; jokes; 16, 26, 57, 85, 96, 100; as love, 119; as marriage, 54, 127, 66–70; mysticism, 108; other types of sisterhood, 25, 56; play, 18, 70; protection, 30, 54, 115;

Sisterhood (*continued*)
  Secret Sister, 92–94; security, 59; stepping back, 117–119, 124; Support Sister, 65–66, 117–119; as temporary, 115, 121–122; threats to, 107–108, 113–116; violence, 30. *See also* Righteous sister; Righteous sisterhood
Social class, 6, 17, 36, 91, 98; middle-class, 104, 126–127; working-class, 26, 43, 79, 91
Subculture, 10; biker subculture, 4, 9; stigmatized subculture, 7; male-dominated, 11, 17; violence, 22

Tattoos, 1–2, 30, 36, 51, 63, 67
Thompson, Hunter S., 5, 9, 21, 24, 30, 36, 54; initiation, 61, 65
Trump, Donald, 24, 139; Bikers for Trump, 38, 139, exile, 110
Turk, Diana B., 15, 25

Turner, Victor, 43; communitas, 111; community as authority, 34; liminality, 64, 111; *rites de passage*, 34

Veno, Arthur, 5, 53–54, 61
Violence, 3, 5, 32; one-percenter, 29, 33, 42; racially-motivated / Anti-Black violence, 6–7, 22; state-sanctioned violence, 5, 37; women, 6–7; turf, 7, 22, 25, 27, 36

Weber, Max, 45; charismatic leadership, 47; *The Wild One*, 4, 55
Wolf, Daniel, brotherhood, 46; class, 36, 79; ex-ethnographer, 127–129; gifts, 88; influence, 8; initiation, 61–62, 65–66; paradox, 57; righteous bikers, 53–55; transcendence, 86; women, 30
Woman biker, 3, 7–8, 10, 36; to righteous sister, 55
Work, 18

Sarah L. Hoiland is Associate Professor of Sociology at Hostos Community College, City University of New York.